IN·SEARCH·OF WILD·TROUT

Fly Fishing for Wild Trout in Rivers

NICHOLAS·FITTON

WARD LOCK

To Charles, John and Bill Fitton,
three great fishermen,
with thanks

Series editor: Jonathan Grimwood

A WARD LOCK BOOK

First published in the UK 1992
by Ward Lock
(a Cassell imprint)
Villiers House
41/47 Strand
LONDON
WC2N 5JE

Distributed in the United States
by Sterling Publishing Co., Inc.
387 Park Avenue South, New York, NY 10016-8810

Distributed in Australia
by Capricorn Link (Australia) Pty Ltd
P.O. Box 665, Lane Cove, NSW 2066

British Library Cataloguing in Publication Data
Fitton, Nicholas
In search of wild trout: fly fishing for wild trout in rivers.
1. Trout. Angling
I. Title
799.1755

ISBN 0-7063-7033-3

Typeset by Computership, Hong Kong
Printed and bound in Great Britain by
Mackays of Chatham PLC, Chatham, Kent

CONTENTS

Introduction
Where to Find Wild Trout

'I care not, I to fish in seas;
Fresh rivers best my mind do please.'
William Basse

This is a book about catching wild trout in rivers. Happily, there are still many places where you can fish for wild trout in this increasingly crowded island. It is not just the cities which are becoming more crowded: many trout–fishing locations are too. These populous venues are mainly ponds, pools and reservoirs stocked with big trout, usually rainbow. But as these stillwater fisheries become more popular, our streams and rivers, with their admittedly often much smaller residents, are increasingly neglected. Many modern trout anglers do not know what they are missing.

UNFAMILIAR TERRITORY

There must now exist a generation of game fishers who have never caught a wild trout and, sadder still, who have never observed a wild trout feeding in his natural environment. Those anglers used to modern stillwater tactics who visit a small river that holds wild fish will invariably find themselves at a loss as to how to proceed. Their rods will be too long, lines too heavy and flies too big. They will frighten more fish than they believe the river could possibly hold, and those few trout they do catch a glimpse of will seem so small that they will pack up in high dudgeon, swearing never again to waste their time on the banks of such a pitiful little ditch. The next day, with their cars securely parked in a friendly tarmac enclosure, they will be back beside their favourite concrete basin, ready to fish shoulder to shoulder with their like-minded comrades.

This book is designed to help the fly fisher to enjoy and find success in the rivers and streams of the British Isles, especially those smaller waters less famous and less fashionable than the bigger ones that get so much attention in books and magazines. Small rivers are extremely important in the education of every trout fisherman. Quite frankly, I don't think there is any substitute for a boyhood spent crawling up and down a small trout brook. In a stream you are able to observe trout at close quarters and build up an intimate knowledge of their behaviour. It is no coincidence that many of the most acute angling intellects of our history have flourished on the banks of small rivers. Walton, Cotton, Halford, Skues, Plunket-Greene and Sawyer were all principally stream fishermen as opposed to big-river aficionados.

Small rivers are also the last reliable remaining haunt of the truly wild trout. Recent visits to the Test and Kennet have greatly depressed me because of the number of stocked brown and rainbow trout those famous old rivers now hold, while some of the celebrated rivers of the North such as the Ure, Ribble and Eden are stocked in places, either to compensate for local pollution or else to satisfy the demands of overcrowded clubs.

THE ATTRACTIONS OF SMALL RIVERS

Little rivers, whether small in their entirety or simply the narrowing upper reaches of great rivers, have other unique attractions too. Isolation, to begin with: you can usually find utter solitude and tranquillity beside a stream. You can fish all day and never see another soul, casting where you like without fear of being disturbed or hurried. There is wonderful scenery with wild animals all about you: deer, stoats, hares, foxes, kingfishers, curlews, buzzards and other surprises. If you are quiet and stealthy you can watch trout behaving naturally in their own undisturbed environment. This tranquillity is among the main attractions of a small river.

Next, the fishing is challenging: every pool is different. Casting is tricky, with rock, tree and undergrowth presenting constant problems. Playing trout in a confined space is often difficult too. Good eyesight and entomological skill are required. There is a constant change, an infinite variety, about fishing in streams, and every trout you catch will be a wild one – a cunning, native inhabitant who will fight with every inch of his muscular, bronze fuselage. It is true that trout in these waters can run small: three or even more to the pound. Here a half-pounder (0.2 kg) may be a biggun, while a pounder (0.5 kg) is a veritable monster. This limitation of size is the only disadvantage of such streams, though as Arthur Ransome wisely says:

> Happily, however, the pleasure of fishing is not strictly measurable in weight of fish.

No less an authority than Charles Ritz, a catcher of many huge specimens, echoes this sentiment, adding a further morsel of wisdom:

> In my view, the sporting qualities of a fish are dependent neither on its size nor its weight, but on the effort of concentration, the skill and mastery it demands from the fisherman.

The fish in many of our little streams may not grow very large but they will tax the brain, the hand (and the heart!) of even the skilled fisherman.

INEXPENSIVE SPORT

I have not yet touched on what may be to many, especially in these costly times, the principal attraction of small rivers and streams – their remarkably cheap fishing. Some of the big reservoirs are expensive to fish, especially if a boat is hired: £20 is not exceptional for a day's sport. Indeed, this would be quite cheap for a day ticket on some southern rivers. I have an acquaintance who pays over £1000 per season to fish a stretch of Hampshire chalkstream. For this sum he is allowed to fish once a week and keep no more than a brace per visit. By contrast many of the little northern rivers I fish cost me less than £2 per day, and quite a few cost me less than £1. On one river this spring the lady who sells tickets was embarrassed to have to inform me that the price had gone up over the close season – from 80p to £1 a day! This is a river, by the way, which gets the mayfly and beside which I rarely meet more than half a dozen other fishermen in a season.

Yet another stream costs me 60p per day, and it is a genuine chalk-stream, a beautiful little brook crammed with fat trout. A couple of seasons ago I caught one hundred and five trout there in ten visits. The best fish was 13 in (33 cm) and weighed exactly 1 lb (0.5 kg); a beautifully proportioned fish with plump, butter-coloured flanks. This stream also gets the mayfly, as well as excellent hatches of olives all through the season. It is cheap not because it is a subsidized public water or because it is maggoted to death by coarse anglers. It suffers neither of these fates but is simply typical of many northern streams – a brilliant little beck very rarely fished. Apart from me, only my friends fish it; nobody else seems to know about its peerless value for money.

Streams like these are by no means unique – they exist in their hundreds all over the British Isles. They are there, flowing peacefully, idyllically neglected, just awaiting your first visit. In Scotland, and even more so in Ireland, you can fish many good streams free of charge. I have also fished quite a few free streams in England and Wales. One of my tricks has been to trace their courses on a map. As a lad I would choose a good private beat or inaccessible club water and follow the river up the valley, stopping at every farm to ask if I could fish. Some said their water was let, others had not let it and told me to scram, but it is surprising how often I scored. Such fishing is often rough, tangly and hard work but it is likely to be most rewarding.

AN UNEXPECTED BONUS

In autumn such stretches come into their own. Trout full of the spawning urge run upstream into these neglected reaches and, quite legitimately, you can help yourself to expensive stock from exclusive clubs downstream. Streams above and below stocked reservoirs or pools are similarly very profitable. I have had some mighty fugitive stillwater trout from little streams in my time. The best was a rainbow trout of 3¾ lb (1.7 kg), from a stream a fit person could leap across.

I have fished some of the most celebrated British trout streams *absolutely free* (admittedly not on prime beats) simply because I had the gumption to ask. Be warned, however: a boy on a bicycle can get away with this kind of enterprise better than a well-dressed person of mature years with an expensive car. If you are such a person, take a son or nephew along, because he is more likely to appeal to the farmer's or landowner's benevolence. Another tip: always offer a kindness in return if you manage to get some fishing on advantageous terms. I always give my host a brace of fish – a courtesy that has reaped dividends for me over the years. In some places I now pay a reduced price or even fish free just because of a few donated trout. At one day-ticket water the lady who runs the fishing was astonished when I offered her a brace. She told me that I was the first angler to make such an offer in the twenty years of her stewardship. I still pay for my ticket when I fish there but any guest of mine fishes free. Another landowner gives me free access to the whole of his river simply because I taught his sons to catch trout. I like to think that I originally performed these kindnesses without an eye to any reciprocal gesture. I have come to learn that in the country, more than any other environment, one kindness begets another.

THE REWARDS OF RESEARCH

I have spent the last 25 years building up a network of excellent little rivers and streams. It takes time to find a wide variety of places but not long to stumble on one or two. All you need is a car, a bicycle or just a pair of sturdy walking boots, as well as a map and some curiosity, and you will find such places for yourself. Some little rivers are ill-kept or even completely neglected, with tangled undergrowth restricting free casting. They are sometimes remote, requiring half an hour's walk or more from where you have parked your car. Yet some are surprisingly accessible. I have fished some excellent cheap water right in the middle of towns. Only last summer I rented a cottage for a week in a charming Yorkshire Dales village through which flowed a tiny stream stiff with trout. Fishing was free. I caught a few unexpectedly good trout from this beck and they were delicious eating. By contrast, on the nearby parent river I paid £5 for a day ticket and caught nothing. It was an overfished – indeed fished-out – stretch; a complete rip-off.

This is one of the frustrations and yet, paradoxically, the delights of the search for wild river trout. Sometimes you do not get your money's worth, but at other times you will be pleasurably surprised. I have to say that after half a lifetime of such searching the delights have very much outweighed the disappointments. It is worth spending time exploring, taking guesses, stopping at farms, country pubs and tackle shops, buying detailed maps and generally casting around for information. In the short term you lose fishing time, but in the long term you will benefit. If you are prepared to invest in your fishing future with hard work of this sort you will reap dividends that lazier, less enterprising fishermen will never even know about.

FISHING GUIDES

Another helpful idea is to buy a where-to-fish guide. Some of these are not much use but one or two are excellent. I can recommend *The Haig Guide to Trout Fishing in Britain*, which gives a pretty comprehensive coverage of the country's river systems. *Where to Fish*, published by Thomas Harmsworth and updated annually, is also worthy of scrutiny. In the angling press, too, guides are published at the beginning of each season (March or April), while magazines such as *Trout and Salmon* run articles throughout the season suggesting new places to visit. But be warned that not all the information in these guides is accurate or up to date. Also, some of the recommendations may prove to be poor, costly, or both. Generally speaking, places off the beaten track in these guides provide the best value for money.

It also pays to keep your eyes open wherever you go, on whatever business, at any time of year. My family and friends are quite used to my eccentric habit of stopping the car (or asking for it to be stopped) every time an unknown bridge looms ahead. Hanging over the parapets of strange bridges, looking down into unfamiliar waters, I have made some of the best discoveries of my fishing career. Some folk on journeys look primarily at the buildings they pass, others at the landscape, the clouds, the vegetation, the farm stock or other cars. I look out for trout streams with unswerving concentration: they are my obsession.

A lad can get away with murder. I have fished many a river whose name I never knew and whose owner I never saw: mostly chance discoveries in wilder areas. Bridges featured prominently in these encounters. Many a plump half-pounder (0.2 kg) has come out from under a nameless bridge over a nameless river. My father and I once stopped in Scotland for a picnic by a bridge over a small, peaty burn. The heather was alive with grasshoppers, and while my father had a nap after lunch I caught a dozen in my handkerchief. Having mounted one on a hook, I fished up 100 yards (90 m) or so of the burn. In every nook, corner and pocket a burly little trout was ready to rush up and seize the bait. I took a hatful, all returned bar a brace which tasted marvellous that night. We were on our way to fish the Deveron. Having studied the map after our delicious supper, my father opined that I had been poaching the headwaters of the Tweed. Mighty oaks from little acorns grow.

Sometimes the acorn yields better bounty than the branch bowed down with fruit. Tributaries can sometimes offer much better fishing than the parent river. This is particularly true in hot, bright weather when water is low. In my experience small, tree-lined rivers usually fish best in very hot weather when the branches teem with terrestrial life. Many insects fall into the water and the trout make hay while the sun shines. Again, in flood time, tributaries run off more quickly than the main river. The wise angler will have learnt the secrets of these burns and brooks and, rain or shine, will know where to go when his local parent river is unfishable. (See Arthur Ransome's essay 'The Local Angler and the Others' for an excellent account of this type of fishing.)

A FRESH CHALLENGE

The benefits of small rivers, then, are considerable, if neglected because of the explosion of interest in stillwater trout fishing. Today's trout angler is a somewhat pampered species: he has got used to instant fishing with its instant results. He can drive right to the water's edge, park, and within minutes take up his 'peg' in a ring of anglers round the pool. But there must exist fishermen who have begun to tire of this stillwater merry-go-round and who seek more challenging targets. For this type of fisherman my book might open up new horizons, while I hope it will offer food for thought to the experienced river angler.

There is some explanatory writing for beginners as well as plenty of technical detail for the seasoned angler. I set out to write the sort of book that *I* wanted to read, the sort of book which I believed needed to be written. So many books on trout fishing cover the same ground with their obligatory chapters on technical innovation, casting, fly tying and elementary tactics. This kind of writing is tedious for the experienced fisherman.

I do a certain amount of hypothesizing to stimulate thought and discussion. Wherever possible I quote from my own experience, as well as quoting other authorities with some regularity to back up my views. I have tried to make most of the book relevant to rivers both small and big, although I admit there is probably a bias towards little rivers and streams because of the many merits already discussed. There is also, I admit, a bias towards the dry fly.

A LIFETIME OF TROUT FISHING

What are my qualifications for writing a book on trout? I caught my first trout over 30 years ago, when I was eight, on a worm. By the time I was 14, I was catching them with regularity on fly. In that year, 1964, I began keeping records, and have done so to this day. I am almost exclusively a Midlands and North of England angler. I was born in the same county as Izaak Walton (Staffordshire), indeed within a dozen miles of his cottage at Shallowford, which is now a museum. I lived for a while in Yorkshire as a boy, where my grandfather, who was a great Yorkshire angler, introduced me to several prestigious northern waters. My father, who taught me four-fifths of all I know about fly fishing, took me all over Scotland, England and Wales to catch salmon and sea trout as well as the native brownies.

Much of my experience has been gleaned from regular fishing in the following celebrated rivers: the Derbyshire Wye and Dove, the Manifold, Ribble, Ure, Rye, Eden, Eamont and Tyne. I have fished other well-known waters, but not so regularly; rivers such as the Exe, Lyn, Teme, Monnow, Wye, Teifi, Kennet, Driffield Beck, Derbyshire and Yorkshire Derwents, the Yorkshire Dove, Lune, Wharfe, Glass, Spey, Deveron and Aberdeenshire Don. But the biggest proportion of my time has been spent on rivers of regional rather than national importance. I have also fished many nameless streams, catching trout in places where no other angler has cast a fly in decades.

As a jobbing English teacher I have worked abroad and fished for trout in Canada, Australia, New Zealand, France, Sweden and Germany. Because my job kept me on the move so much in my twenties, club membership was hardly worthwhile. Most of my fishing, then, has been done on a day-ticket basis. You do not need to be in a club to get good trout fishing: there still are countless rivers where cheap day permits can be bought. It is to these rivers that I hope you will go, and find as much enjoyment as I have found over the years.

1

Wry Fly
The Forgotten Deadly Weapon

'We darkly know, by Faith we cry,
The future is not Wholly Dry.'
Rupert Brooke

There is a method of fly fishing that is hardly ever mentioned in fishing books and receives little or no attention in the angling press. Why this is so remains a mystery to me, for the technique is a deadly one. On its day it is marvellously efficient and will beat any dry fly or wet fly tails up. Nor is it a forbiddingly difficult system to learn. Indeed, this way of fishing greatly simplifies the difficult skill of upstream wet fly fishing. It is fishing with a dry fly *and* a wet fly on your line at the same time. It has no recognizable name (because the technique is not widely recognized) so I have christened it 'wry fly'.

THE DRY-WET DIVIDE

Like many other innovative ideas, the concept of fishing with a dry fly and a wet fly simultaneously is a simple one, but, paradoxically, like many other simple ideas it may take a while to become accepted. Historically, fly fishing has tended to divide into two camps: the dry fly fishers and the wet fly fishers. Perhaps this polarity has been responsible for rigid thinking. At any rate, I, like countless other anglers, grew up thinking of fly fishing as something you did either with a dry fly on your line *or* with wet flies on it, and it was not until recently that another approach dawned on me.

Of course, there are times when though you are technically wet fly fishing you do momentarily use a 'dry fly'. Two such occasions spring to mind. When fishing the bob fly from a boat, as you dibble or bob the top dropper fly on the surface of the loch you are actually fishing 'dry'. Again, if when fishing an upstream wet fly you have a bushy wet fly on the top dropper (which many upstream experts insist on) you may find a trout comes up and takes it 'dry' before it has sunk. This also sometimes happens if you have just tied on a new fly and it has not yet become wet enough to sink, or if you have just had lunch or a smoke and your wet flies have 'dried' in the meantime. However, these are haphazard and temporary examples of wry fly, far removed from any deliberate use of the technique.

AN ACCIDENTAL DISCOVERY

My own adoption of the method was similarly haphazard. I cannot say that I sat down and logically thought it out. Rather, I stumbled on it through a series of accidents and coincidences. Fishing is essentially a practical skill, and though the intellect is useful in the process, most developments are the result of trial and error. I had noticed, for instance, that sometimes when I was fishing with two dry flies (of this practice, more in the next chapter) the smaller of the two would sometimes become waterlogged and fish almost awash. This mattered not a jot as far as the trout were concerned – indeed there were occasions when the slightly immersed fly appeared the more appetizing of the two. I was slow to see the implications of this fact. I was also slow to strike on those occasions when a fish did take the submerged fly. Employing the more leisurely dry fly strike (because I was ostensibly fishing dry) I took a while to realize that by the time I saw the surface boil in the vicinity of my sinking fly the trout had already taken it milliseconds ago and I was, in consequence, infinitesimally late in striking. My mind had not yet become trained to the idea of the 'dual strike' which wry fly requires – but more about this later.

SUPPORTING EVIDENCE

It took several seasons before any kind of deliberate policy began to form, but then, just as my ideas on the subject began to crystallize, a beginner friend of mine asked my opinion of a book he had recently acquired. It was *Teach Yourself Fly Fishing* by Maurice Wiggin, in which the method of simultaneously fishing dry and wet was mentioned. This encouraged me to experiment with the technique more seriously. Following Wiggin's suggestion, I was fishing with the dry fly on the point of my cast and the wet fly on the dropper, but I still found that I missed many of the fish that took the wet fly. It was not until the beginning of the following season that I took the next step in my wry fly education.

That spring I was resolved to fish with a wet fly, not a dry fly, on the point. April was not very kind to me (wind and high water) so it was early May before I found the conditions right for this experiment. The sixth was a bright, cloudless spring morning. I remember it as if it were yesterday; no need to refer to my fishing log book. I was up in the North Riding of Yorkshire on a beautiful upland river, running clear and at medium level.

TESTING A THEORY

I had a Medium Olive Dun as my dry fly on the dropper (size 12) and a Pheasant Tail Nymph (size 12) on the point of my leader, a no. 5 floating line and, just to complete the picture, my 8-foot (2.4 m) Cummins split-cane rod and Hardy Perfect reel. I was fishing by ten o'clock and I began to catch trout immediately – all little ones, which I returned. Fish were taking the point nymph almost exclusively but as the day advanced the trout grew bigger and the dry fly began to attract them. Fly was hatching: olives in dribs and drabs, some smuts and some red ants. I was able to stalk some individual fish I spotted; in other places I just fished the water hopefully. It was fascinating fishing. By the time I stopped for a late lunch at 3.45, I had caught 24 fish, though I did not keep them all. Of the trout I kept, several were big for the water – it was a wonderful creel.

Later I added another brace, so I ended up having caught 26 trout and grayling, of which 15 had taken the nymph and 11 the dry fly. But though I had proved this technique had much to offer, there was still a long way to go before I could be certain about it. I was brought down to earth with a bump exactly one week later at the same place when, using exactly the same tactics, I could only manage seven trout all day, of which four were keepable. Admittedly, on this second occasion the water was up after rain, and I was casting into an eye-watering downstream wind all day, but my confidence had been shaken.

However, extensive experimentation since then has convinced me that the method is indeed a winner. That first day's success turned out subsequently to have been no fluke. The whole episode also showed me how slow we anglers are to adapt to new ideas. It took me several seasons to see the significance of what I had stumbled on. We might be inventive about new fly dressings, but that is merely jumping through hoops, for one fly is more or less as good as another. By comparison with inventing a new pattern, fishing one dry and one wet fly simultaneously is a quantum leap.

HISTORY OF THE WRY FLY

The more I fished with this method, the more convinced I became that it was the 'forgotten' deadly weapon of fly fishing, a device so lethal it had been shrouded in secrecy. I began to try to trace its history, but I must admit that I have not got very far. Apart from Maurice Wiggin's description of the technique, I have come across only nine other direct references to it in print. The earliest comes from a book published in 1931, *The Art of Fly Fishing* by Colonel W. Keith Rollo. When talking about the usefulness of employing two flies at once in dry fly fishing, the author mentions the following variation: 'If trout are nymphing, a nymph or wet fly could be mounted on the point, whilst a dry fly could be mounted on the dropper.'

This is as far back into angling history that I have, as yet, been able to trace the wry fly. Unfortunately, Rollo elaborates no further – he clearly did not rate the method as highly as I do.

The second reference is found in that repository of much wisdom *The Fisherman's Vade Mecum* by G.W. Maunsell, published in 1933. As early as page 9 the method gets an airing.

Next comes W.H. Lawrie in *Border River Angling*, published in 1939. This author advocates a nymph on the dropper, saying that 'in desperation' he had tried a new idea on the Tweed one day: 'a small wet dotterel spider was knotted on to the cast as a dropper, about 24 inches [60 cm] above the dry fly.'

DISPUTED ORIGINS

Lawrie claims to have originated the system, telling us that it was 'entirely new' when he discovered it, but Rollo's 1931 reference proves that the technique was already known. I suspect the wry fly predates 1931 and that we will never learn who truly was its originator. However, Lawrie is in no doubt about its effectiveness, calling it 'the most deadly of all the available methods of nymphing' – and I agree with him.

Fourth, the technique is mentioned in a slim volume by Richard Clapham, *Trout Fishing on Hill Streams*, published in 1947.

In 1957 Dermot Wilson published a book that was re-issued in 1970 under a new title, *Fishing the Dry Fly*. In my copy (revised 3rd edition, 1987) is the reference:

> Some experts in the West Country fish dry and wet at the same time and this can be a very successful method. They use two flies on their cast, a wet fly as a tail-fly and a dry fly half way up as dropper. They cast upstream and the trout can take their choice. If they prefer the dry fly, the fisherman sees them rise. If they choose the wet fly, the dry fly acts as a sort of float which bobs visibly so that the fisherman knows when to strike.

The exact method I advocate. There is evidence here too that the West Country, as opposed to the North, might have been the breeding ground of wry fly. Wilson, however, says no more on the subject, maybe because his brief is dry fly.

In 1958 came Maurice Wiggin's book and, like Lawrie, he points out the importance of wry fly. He calls it 'neither dry nor wet, but more effective than either'. He was also rather puzzled that the technique was not more widely practised. Like Lawrie, Wiggin advocates dry fly on the point, nymph on the dropper, and he points out how the system makes upstream wet fly less problematic: 'It makes upstream wet-fly fishing as easy as upstream dry-fly fishing – but much more productive.'

The seventh and eighth mentions that I have been able to find both come from the pen of William B. Currie. In *Game Fishing* (1962) and *The Art of Trout Fishing* (1963) he describes this technique, naming it 'tired nymph' because it imitates the actions of nymphs in the exhausting process of struggling up to the surface and freedom. He advocates this as a loch tactic, but it has just as much relevance as a river method.

A MODERN VARIANT

An oblique reference to wry fly, and a variation of it, is to be found in John Roberts's *The Grayling Angler*, published in 1982. Roberts admits to tying a bit of wool on to his line to aid detection of the grayling take when he is fishing a deep nymph, especially in turbulent water or in poor light. He also touches briefly on the idea of a dry fly acting in this capacity, as a bite indicator. Roberts is clearly describing the dry fly here in a passive role only – quite different from my approach, where the dry fly also has a crucial active role. You can now buy horrid little fluorescent bite indicators for nymph fishing. Why not try a dry fly instead?

Finally, an article entitled 'The Best of Both Worlds' by James Langan appeared in *Trout and Salmon* magazine in June 1986. Langan prefers the Lawrie-Wiggin system of dry fly on the point. I was very interested to read this article, especially as I had been planning to publish one on the same subject for some time, but was depressed to see that it provoked absolutely no correspondence. Then, in October 1986, *Trout and Salmon* published an article of mine on the subject entitled 'Wry Fly Revolution', in which I put forward the value of the Rollo–Wilson system of nymph on the point. Once again, alas, the article elicited no response from readers.

It does seem that the majority of fly fishermen remain indifferent to the technique of wry fly fishing. However, the fact that such eminent angling brains as Rollo, Lawrie, Wiggin, Wilson and Currie have attributed importance to the method should be enough to convince readers of this book that it is worth trying.

A CAREFULLY GUARDED SECRET

I am inclined to think that wry fly has its origins in upstream wet fly and was first evolved during the last century. Furthermore, I think it is a method so deadly that those anglers who mastered it kept it to themselves – a jealously guarded secret which separated them from the run of anglers who took ordinary baskets. I also believe that it must be a technique which quite a few upstream fishermen discover for themselves. It probably spreads by word of mouth, especially as most publishers and editors do not seem interested in the technique. Maurice Wiggin admits that he was told of the method by 'a countryman who never reads a book'.

THE TWO METHODS OF WRY FLY FISHING

There are two ways of fishing wry fly. The first is to fish with the nymph on the point of the leader and a dry fly on the dropper. The second is to fish with the dry fly on the point of the leader and a nymph on the dropper. Each has its merits, but I believe the first method has more profound implications for the development of fly fishing. It was not until I put a nymph on the point of my leader that I began to realize the murderous efficiency of wry fly fishing.

Times have changed since Lawrie and Wiggin, who were both champions of the second system, published their books. Two subsequent developments have taken wry fly fishing a stage further: the light filmy nylon now on the market and the Frank Sawyer nymph. In 1958, the year that Wiggin's book was published, Frank Sawyer's *Nymphs and the Trout* appeared – a watershed in angling history. Just as Sawyer nymphs have revolutionized nymph fishing, so have they radically changed the much more secret world of wry fly fishing. When his book was published, Wiggin was clearly unaware of the new Sawyer technique, for the illustration in his text of the Pheasant Tail Nymph is the old standard pre-Sawyer pattern. Furthermore, the following sentence occurs in the nymph fishing section:

> Since the nymph fishes so close to the surface, you have a fair chance of seeing any rise to it.

This was clearly written under the influence of G.E.M. Skues's earlier system of nymphing.

Where our grandfathers and great-grandfathers used to fish upstream with cumbersome gut and lightly dressed, slow-sinking flies, the modern fisherman has the use of weighted, hackleless nymphs and almost unbelievably fine leader material. This tackle gives a sensitivity to and control of a wet fly that would have astonished the likes of W.C. Stewart and his generation (and doubtless a good many anglers since then). I was only eight when Sawyer's epoch-making book came out, but even I can remember using gut casts when I first fished with fly. The quality of nylon has improved immeasurably just in my short lifetime.

Let us now look in detail at the two methods of wry fly fishing.

WRY FLY WITH NYMPH ON THE POINT

Instead of putting a dry fly on the point and a nymph on a short dropper 2 ft (60 cm) up the leader I use a Sawyer nymph on the point and a dry fly on a longish dropper of about 4 in (10 cm) *at least 3 ft (90 cm) further up the cast.* See fig. 1.

The beauty of this method is that as you fish upstream the dry fly remains perkily aloft while the weighted hackleless nymph sinks deeper below. You are fishing at the same time for two quite different

Figure 1 Wry fly – first method (nymph on the point)

Figure 2 Advantages of first method

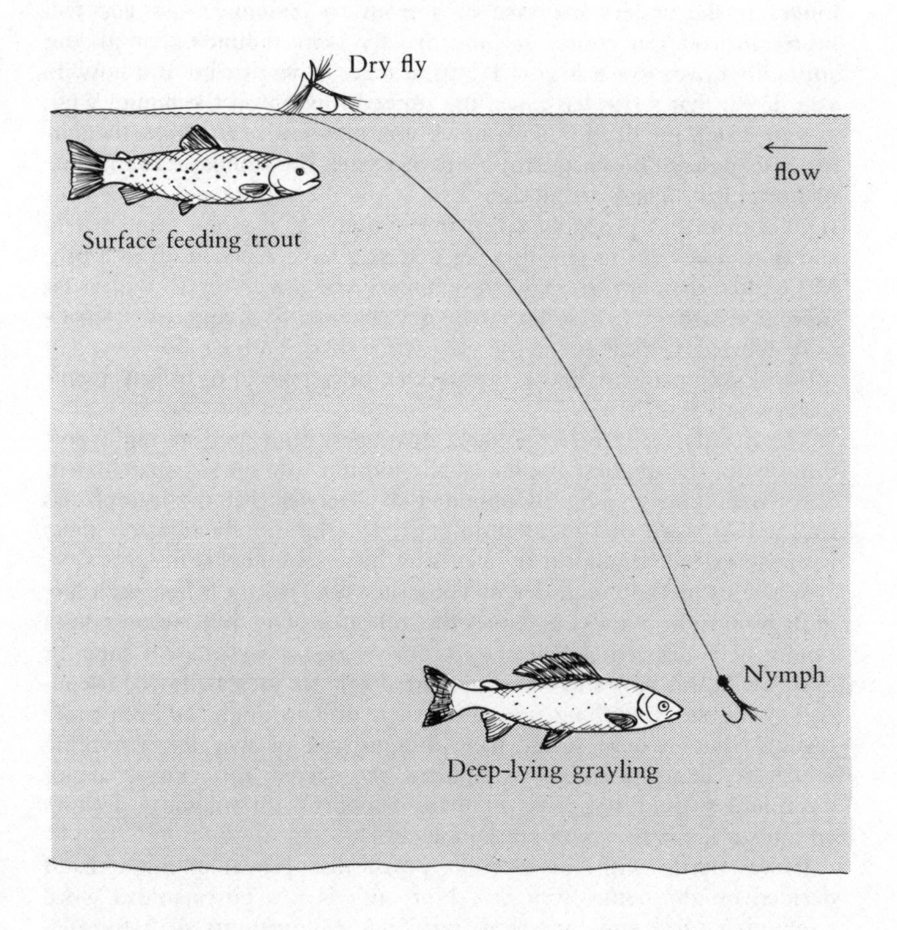

With a dry fly on the surface and a nymph near the bottom, both the surface-feeder and the deep-lying fish can be tempted.

types of feeding trout: the surface feeder and the deep feeder. There is no need to fish up a pool first with a dry fly and then with a nymph: now you can fish with both dry fly and nymph at once. When we are fishing with either a dry fly or a wet fly, we often fail to catch the biggest fish in the pool because we used a dry fly when he was lying deep, or used a deep nymph when he was scanning the surface. With wry fly this familiar twist of fate is far less likely to occur: wherever he is lying our system can attract him. See fig. 2.

EFFECTIVE TAKE INDICATION

This is just the first of several advantages of fishing wry fly in this way. The second is that wry fly greatly simplifies the hitherto rather complex and ambiguous techniques of nymphing and upstream wet fly. No longer is the underwater take of a trout so intangible. As you fish upstream you can clearly see the dry fly come bouncing or gliding smoothly down towards you. If a trout takes it, you strike. But how do you detect that a fish has taken the sunken nymph on the point? Well, as you watch the dry fly like a hawk you may notice a slight irregularity in its passage downstream: it might twitch or wobble or even come to a brief halt. These are all signs that below the surface and out of your sight a trout has probably taken the nymph. You strike immediately and nine times out of ten discover that you have fastened on to a fish. More often than not, though, the evidence you are presented with is far more spectacular. In fast water the dry fly usually disappears dramatically when a fish takes the nymph, while in smooth or slow water it often skids upstream like a water-skier or a pike bung when a pike seizes your dead bait.

The dry fly really behaves like a float, or a buoy, registering everything from the gentlest lipping of the nymph to a greedy snatch at it. Sometimes you will be disappointed to discover that the nymph has snagged in weed or caught on a rock, for the dry fly registers these happenings too, though it is surprising how seldom this occurs.

With this method your dry fly takes on a dual role: it is not just a lure in its own right but also becomes the indicator of an underwater take. I cannot help suspecting that dry fly purists might well raise a superior eyebrow at this new and rather perverted role for their hallowed friend, and as for the nymphing fraternity, their disdain might be even more severe. Skues would surely have disapproved of wry fly. Anything which so demystified and simplified the sacred and elusive art of nymphing would not have won his support. But maybe I do him an injustice, for he was a great innovator.

It was partly with this possible purist disapproval in mind that I decided on the name 'wry fly'. Not only is it a portmanteau word combining 'dry' and 'wet' but 'wry' has connotations of 'perverse', 'distorted', 'crooked', and 'in the wrong direction'. All this is more than enough to make a purist pull a wry face! There is finally another more personal reason for choosing the term. It is a pun on Rye, the Yorkshire river on which I perfected the technique.

A SPRINGBOARD TO UPSTREAM PROFICIENCY

The third advantage of wry fly is that it is an ideal training method, helping you to come to terms with the more subtle wiles of nymphing and upstream wet fly. I would advise any beginner who wishes to learn these latter two methods first to spend some time fishing wry fly. Because the technique makes it so easy to detect the sunk-fly take, it provides an ideal springboard from which to progress to other upstream skills.

Wry fly's fourth advantage is its especial appeal to grayling, which lie deeper than trout. Big grayling seldom rise to the surface: they are almost exclusively bottom feeders. With a deep-sunk nymph on the point you will catch grayling that a dry fly or surface nymph would never tempt. Time and time again I have ended the day with a grayling or two nearly twice the size of any trout in the creel. These big specimens always take the nymph.

The fifth benefit of wry fly fished this way is that it allows you to fish more quickly, to cover more water than with other methods. Instead of fishing pools twice – once dry, once wet – you save time by fishing once with both. You not only fish more quickly but more thoroughly, because you cover both the surface and the bed of the stream.

REDUCING UNCERTAINTY

Finally, this first method is invaluable when you do not know what is happening on a river: when there is little fly life evident and no trout are showing. Likewise, it is a very effective way of searching out unknown water, a highly recommended tactic for first visits to rivers. It is a great stand-by on hot, cold, dour, dismal and difficult days, as well as a great saver of blank days. There is never any need to resort to desperate remedies if you know how to fish a wry fly.

Nor is the deep nymph your only saviour on days when nothing is rising; and it is by no means exclusively the big-fish taker. The dry fly on your cast, particularly in early season, will often lure big trout. Time and again I have caught the biggest trout of the day on the dropper dry fly in cheerless spring weather, having not seen a rise all day – unless it was to my fly. No matter how dull and dreary the day, there will always be the odd opportunistic fish that cannot resist a bushy morsel bobbing down on the current.

I find the method most effective between mid April and the end of May. Early in the season trout seldom come to the surface and rise, unless there is a good hatch of black gnats, March browns, iron blues or dark olives. These hatches are often short-lived and the last thing you should do is switch flies about, wasting valuable minutes during these vital flurries of activity. Taking a wet fly cast off, greasing your line (or even changing reels) and then putting on a dry fly is profligate of time. Some anglers carry two rods to facilitate rapid switches, but these are usually stillwater fishers static at their pegs. On moorland rivers or heavily wooded streams where you normally cover several miles of water in a day, you are really forced to carry only one rod.

Wry fly with nymph on the point is an extremely useful compromise. By fishing a bushy Rough Olive, March Brown or Greenwell's Glory on the dropper and an Olive Nymph imitation on the point (Pheasant Tail is as good as any) you have an ideal combination to attract trout early in the season. The dry fly is already there on your line if a rise should occur, and it is also very handy to have there in the periods just before and just after a rise when either the pre-emptive trout or the greedy lingerer can be picked up.

THE DRY FLY'S ASCENDANCY

As the season progresses the dry fly comes more and more into its own. A typical division of capture using wry fly in early April might be: twelve fish caught – three on the dry fly, nine on the nymph. By the end of May this situation is quite likely to be reversed: twelve fish caught – nine on the dry fly, three on the nymph. There will be odd exceptions to this rule but I have found that it generally holds good. Here is an example from my own records, based on the month I first used the method of wry fly with nymph on the point:

Date	Fish caught	Dry fly	Nymph
6 May	26	11	15
12 May	7	0	7
17 May	20	11	9
18 May	24	11	13
25 May	18	14	4
29 May	10	7	3

There is one discrepancy in the middle of the month, but the overall picture shows the increasing efficacy of the dry fly as summer nears.

A more recent example, from April 1987, is an even neater illustration (though somewhat less impressive in terms of fish: I fished mainly with three wet flies because of the chill conditions):

Date	Fish caught	Dry fly	Nymph
4 April	11	2	9
5 April	9	3	6
19 April	5	3	2

This analysis raises an important point. While wry fly is a very important method of fly fishing, either as a 'utility' method on some days or as unquestionably the best one on others, it is by no means always the best approach. There are many occasions when it is better to fish with either a dry fly or a wet fly. The spring of 1987 was cold, wet and blowy, and I found the traditional team of three wet flies fished downstream was the most successful method. In the latter part of May, however, it was with a traditionally fished dry fly that I did best.

VARYING PATTERNS

As the season progresses you will find that the patterns of dry fly used with wry fly will also change. By May, gone will be the Rough Olives; now the Gold Ribbed Hare's Ear comes into its own and fancy flies such as the wondrous Wickham's Fancy. Other good dry flies to try are: Coch-y-bondhu (especially in tree-lined stretches where terrestrial insects are prone to fall into the water), Blanchard's Abortion (an excellent 'floater' in rough water), Silver Sedge, Black Gnat or Alder, John Storey, Ginger Quill, Red Palmer, Baigent's Brown and Blue Dun or Tup's Indispensable, while Greenwell's Glory also remains wonderfully successful all season.

With the nymph I find less need for variation. Sawyer's Pheasant Tail is as far as any angler need look. With this basic pattern, on varied hook sizes from 10 to 16 (12 and 14 being the most useful), you can fish successfully all season. A few long-shank variations of this great fly might also come in handy, for I think many fish mistake them for caddis larvae. I would personally add only one other nymph: Sawyer's Killer Bug, which is an immensely effective fly when fish are lying deep on chill, dismal days. You may prefer to try your own favourite patterns, but if, after objective experiment, you stumble across a more killing nymph than those I have suggested then please let me know. My own personal favourite combination is dry Gold Ribbed Hare's Ear on the dropper and a Sawyer Pheasant Tail Nymph on the point, both size 12 or 14. I would be quite happy to fish this duo all season.

I find that May is the great wry fly month. Trout are becoming increasingly likely to rise and yet there is still a great deal of deep fodder for them. In the rivers I visit caddis larvae make up a large part of the fishy diet (especially for the grayling) so that the deep nymph elicits many takes even when trout are rising all over the place. Once May has gone, you may find that it profits you to fish exclusively dry fly or nymph, though wry fly will continue to reap dividends all through the season.

VARYING FISHING DEPTH

One last advantage offered by this method of wry fly is that you have the opportunity to vary the depth at which your nymph fishes. Wry fly is not unique in this, for greasing of the leader when nymphing gives you similar control, but it does provide a pleasantly simple alternative. I suggested earlier that the distance between dropper and point of the cast should be no less than 3 ft (90 cm), but you can make it *more* than this. I often use an interval of 4 ft (1.2 m) when I am fishing the deep parts of a river, or a stream running high after rain. It stands to reason that the longer you make the length of nylon between dropper and point, the deeper your nymph will fish. What wry fly enables you to do is to control exactly how deep the nymph sinks, for the dry fly, acting as a buoy, allows only the end portion of the nylon to sink.

There is nothing to prevent you using lengths of 6 ft (1.8 m) or more beyond the dry fly, but such experiments are probably only necessary on big rivers. For small rivers and streams, very long distances between dry fly and nymph are rarely necessary and I do not recommend them. Indeed such long distances provide the angler with considerable problems: for instance, casting becomes tricky because long leaders are unwieldly and prone to form bird's nests.

PROBLEMS OF WRY FLY FISHING WITH A NYMPH ON THE POINT

I have so far concentrated on the advantages of this method of wry fly fishing, but it does have its drawbacks. The first problem you will encounter is the necessity for two different strikes. You must strike immediately you receive evidence that a fish has taken the nymph, but you may have to delay the strike when the dry fly is taken, especially in slow-flowing water. Generally speaking, the slower the water the greater the difference between the two strikes. In fast water you will have to strike at dry fly takes as quickly as you do those to the nymph. This is no easy thing to master.

Considerable discipline is required in order to become adept at the technique. When fishing a dry fly up a smooth stretch of river you adjust yourself to the tempo of the business and use a delayed strike. When fishing with a nymph or wet fly you adjust to a rapid strike. But with wry fly you can never settle into a rhythm, since you never know which fly will be taken next. One minute you are required to react like lightning as the nymph is taken, the next to exercise self-control and pause before striking as the dry fly is unhurriedly swallowed. You will miss lots of fish until you learn this see-saw discipline. Personally, I find I miss more rises to the dry fly than I do to the nymph because a reflex response is generally a quick one and this suits the nymph strike better.

CASTING PROBLEMS

The next disadvantage involves the extra problems wry fly creates for casting. With a small lightly dressed nymph on the point and a manageable leader length (totalling 8–9 ft/2.4–2.7 m) you will not find casting difficult, but with a heavy nymph on the point your hazards increase. Tangles are more likely – remember you have two flies on the line. Sawyer Bugs are very deadly but they are not ideal flies for casting on light lines. A dry fly halfway up the leader unbalances the outfit even more. Heavy point flies also hinder false casting, which you need to do to keep the dry fly nicely fluffed up. The extra effort false casting requires with bugs on the point multiplies the chances of tangles and bird's nests. A vicious circle!

Good though bugs are, they do create extra problems in wry fly fishing. You will find that if you fail to keep up the false casting scrupulously (which requires great vigilance) your dry fly will soon get inundated and you will be fishing with two wet flies on your line. Pheasant Tail Nymphs are more easily handled and you might find them preferable on purely technical grounds. It is better to limit your use of bugs to the odd deep pool, or to those places where you have located a shoal of grayling.

It also stands to reason that long, unwieldy leaders multiply all the problems I have just discussed. The 4-foot (1.2 m) length I mentioned earlier is really the comfortable maximum distance between the two flies, but 3 ft (90 cm) is ideal. Of course, a big rod and heavy fly line help with these snags – a 9-foot (2.7 m) rod with no. 7 WF (Weight Forward) line can manoeuvre Sawyer bugs without any difficulty – but many of the rivers I propose you should try require much finer tackle. On an 8-foot (2.4 m) rod with a no. 4 or 5 line and a 3 lb (1.35 kg) b.s. tippet a heavy bug will feel like a hand grenade, and is potentially as lethal! Add to all this the problem of trees and the necessity of using side casts and you can begin to imagine the difficulties involved.

PRESENTATION PROBLEMS

The third disadvantage of this type of wry fly concerns presentation. Two flies make more disturbance when they land on the water than does one. There is unquestionably a sacrifice in delicacy with wry fly. In still parts of the river where gossamer presentation is necessary it is best to switch to either dry fly or nymph. Sometimes the sight of a fluttering dry fly disturbs the nymphing fish in a still pool, and likewise the plop of a bug can frighten the surface feeder (though it can also induce him to snatch it greedily). As a general rule wry fly has its limitations in clear, still parts of the river but comes into its own in the streamy, ripply places.

A further presentation problem occurs when you want to cover a rising fish just off the opposite bank. With a nymph 3 ft (90 cm) or so beyond, obviously you cannot put your dry fly on the trout's nose without fouling the bank. At such moments the best solution is to take off the nymph, put the dry fly of your choice on the point and then cover the rising fish.

SNAGGING

The fourth disadvantage is that if a trout takes the dry fly the trailing nymph may catch on underwater vegetation or rocks during the fight. The heavier the nymph, the greater the hazard. Furthermore, the longer the length of nylon between the two flies the more vulnerable you are. Once or twice a season I lose a fish this way and you must just accept it as one of the risks of wry fly fishing. On the other hand there will be occasions, admittedly rare, when the same tendency works to your benefit. From time to time when I have hooked a trout on the nymph, another has taken the dry fly submerged during the fight. Indeed, I once took the best trout of the day like this. Playing two trout on your line at once is always likely to quicken the pulse.

UNWIELDY METHOD

The fifth and final disadvantage of wry fly fished this way is really a combination of its other major drawbacks. Deadly though the method is, it is more cumbersome and unwieldy than a single fly attack. You do not have quite the same control, or access to tricky places, as you do with a solo dry fly or solo nymph. Therefore, for the most delicate or ambitious tasks I do not recommend wry fly.

In summing up, I urge you to try this method if you have never done so before. Wry fly with nymph on the point has revolutionized my fly fishing and trebled my baskets. In the May I first tried it I caught over one hundred wild brown trout on that method alone. It is best used as a way of fishing the water, as opposed to fishing the rise, though I have successfully used it to cover individual trout that I have spied on numerous occasions. It is tailor-made for rushing, tumbling, rippling or streamy kinds of water and is ideal for the rivers of the North and West. It is generally most effective in the first half of the season but remains a valid method throughout the fly fisherman's calendar.

Finally, this method is an immensely enjoyable way of fishing: you never know quite what to expect. But you can depend on it being always varied, always exciting and always profitable.

WRY FLY WITH DRY FLY ON THE POINT

The second method of fishing a wry fly is with a dry fly on the point of your cast and a nymph on the dropper. This is the method favoured in the most recently published references to wry fly. However, though it is a good system of fishing, I regard it as by no means as revolutionary – or as effective – as the method I have already outlined.

You put a dry fly on a cast of standard length, 8–9 ft (2.4–2.7 m), and a nymph or traditional wet fly on a dropper about 2½ ft (80 cm) distant from it. I say 'about' because this distance is not so critical as with the other method. However, it should not be more than 3 ft

Figure 3 Wry fly – second method (dry fly on the point)

Both flies are fished near the surface: the point dry fly just above, the wet fly just below.

Figure 4 Advantages of second method

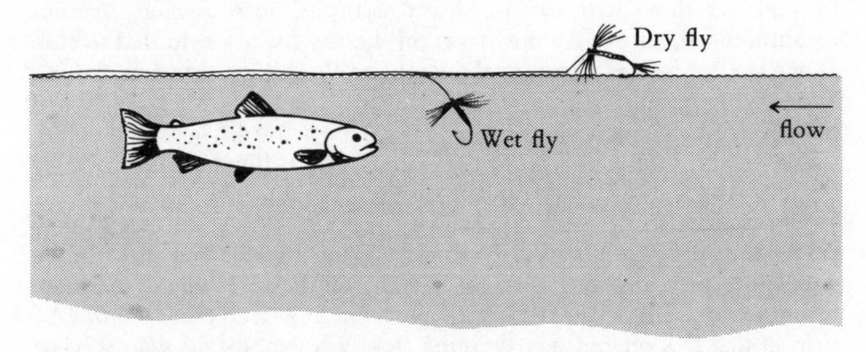

The buoyant dry fly transmits an attractive bobbing action to the wet fly below. A trout can choose between the two.

(90 cm), for reasons I will explain shortly. The length of the dropper should be 2–4 in (5–10 cm), according to preference (and your skill in casting, since the longer the dropper the more vulnerable it is to tangles). A good compromise is 3 in (7.5 cm). See fig. 3.

SHALLOW METHOD

It becomes immediately apparent when you fish with a dry fly on the point that the nymph cannot sink deep at all; indeed, it can only sink to a depth corresponding to the length of the dropper. For this reason wry fly of this type is more attractive to surface-feeding fish than to deep-lying ones. Deep-lying trout and grayling may well be induced to dash up and take the dry fly but are less likely to rise to the nymph. As for the biggest grayling, they will most likely spurn all efforts to attract them with this method. See fig. 4.

This method of wry fly fishing is just a variant of dry fly fishing. You fish carefully upstream, searching out the water exactly as you do with orthodox dry fly. You can cover the opposite bank without difficulty, unlike the other system. Indeed, wry fly with dry fly on the point is altogether easier to handle, being less cumbersome. Casting presents no extra problems, nor does false casting, so it is far easier to keep your dry fly fluffy and floatable this way. This method of wry fly fishing has fewer of the drawbacks of the other method, though fewer of its great advantages either.

FLY CHOICE

For the dry fly, standard patterns, or any pattern of your choice, can be used, but with the nymph you face constraints. The Sawyer type of nymph is clearly unsuitable for it is designed to sink, but here the dry fly will not allow it to do so. Heavy nymphs, such as bugs, are not recommended, since they put strain on the dry fly and help that to sink as well. Use instead traditional North or West Country wet flies or Skues-type nymphs. You could also try Buzzers, especially when midges are hatching.

Personally, I think a dark, spidery kind of fly is the most effective for the job. As the dry fly bobs up and down on the current it transmits the same impulses to the sunk fly, which must also bob about attractively below the surface. Spiders have long, waving hackles and these prove irresistible to many fish that catch sight of them. I would therefore recommend a Black and Peacock Spider or Stewart Spider – indeed I suspect that this type of wry fly quite closely resembles the way Stewart must have fished his wet flies. I think he would have approved heartily of wry fly, and had he stumbled across the method in his lifetime I believe he would have been one of the greatest wry fly exponents.

Another great fisherman, a much more recent one, invented a type of fishing all of his own. Eric Horsfall Turner's Beetle, fished just submerged with a greased leader, brought him tremendous results, and many North Country fishermen still emulate his initial success with the method. Actually, Skues discovered an almost identical method of fishing the century before Turner, when he learnt to fish an Alder slightly sunk. Both of these discoveries were in effect pre-empted by Stewart and are variants of that energetic Scotsman's spiders.

Thus Eric's Beetle, or an Alder, are also splendid flies to try on your dropper. I myself rather favour simplicity in all things and often do not trouble to open my nymph box at all. A small dry fly pattern of Black Gnat, if not treated with floatant, fishes wonderfully well as your wet fly. I took a splendid bag of trout recently on the River Dove in Yorkshire using exactly this method.

Three other patterns are worthy of mention. Waterhen Bloa and Snipe and Purple are deadly on the dropper – especially the latter – as is a Coch-y-bondhu (a pattern very similar to Eric's Beetle).

It has been suggested that this method works well with matching dressings. If, for instance, dark olives are hatching then a Greenwell's Glory nymph and dry fly should be fished to represent both the hatching nymph and the newly hatched dun. This is neat thinking, a very pretty idea, and no doubt worth trying, but I believe you will find that wavy spiders will beat most 'representative' nymphs on all but the stillest of waters.

RISE DETECTION

Detecting a rise to the nymph with this method is not quite the clear cut thing it is with the other. Sometimes there is no problem whatsoever: you see the dry fly jerk, then strike to find the fish is hooked. But it does not always happen like this. With the first method, as soon as a trout takes the deep nymph the progress of the line downstream is immediately arrested. If the fish is big and powerful, the take violent, or the current rapid, the dry fly usually obligingly disappears. The same is not so with dry fly on the point. Visualize it: a fish sedately takes the dropper nymph in streamy water and stays in his station. The dry fly continues to drift downstream towards you without registering any twitch or shudder. You miss the fish for you never even knew it had taken. I suspect misses of this kind are quite common with this form of wry fly. I certainly miss trout to the nymph this way but rarely do I miss them the other way.

To be on the safe side, you must not only watch the point dry fly when you use this method but keep an eye on the patch of water where you believe the sunk nymph to be. If you see a slight disturbance at the surface, a bulge or a dimple, then strike straight away. I often connect with fish this way before I ever see any clue from the dry fly. The greater the distance between dry fly and nymph the more difficult it is to keep an eye on both; hence a suggested length of around 2 ft (60 cm) between the two. Experiment to find your own ideal visual tolerance.

SEASONAL FACTORS

As to the best time of the year to use this second method of wry fly, I suggest later in the season rather than earlier. Though it will work in spring it is really only effective during hatches then, which can be pretty short. It comes into its own in high summer when all kinds of different feeders are on the prowl – every trout from the greedy sucker to the fastidious nibbler, from the fish steady at his station to the cruiser. It is good in the dog days of a hot summer, and on lazy August afternoons in low water. On chill, dismal spring days it is not much good at all.

This second method is good and will often beat a well-fished solo dry fly or nymph. But the first, especially on its day, is sensational. Each has its charms and its drawbacks, and I would not be without either. As

Figure 5 Comparison of the two methods

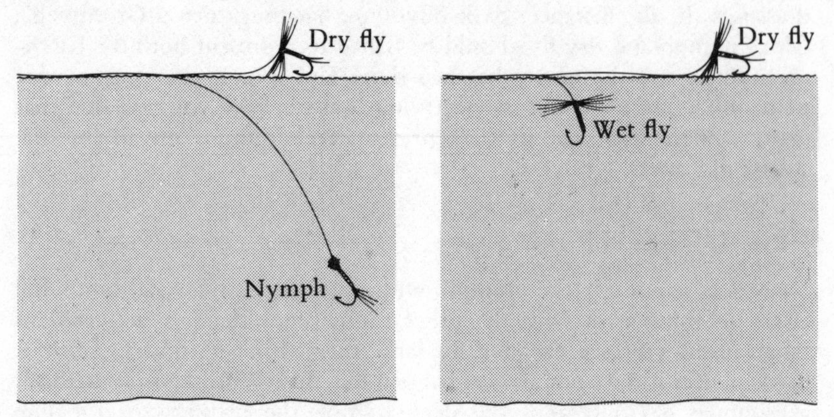

Fishing with the nymph on the point has the advantage of attracting both the deep nympher and the surface feeder. The deep nymph could lure bottom-grubbing grayling of size.

Fishing with the dry fly on the point is basically for surface-feeding trout, though deep-lying trout may dash up to take the dry fly. Big grayling rarely venture up for either fly.

Figure 6 Choice of fly to present to a fish

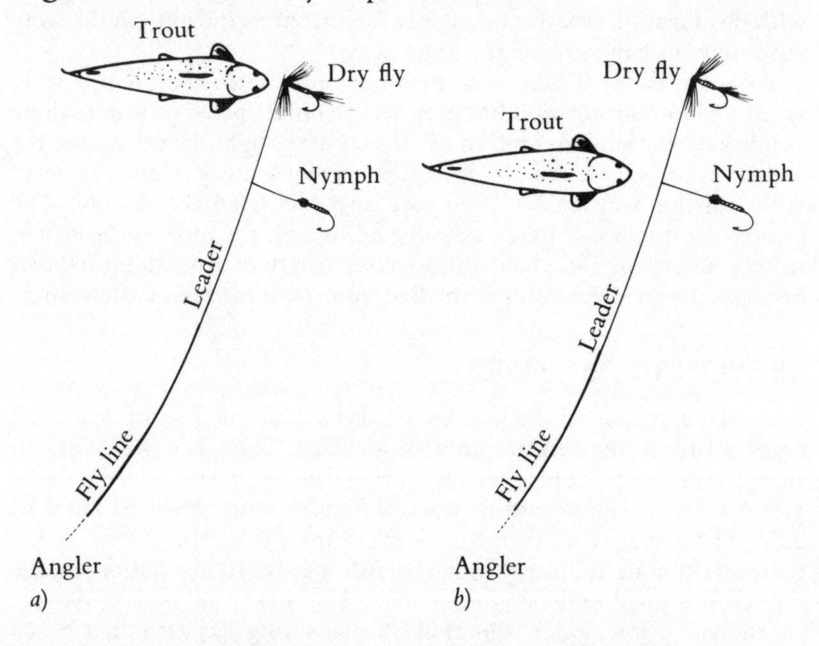

You have a tactical choice when fishing two (or three) flies. Either a) present the point dry fly first, or b) present the dropper nymph. The point dry fly presentation (a) has the advantage that the trout will see less nylon.

I am primarily a dry fly man I should prefer the second method, but I prefer the first, because it is so deadly and so mysterious. It fascinates me to think I am combing both the surface and the bed of the stream with every cast. See fig. 5.

A few final points on the differences between the two methods. While both are ideally suited to fishing the water, the second is perhaps better for fishing the rise. If you do see a rising fish you have two options – which fly to cover him with first? If the fish is lying directly upstream of you it is probably best to throw both flies above him, giving him two chances. With a fish lying opposite your position you have a rather different tactical choice. Perhaps it is best to cover him with the dry fly first as you will be presenting him with less nylon. At any rate be aware that you have a nymph on your line (because it is sunk and invisible) and if you believe you are covering a fish with the visible dry fly first, he may in fact see the nymph first and take that. Keep on your toes! Wry fly will make you a more exact judge of distances than you have ever been before! See fig. 6.

Finally, you must fish both methods of wry fly with a well-greased floating line. There is no need to grease the leader, though I normally grease the first 1 ft (30 cm) or so adjacent to my fly line, just to ensure maximum buoyancy. I shall return to wry fly later, but first let us look at another method that uses two flies on the line: the productive practice of fishing two dry flies at once, or, as I call it, twin dry fly.

2

Twin Dry Fly

'But yet I'll make assurance double sure.'
Macbeth

I cannot remember when I first fished with two dry flies on my line; it was a long time ago, but, rather as with my wry fly experiments, it was not until comparatively recently that I realized the full potential of the method. For years I messed about with the method at idle moments without thinking deeply about it.

A few seasons ago I went to fish the Aberdeenshire Don as the guest of Alan Bell-Tawse of Culquoich and talked with him at length about the technique of fishing two dry flies on the same cast. In his youth this gentleman had been taught to dress his flies by the celebrated Dr William Baigent of Northallerton, who used to fish the Don regularly, for which river his famous Variants had been specifically designed. Of course, as a North Country fisherman I was acquainted with the dry fly known as Baigent's Brown, but had not realized that the great doctor used to fish with two dry flies, the Black and the Brown Variant, on the same cast. My host tied me up a few of these lovely flies – in his fingers as Dr Baigent had taught him (Roger Woolley never used a vice either, like many other professional dressers in the past) and then took me down to the water, where he fished with two dry flies simultaneously. I followed suit.

The Don is a rocky, rapid, rushing river in its upper reaches; streams and pools tumble into one another with uniform vigour. The dry fly fishing here is a rather remorseless affair. You fish from pool to pool without much relief. There are few quiet glides, smooth flats or restful reaches; instead the current bubbles and surges down towards you, bouncing through the rocks with which it is strewn. Trout lie in every pocket, hollow and sweep and rush up to seize your fly with a wild eagerness which has to be seen to be believed. Once hooked, they leap about with a savage intensity, and they run big – I had nothing under 1 lb (0.5 kg) on this visit. It is an utterly different affair from the serene calm of the Kennet (which I fished for the first time a few seasons ago) with its lush, buttercup-filled meadows criss-crossed with canal-like side channels. Here the calm seems to rub off on the trout for in comparison they are sluggish and apathetic when hooked.

Yet, despite their differences, both rivers are dry fly waters, though the skills and techniques required to fish them remain very different. William B. Currie (a favourite modern writer of mine) summarizes perfectly the often subtle differences between the many varied types of dry fly fishing.

> There is obviously a scale involved in dry fly fishing. At one end is the rough stream fishing which looks like a version of nymphing upstream, where the fly may disappear or where the water may be fished at random. At the other end is the delicate art of stalking rising trout on chalk streams or on the clear glides of a limestone river where individual fish are noted, studied, stalked and covered, perhaps for fishing day after fishing day until someone gets the pattern and the range and the drag problem sorted out, and he is on. What satisfaction that gives! Between these extremes is the whole range of dry fly fishing, some of it inclining more to the accurate placing of a long line, and some of it more characterised by short line fishing and wading. Dry fly fishing is a single category of fly fishing in most books, but it is certainly not a single art in practice.

My experience on the Don brought home to me the sense of using two dry flies at once. On rough, turbulent water each fly helps to buoy up the other and with two flies you have more of a target to look for should you momentarily lose sight of the end of your cast. I had not worked out all the subtleties and advantages of the method by the end of this visit but I had begun to think about it seriously, deciding to test it rigorously on other rivers. Thus began my enquiry into the practice of what, for the sake of convenience, I call twin dry fly.

THE ADVANTAGES OF TWIN DRY FLY

There are, by my reckoning, a dozen advantages to fishing twin dry fly. Here they are in rough order of merit. The first advantage, probably the most obvious one logically, is that with twin dry fly you have twice the chance of rising a trout that you have when fishing orthodox dry fly. This advantage is particularly heightened in streamy water, where even the most suspicious trout is unable to perceive that the two flies are in any way connected. Any method which doubles a fisherman's chances is bound to be of interest to him!

The second advantage is that with this system each dry fly acts as a buoy for the other and they become even more unsinkable as a result. This benefit must not be under-estimated, especially in very rough, turbulent water. On rushing, surging rivers such as the Don, where it is always a problem keeping your dry fly afloat, twin dry fly is a superior system to orthodox dry fly, as Baigent discovered.

ELIMINATING DRAG

The third advantage is that twin dry fly is invaluable as an eliminator of drag. Of course, it will not counteract the most troublesome drag (no system will) but it is certainly more robust than a single dry fly. In boisterous water full of cross-currents it is surprising how nicely two flies can be made to fish. If you can place one fly in one current and the other in another current adjacent to it then the pull of one fly on the other steadies the progress of each. It takes a bit of practice to get the best out of this method; basically you use each fly to adjust the other. Much of the process is hit or miss, and explanatory diagrams would be almost impossible. Far more valuable is experimenting and working out the possibilities for yourself.

You may find altering the size of fly will help: the bigger the fly the more of an anchor it makes. For fishing tricky backwaters protected by a strong current, you could try putting a really big dry fly on the dropper and then placing the point fly of your choice into the eddy beyond. Sometimes, but not always, the anchoring dry fly will stabilize your point fly for just long enough to allow a trout to take it.

USING A SMALL FLY ON THE DROPPER

The fourth advantage, and a very crucial one, is that twin dry fly enables you to fish a small dry fly, smaller than would be feasible with single dry fly, in fast or broken water. By using a big fly as a marker on the point you can fish in difficult places with a tiny fly on the dropper, a fly so small that you cannot see it. The trout will see it though! There are infuriating days when they will only take minuscule flies such as smuts, caenis, and the like. All you do is not only watch the big marker fly on the point but be aware also of the patch of water where you estimate your dropper is (about 2 ft/60 cm up the cast). Should you see any disturbance in this vicinity you strike, for it may well indicate that a trout has taken. So too the marker dry fly may skate backwards or under – a sure sign that the tiny fly on the dropper has been taken.

This technique is also very useful on still or smooth water in poor light, or if you have to make a long cast with a small fly. You select a marker fly which will be visible in the particular conditions and present the fly on the dropper to the rising trout you are after. The marker will help you register the take. Also be prepared for the trout to take the big marker fly, which they sometimes do, often slashing at it savagely and causing the angler to miss a heartbeat and strike too slowly.

The evening rise is a time when this policy may reap dividends. The fish may be taking a fly so small that you cannot see your imitation in the failing light. With a big pale marker on the point you find that you get round this problem. You might also obviate that frustrating situation in which having at last hit on the killing fly, you find that it is becoming too dark to see it any longer. Be ready for a fish to take the marker though, for in the gloom your big, bushy point fly will often be mistaken for a moth.

IMPROVED VISIBILITY

The fifth advantage is that of visibility. In disturbed water where it is difficult to see even a big, fluffy dry fly, two flies are more visible than one. As soon as you catch sight of one fly you will know the other is nearby. It is important not to set your flies too far apart on the line for this very reason. The suggested distance is 2 ft (60 cm), but you could try 18 in (45 cm) in very rough water. Another trick is to select two flies of radically different colour, one pale, the other dark (for instance, a big Tup's Indispensable or Jock Scott and a bushy Coch-y-bondhu or Knotted Gnat) so that at least one will be visible at any one time, whether it is glary or gloomy. Baigent used this system. The Baigent Brown is mid brown in appearance with a pale body, whereas the Baigent Black is a very dark fly.

DOUBLE APPEAL

The sixth advantage of twin dry fly is that you can appeal to more than one side of a trout's personality at once. If you put both an imitation of a natural and a fancy fly on at the same time, the first will possibly deceive a trout with its realism, while the second may excite him by arousing his curiosity, jealousy, greed or aggression. With a fly such as a Greenwell's Glory, Orange Quill, Lunn's Particular or Sherry Spinner on your cast as imitations of ephemerids, you could try, as contrast, attractors such as Wickham's Fancy, Sturdy's Fancy, John Storey, dry Peter Ross, dry Jock Scott, Blanchard's Abortion or Grey Wulff. How often have I seen a trout or grayling come up to take one of the flies on the cast, spurn it, then promptly take the other! The two flies, if carefully chosen, work well as a team in this respect. Sometimes a fish is attracted initially to the fancy fly but takes the ephemerid copy; at other times a fish scrutinizes the copy then suddenly sights its meretricious companion and snatches greedily at that.

This throws up a question of tactics: is it better to put the imitative fly on the point or on the dropper? I favour its position on the dropper with the flashy fly on the point, especially for fishing the water speculatively. However, there may be occasions when the imitation is best on the end of the line, where it can be presented to a rising fish more delicately with less nylon on display.

IMAGINATIVE TACTICS

The seventh advantage is that you can fish a fly that is a proven success on the type of water you are visiting at the same time as another less tried one. This might involve you choosing not necessarily the fly the fish are taking but the one you think they *ought* to be taking. This is not as daft as it sounds. Imagine you are fishing a river about which you have extensive local knowledge. It is the time of year when you know one pattern of fly to be particularly deadly. On arriving at the river you perceive that there is already a rise in progress but not to the type of fly you had expected. Orthodox dry fly theory dictates that you put on whatever fly you perceive these fish to be taking. With twin dry fly, however, you can still use this fly but also have the luxury of knotting on to your cast the fly you *imagine* they should be taking. It is surprising how often this tactic pays dividends and I can commend it.

The fly that I use most often in this role is the Black Gnat. I seldom examine a trout's stomach, at any time in the season, without finding some members of the order Diptera contained within it. A Black Gnat is more than a mere representation of its actual namesake, but it can also be mistaken by trout for various midges, houseflies, hawthorn flies, bluebottles and any small terrestrial insects which stray on to the water such as spiders, ants or beetles. I find the Black Gnat a very deadly fly throughout the season, especially on tree-lined rivers where insects fall from branches. It is one of my constant stand-bys. I very often fish with the Black Gnat on the dropper and either an ephemerid copy or a fancy dry fly on the point.

The eighth advantage: twin dry fly is a great time-saver. You can change two flies at a time in your quest to find out what pattern appeals to trout on any particular day. This way you often find out which fly to use more quickly than does the solo fly, orthodox fisher.

TWO OPTIONS

The ninth advantage is a tactical one. As you approach a rising trout you have the choice of two flies to present to him, whereas the orthodox fisher only has one. This bonus can prove a time-saver too. The choice of which fly to present first also has important tactical implications. For instance, do you try the imitative fly on your cast first, or do you try to appeal to the trout's greed or aggression and show the fancy fly first? Speed is sometimes of the essence in fishing and with twin dry fly you have options denied to the solo dry fly purist.

The tenth advantage is the usefulness of twin dry fly in mayfly time. I do not advise two different patterns of mayfly (though there is no reason why you should not experiment) but the use of a much smaller dry fly on the dropper than the big mayfly on the point. The ideal smaller fly is a Black Gnat or Knotted Midge. There are two reasons for this tactic. The first is that I have often noticed trout at mayfly time suddenly switch to smutting or taking midges, even when a good supply of drakes or spent gnat are still on the water. Sometimes we are slow to spot such a switch, and so to start off with a little midge on your dropper is no bad idea, for you are prepared for this phenomenon should it occur. Incidentally, this often happens in early evening.

The second reason for this practice is that fishing in mayfly time is not always easy. 'Duffers' Fortnight' can be rather a misnomer. Not every day in the fourteen is a cinch. Once trout get glutted on mayfly they can become quite sniffy about your artificial Grey or Green Drake, but you might find that your small, insignificant Black Gnat or Knotted Midge proves very appetizing.

Harry Plunket-Greene states that he often used his beloved Iron Blue Dun at mayfly time with excellent results. I think his shade would shudder at the idea of twin dry fly, for he was the purist supreme, but you could try knotting his suggestion of Iron Blue on your dropper. A good standard ephemerid copy such as Greenwell's Glory could also prove effective.

MIDGE AND GNAT IMITATIONS

This trick of having a Black Gnat or Midge on your dropper so as to be ready for midging or smutting trout is not just advisable during mayfly time, but at the tail end of any big hatch. Trout, once they get glutted on any biggish fly, often suddenly switch en masse to taking smuts or midges, almost as if they regarded these humble offerings as a tasty dessert. Watch out for this in early spring too – at the end of good hatches of iron blues or dark olives the trout can often go mad on midges or gnats.

One of the most spectacular spring rises that I have ever seen was, I suspect, a chironomid or black gnat rise. Both dark olives and iron blues were hatching but no copy of either of these appealed to the trout. In my inexperience I never tried a small black fly. I fancy I might have made a wonderful discovery had I done so. How many superb rises I witnessed in my youth that I should like to re-fish now!

GRAYLING ATTRACTORS

The eleventh advantage pertains to those rivers that contain a good head of grayling as well as trout. You might well find it advantageous to use a known grayling attractor as one of the two flies. Such a fly which springs instantly to mind is Sturdy's Fancy. Other stalwarts are the Red Tag, Grey Duster and Treacle Parkin. A dry Peter Ross is also a deadly grayling fly. This tactic can help make your basket heavier and your day more interesting. A combination of flashy grayling fly and more sedate ephemerid copy (for instance, Sturdy's Fancy and Greenwell's Glory) beats the approach of the solo fly fisher, who must choose either one fly or the other.

I had a curious experience on the Eden years ago when I found trout and grayling rising avidly side by side in a strong run. The grayling would only take a white fly and the trout a brown one. By the time I had sorted out this perplexing discovery I had missed many good takes (principally because two different strikes were required – a rapid one for the umber, a more deliberate one for the trout) and caught only a quarter of the fish I felt I should have taken. Had I been fishing twin dry fly on that occasion I would probably have cottoned on more quickly and taken more fish.

I might add here that despite the advice I have received over the years about the necessity of always having something red in your fly when fishing for grayling (thus Red Tag or Bradshaw's Fancy) or that grayling prefer a pale fly to a dark one, experience has taught me otherwise. I have no hesitation in naming the Black Gnat as the most deadly fly I have come across for grayling. It is always my first choice when I suspect grayling are about, at least while their season coincides with that of the trout. Later in the year, I have found, fancy reds and whites come more into their own.

FLEXIBILITY

The final advantage of twin dry fly is that, with a dropper already tied on my cast, I can switch in under a minute to wry fly if I so wish. This is really useful. Speed is often required in fishing, especially when light is fading or bad weather threatens. Flexibility is often required too. If you can make your tactical changes swift then, like a good general, you win the battle. For example, if you are fishing twin dry fly with a Black Gnat on the dropper you can suddenly change to wry fly by merely allowing the Black Gnat to sink. This can be done either by not applying floatant to the fly, or by soaking it for a second or two in your mouth – saliva is an excellent sinking agent. This is a tacitc I have often employed, and it can be almost immediately exploited when you are fishing with twin dry fly, though the orthodox fisher has no such instantaneous flexibility.

THE DISADVANTAGES OF TWIN DRY FLY

Acting as a counterbalance are four disadvantages to this technique. The first is the greatest: two flies are more visible than one and sometimes can frighten trout. Two flies alighting on the water together make more disturbance than one fly alone, so that in the stiller pools of rivers you may find twin dry fly a liability. One temporary solution is to remove the dropper fly until you have fished the slow pool. I sometimes do this, still leaving a few inches of dropper on the cast so that I can retie my second fly on whenever I wish.

The second disadvantage is that just as twin dry fly can help to eliminate drag, so it can on occasion create extra drag. Two dragging dry flies obviously give more of a scare to a trout than does one, so this danger must always be borne in mind.

The third disadvantage is that two flies on your line are slightly more vulnerable to tangles and bird's nests (even more so for beginners) than is a solo fly.

The fourth disadvantage is that it is easier to snag in trees and other clutching riparian vegetation when you are using two flies rather than one. For casts into very tricky and inaccessible places solo dry fly beats twin dry fly. Again, nip off your dropper fly before attempting a particularly adventurous cast.

ADAPTABLE APPROACH

In my view, the merits of twin dry fly heavily outweigh these drawbacks, and I have no hesitation in suggesting you try it out. While it is true that twin dry fly is probably of more use to you on a Don-type river than on a Kennet-type one, I prefer to avoid cast-iron generalizations. For example, if I were casting to a shy fish in a smooth glide on the Don I would choose orthodox dry fly. Likewise, when fishing up a rapid, bubbling channel through the cress beds in Kennet country I would plump for twin dry fly, if club rules did not disqualify this. Better to decide your tactics by the side of each individual pool or run than make rash generalizations about rivers as a whole. Flexibility is the recipe for success.

Some clubs, associations and day ticket waters have long lists of prohibitions among their rules. Sometimes I can see the sense in these – the forbidding of maggots, for example – but some such interdicts I find footling and idiotic. There are still clubs which will not permit nymph fishing. This is not progress – it is atrophy. Once upon a time, to the hidebound and narrow-minded, nymph fishing seemed the thin end of the wedge, but it has not proved to be so. Indeed it has lifted fly fishing to a new plateau of skill, enriching the sport rather than killing it.

The same is true, I believe, of twin dry fly and wry fly. They are not the beginning of the end but show a new way to more interesting fishing and even higher levels of skill. Nevertheless you might find that some clubs stipulate a one-fly-only rule. This will exclude twin dry fly, and you must comply with the regulation. We can only hope that enlightenment will ultimately come to these doddery and archaic institutions.

AN ESSENTIAL WEAPON

If I had to limit myself to orthodox, single fly dry fly fishing I would feel like a modern batsman facing a fast bowler without his protective helmet, or a Grand Prix driver deprived of his eight-second tyre change. Once you have learnt to live with these things it seems you cannot do without them! Twin dry fly is a vital part of dry fly fishing, an essential weapon in the modern fly fisherman's armoury. I did not invent the technique – cleverer, more original men than I did – but I am an ardent champion of it.

Near the beginning of this chapter I quoted William B. Currie, who points out that there are several different types of dry fly fishing, each one evolved for different kinds of river (or parts of rivers). Twin dry fly

Figure 7 Twin dry fly

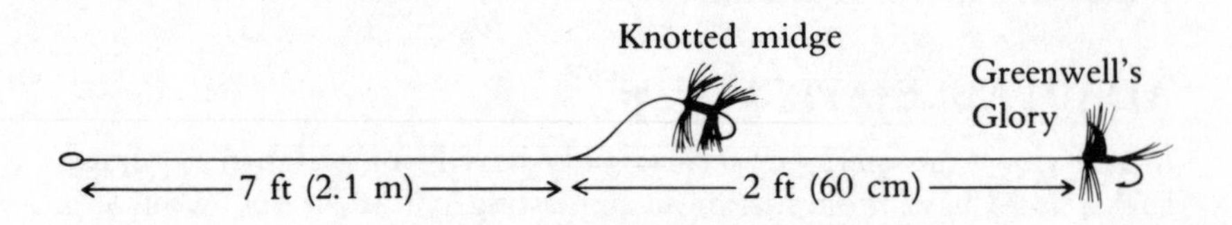

With twin dry fly, beware of leaving too great a gap between the two flies. A distance of 2 ft (60 cm) is suggested. Much more than this and you will have difficulty keeping an eye on both flies in rough water.

is but one of these branches of dry fly technique. It is a method which has not been written about often, or much publicized, but the time has come for its efficacy to become more widely known. The earliest reference to twin dry fly that I can find is in *Dry Fly Fishing* by R.C. Bridgett, published in 1922, but the fullest account of the technique that I have come across is in W. Keith Rollo's *The Art of Fly Fishing* (1931). In this book you will also find out more about Dr William Baigent's dressings and theories. Charles Ritz, in his book *A Fly Fisher's Life* (1953), touches on the subject briefly, because one of his friends apparently used the method.

Finally, a technical point (see fig. 7). It is best to fish twin dry fly with quite a lengthy dropper, 3 in (7.5 cm) at least, even 4 in (10 cm). This allows the dry fly to sit properly on the water. Beware of tangles, however, for the longer the dropper the more prone it is to bird's nests. If the dropper is too short, though, your fly will not sit naturally on the surface. It is best to devise your own method, one which suits your level of skill.

3

Wry Fly
Further Tactics

'There's more than one way to skin a cat.'

Proverb

The last two chapters have concerned themselves with fishing with two flies on the line. This chapter introduces the idea of using more than two flies at a time. The traditional North Country team of three wet flies is an historic and still often used formula. Above the border, teams of more than three flies are used. In my boyhood I met several Scots anglers who fished with four small wet flies on their casts (of which a typical team was: point – Dunkeld or Hardy Gold on a double hook; dropper no. 1 – Blae and Black or Black Pennell; dropper no. 2 – Peter Ross or Bloody Butcher; top or bob dropper – Mallard and Claret or Mallard and Black). And I know for a fact that last century some Scotsmen fished double this amount – more like mackerel fishing with feathers than trout angling! Clearly, multi-fly casts are nothing new.

TWO SEASONAL COMBINATIONS

The application of a little lateral thinking to wry fly suggests the idea of more than two flies on the cast. If so, how many of the flies should be wet and how many dry? The answer is: it depends. I will only speak here of the experiments I have myself conducted. There are two combinations that I recommend. The first involves one dry and two wet flies. On the point you place a Sawyer Pheasant Tail Nymph or Killer Bug; on the middle dropper a less weighty fly – a Snipe and Purple, Waterhen Bloa or Partridge and Orange, for instance; while on the top dropper you knot some big, fluffy dry fly such as a March Brown, Rough Olive, Greenwell's Glory or dark pattern Blanchard's Abortion. See fig. 8.

This outfit fishes splendidly in early spring. The point nymph attracts any doggo, deep-lying fish; the middle fly fishes nicely in mid-water and appeals to any active trout; while the prominent dry fly acts as a temptation to greedy fish at any level. What is noticeable about this combination is that the best trout of the day nearly always takes the dry fly. (The biggest fish of the day, taken on the point nymph, is often a heavily gravid female grayling, which at this time of the year must be

Figure 8 Wry fly with three flies (two wet)

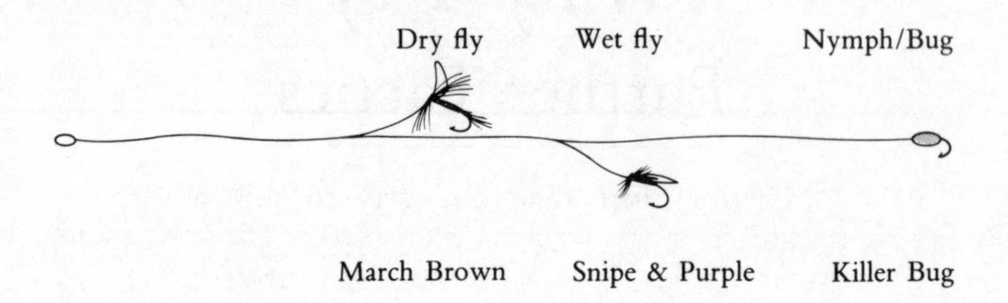

An excellent method for early season, especially on cold, cheerless days.

Figure 9 Wry fly with three flies (two dry)

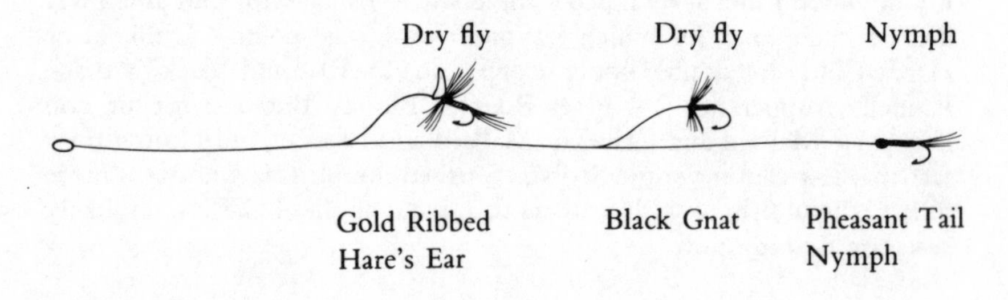

A good combination for summer days, especially early in the morning.

gently released back into her spawning element.) But the dry fly will bring you some good trouty surprises. You might only get half a dozen takes to the dry fly all day, but, odds on, your biggest brace will come this way. It certainly helps to enliven an otherwise perishingly cold, rather dismal April day.

My second three-fly combination is for use in high summer. This time two are dry and one is wet. On the point you place a lightly dressed Sawyer Pheasant Tail Nymph on a no. 14 hook, or any nymph of your fancy. I often try a traditional Snipe and Purple. On the middle dropper I suggest a small Black Gnat or Knotted Midge, and on the top dropper an ephemerid imitation – a Greenwell's Glory, Medium Olive, Blue Upright or, my own personal favourite with this set-up, a Gold Ribbed Hare's Ear. If, for example, pale wateries were hatching, it would not be a bad idea to tie a Tup's nymph on the point and place a dry Tup's on one of the droppers. Experiment with your own *ménages à trois*. See fig. 9.

While the first combination, excellent for spring fishing, is basically an upstream wet fly variant, this second team is biased towards the dry fly. It is good on big pools and runs in late May and on into June and July. Furthermore, it pays dividends on days when lots of different types of fly are hatching and trout seem spoiled for choice. But it is rather a cumbersome rig for delicate work and I would not consider using it in low water or on overgrown tree-lined stretches. In short, the first combination is very much the more useful.

FOUR-FLY TEAMS

Why stop at three flies? Why not four flies, like those canny Scots loch fishers, but instead two dry and two wet? The logical combination would be a kind of mixture of twin dry fly and wry fly – two dry flies on, on the top droppers, wet flies/nymphs on bottom dropper and point. Though I have never tried this method I can imagine it being most effective, especially on really big rivers. I can visualize it as being most relevant on broad rivers such as the Tweed, Tay, Tyne, Eden, Ribble, Teifi and Wye. Here you could indulge in leaders of 12 ft (3.7 m) or so with the flies spaced 3 ft (90 cm) apart.

In April on the Spey, Tweed or Eden I think this combination could well be worth a whirl. You could even complicate things further by alternating the dry and wet flies: top dropper – dry fly, next dropper – wet fly, next dropper – dry fly, point – weighted nymph. The danger of this is that if the dry flies were too far apart an angler might have difficulty in keeping his eye comfortably on both. Therefore a standard 9-foot (2.7 m) leader might be necessary with this arrangement.

None of the ideas in these last two paragraphs are of any practical value for brook and stream fishers, but I will go further by indulging in a little speculation quite outside my brief. First, what exactly are the implications for wry fly on lakes and reservoirs? Exciting, I would say. Here is a chance for *real* long-leader experiments. How about a dry fly (Diptera copy) on the surface and a nymph 15 ft (4.6 m) beyond and below? Nonsense? Try it! Second, what is the potential of wry fly in migratory fishing? Limited as far as salmon are concerned, but really rather exciting for sea trout, I would suggest. Imagine fishing up a run full of fresh sea trout with a bushy dry fly on the dropper and a size 10 Dunkeld, Black Pennell, Alexandra, Butcher or Invicta sunk on the point. I shall try this when I next get the opportunity.

So, I issue a challenge to the whole trout fishing world. In his book *The Grayling Angler* John Roberts says, when discussing the fishing of very deep nymphs in rivers, 'bug fishing is in its infancy'. This is not the only under-investigated branch of fly fishing. Wry fly fishing is in its infancy too. Hence all you curious and clever anglers wherever you are, give some of these ideas an airing. Let us take wry fly into its adulthood. Though already a long-established practice, it has received only individual, uncoordinated attention and has therefore remained retarded. It has been too long either taken for granted by ingenuous anglers or been kept a jealously guarded secret by the uncharitable. The time has come for many anglers' minds to fix on the technique and for wry fly as well as twin dry fly to become the universal heritage of the fly fisher.

LEVEL VERSUS TAPERED LEADERS

Finally, a word about leaders. Most modern writers stress the importance, indeed necessity, of using tapered leaders. I must admit to being a heretic on this subject, never having found tapered leaders necessary for river fishing except on the windiest of days.

With my preference for flexible tactics – which involves the rapid switching from wet fly to dry fly to wry fly, and so on – it does not serve me well to have a tapered leader. With the kind of multi-fly combinations I have spoken of in the last few chapters I need light nylon adjacent to my fly line in order to deceive trout with any regularity. If your leaders for river angling are only 9 ft (2.7 m), as mine usually are, then with three flies on your cast there is no space for tapering. My no-taper system is simple. It is less fiddly than making up your own tapered leaders (and cheaper than buying them) – you need only one spool of nylon in your bag, for instance.

Nevertheless I do not claim that mine is the only way to proceed. I am at variance with orthodox modern views when I say that tapered leaders are not necessary, but it is no more than an opinion. I personally do not rely on them: I prefer level casts. Fishing, like any other sport or practical pastime, embraces a variety of techniques and all kinds of individual whims. This book simply describes the way that I fish. It is up to the reader to decide which of my whims to copy and which to ignore.

4

Selecting the Right Fly

Part One

'It's not only fine feathers that make fine birds.'

Aesop

The talk in the bar was quiet and friendly as the tall fisherman came in from outside. He limped nonchalantly to the counter and ordered a scotch.

'Did you do any good, Mr Smythe?' the barman enquired with a hopeful smile.

'No, I'm sorry to say that I didn't touch a thing, Willy!' the fisherman replied, taking a much-needed snort of his scotch. He gave a laconic sigh and stared disconsolately into his drink.

'That's because you weren't fishin' with a Jenny Spinner!' a bluff voice barked from a few yards down the bar. 'I got all my fish today on a Jenny Spinner – iron blues hatchin', you see!'

The tall newcomer looked up to see who had spoken. His eyes fell upon a ruddy-faced man in tweedy late-middle age. He had bushy eyebrows and an aggressive set to his big, hunched shoulders. He had spoken loudly both to humiliate and boast. But he had not finished.

'Common mistake at this time of year! Got to watch carefully and pick the right moment to change from the dun to the spinner. The Jenny Spinner does for many a guest!' Before the tall fisherman could reply to this piece of belligerent rudeness, another voice cut across the now silent room.

'Och, to hell with your bombast, man. I had a basket this morning on a wee Black Gnat, so there's an end to your Jenny Spinner theory!'

Everyone's gaze turned to the opposite end of the bar where a hitherto unnoticed drinker was sitting on a high stool. He was a diminutive Scotsman with a brown weather-beaten face and also impeccably turned out in Norfolk jacket and Paisley-patterned kerchief.

Before either of the former speakers could retort to this observation, a young lad in his mid teens, sitting with his father at a corner table, piped up:

'And my father and I had fifteen fish between us this afternoon on a dry Gold Ribbed Hare's Ear!'

THE KILLING FLY

I will not pursue the upshot of this conversation, but I have witnessed many similar conflicts about what is the killing fly. How often have I met a friend at lunchtime and tipped out my catch on Greenwell's Glory (or Wickham's Fancy) only to be shown his creel full of fish caught on John Storey (or Tup's Indispensable).

The 'right' fly is less often a particular pattern than a well-presented one. In the rough northern streams a variety of well-fished flies will on most days take trout.

When I read of assertions of the type Skues relished in, that only a dun with a body dubbed with moleskin, as opposed to water rat or seal, was on some particular day the *only* killing fly, I do not scoff, but regard it as a phenomenon that must have occurred in an alien world far removed from the trouty one that I know!

I think we can get over-refined about dressings. I am a terrible heretic about the need for scrupulous realism in fly dressings; likewise about the necessity of using only the very best materials. In the final analysis, flawlessly tied flies have more appeal to other admiring fly-tiers than to any trout, which are far less discriminating. I have been lectured many a time about the inferiority of some modern commercial hackles, or about the absolute prerequisite of using really superior hackles. Why then do those superior creations, of which I have acquired a good many over the years, prove no better than either my own clumsy tyings or the many utterly ordinary commercial patterns I have purchased?

I have no illusions whatsoever that flies tied to absolute perfection with top-class materials have, for the trout, any supremacy over much rougher and readier specimens. Far too much is written in the modern angling press about countless new fly patterns, many of which possess the telling design flaw of being tied more for human than trout approval. As Frank Sawyer says, 'It is the fish, not the human who has to decide if they are attractive.'

THE PSYCHOLOGICAL FACTOR

Another important point is that fly-tiers often fail to appreciate the 'psychological' factor in a fly's construction. There is no doubt that some patterns are so successful because instead of imitating faithfully some species of fly, they highlight or exaggerate a mere *feature* in the species they are mimicking. Just as a mother meadow-pippit or hedge-sparrow reacts frantically to the oversized cuckoo in her clutch because it arouses a stronger stimulus than the ordinary chicks in the nest, so a trout attacks a bulky Gold Ribbed Hare's Ear because it is more attractive than some exquisite but dull Olive Quill. Experiments have been done throughout the animal kingdom to test this behavioural trait. Male robins will attack anything red, despite its size, as will male sticklebacks.

Experiments have been done with moths where models of grotesquely huge females drove males into a frenzy of mating simply because certain colours and patterns were exaggerated. Successful flies are not necessarily the most realistic therefore, but sometimes the most *stimulating*. Fly-tiers should perhaps bone up on psychology rather than concern themselves with endlessly attempting to mirror Nature.

THEORY V. PRACTICE

I have come to believe that fly-tying and fly fishing are utterly unrelated disciplines. The best makers of snooker cues or cricket bats are not the best players of those games. Theory is one thing, practice another. There seems to be almost universal agreement among fly-tiers that only the very best materials will do, but more significant to me is that there is no such consensus among practical anglers. Practical experience has taught me that fly dressings are of less importance than skill in presentation.

The fact that a new pattern works does not make it a necessary one. Almost any fly will work at some time on most days. It is better to find the really good, time-proven dressings and stick to them. (No less an authority than Conrad Voss Bark argues along these lines in an article in the April 1987 issue of *Trout and Salmon*.) Modern technology changes rapidly, but the trout's diet does not. Our indigenous trout have been eating the same insects not for hundreds of years, nor even for thousands, but millions of years. (The first salmonids are fossilized in cretaceous rocks dating from one hundred million years ago.)

Many of our trusty traditional fly patterns cannot be bettered (for example, the Mallard and Claret, Greenwell's Glory, Tup's Indispensable, Red Palmer and Wickham's Fancy), though this does not mean that there is no room for new patterns. We should experiment with new dressings, but should also retain the right to be sceptical. Fashionable contempt for tradition is as much a dead end as narrow-minded adherence to all that is traditional.

INADEQUATELY TESTED DRESSINGS

The Black Chenille, invented by Bob Church in the 1970s, is a wonderful fly, and my favourite stillwater lure. In the previous decade my favourite lure was the Jersey Herd (which I still value highly) but once I had started to use the Black Chenille, Bob Church's invention became my stand-by. This, I hope, shows that I am not blind to progress, nor against it. What I am against, though, is the array of second-rate scribblers rushing into print before they really understand many of the complexities (and, ironically, simplicities) of trout fishing and being allowed influence over beginners hardly less experienced than themselves. Too much of the trout angling press is taken up with new dressings that have not been rigorously tested, and not enough on practical tactics. But then new dressings are easier to write about than new tactics. It is easier to become a good fly-tier than a good fisherman – you need not even go near the water!

Modern stillwater fishing in stocked lakes is in its infancy compared to river angling for trout, which has had over four hundred years to perfect its fly dressings. This is perhaps why stillwater fly-tying is such a growth area. I keep my eyes out for new river trout flies but already know that my fly boxes contain patterns to meet adequately any eventuality. Hence my heretical stance on some issues, and my scepticism.

EXPERIMENTAL PATTERNS

I have experimented with my own 'alternative' dressings but do not flatter myself that I have improved on any existing pattern nor even invented anything of any merit, with the exception of a single fly, the Hotspur. Most of my attempts have been with fancy flies or with non-ephemerid insect imitations. I have, for instance, tied a very tolerable copy of a green fly, for I once witnessed a rise to aphids. I had no green fly with me at the time but Black Gnats and Buzzers did just as well. Though I have carried these aphid look-alikes ever since, I have never once needed them. The moral is clear: we tend to carry more fly patterns than we ever need in practice. There is a Yellow Sally or two in my collection but they have never been used. I have twice seen a huge hatch of Yellow Sallies. On the first occasion I did not have a copy with me but the ubiquitous Black Gnat appealed just as much to the trout, and on the second, the fish ignored the fly, so I did too!

As for bugs and beetles, I have done experiments galore with these. I have a successful dressing of a Violet Ground Beetle (which accounted for my first trout on the dap) but in truth it is no better than a Coch-y-bondhu – indeed nowhere near so good. Eric Horsfall Turner's Beetle cannot be bettered and the Alder takes some beating. For deep-lying fish Sawyer's Killer Bug has no equal, and I am certain Stewart would have backed his Black Spider against any copy of a drowning terrestrial insect.

I would, as a practical chap, have altered my attitudes if I had found them to be in error. The guiding principle throughout my fishing life has been: what is the best way to catch trout? After 25 years of both fishing and fly-tying I think I can claim not to be one-eyed about all this. My considered opinion is that a good half of what I have heard from the lips of fly-tiers, or read in the angling press, is hugely at variance with what I, as a practical angler, have learnt for myself beside the hurly burly of the trout stream. I have reached the depressing conclusion that most editors of fishing magazines must be firstly journalists and secondly anglers. Were it the other way round, more sense would be on display in their publications.

SELECTING THE RIGHT FLY

How then am I to throw any light on all this obfuscation? I am aware that as I write I am adding to the cacophony! How do you select the right fly? Many fishing books are meticulous in the advice they give about fly patterns and their selection. Fishermen themselves often strive to find the 'right' fly with increasing frustration, while some experts go to the lengths of sieving the surface film with a fine net in an attempt to learn what the trout might be taking. In all this hectic activity and analysis one single, basic fact is taken completely for granted: that flies are chosen for the trout's sake. I would like to challenge this obvious assumption by suggesting that it is not the trout but the fisherman who must be taken most into consideration when it comes to picking the right fly.

I do not make this statement to be provocative or contrary, but am entirely serious. It would perhaps be rather predictable if I claimed that if a good fisherman with a Greenwell's Glory on his line and a bad fisherman with a Tup's Indispensable were to fish a confident rise to pale wateries, the good fisherman would catch more trout even though he had the 'wrong' fly. But this raises an interesting point – namely, that it is skilful fishing rather than skilfully tied flies that is the real essential in catching trout.

What is the 'right' fly? Clearly, it is the closest representation we can find in our artificial fly collection to the natural fly the trout are eating. However, often it does not profit us to fish with this fly. The light may be too bad for us to see the fly clearly if it is a very small pattern. Or the water may be too fast-flowing and streamy to see the tiny fly or keep it afloat. In these circumstances if we use the 'right' fly we will not see the trout take it and will therefore rise fish unwittingly. Thus the 'right' fly is in fact the wrong fly. It may be right for the fish but if it is not right for us as well we are defeating our own purposes.

So the 'right' fly becomes the smallest close representation that is visible to us as well as to the trout, or it becomes a pattern sufficiently fluffy to float in the rough water where the trout are rising. In each case the fly may be much larger than the real fly that the trout are feeding on, but that does not matter because when we do rise a fish or two at least we can see that we have done so. It is far better to rise two fish and stand a chance of hooking them than to rise ten fish but have no chance of contacting them at all.

DIFFICULTY IN IDENTIFYING DIET

Another point on which I am certain is that we cannot always be absolutely sure about distinguishing correctly what fly the trout are taking. The fact that an expert skims knotted midges off the surface of the water in his entomological net and then catches a brace on a Knotted Midge does not prove that the trout were tucking into a glut of knotted midges (though an examination of stomach contents might do so). Yet such slender evidence is often enough to prompt an 'expert' to pontificate about the behaviour of trout on that particular afternoon, or even to write an assured article containing a great deal of technical jargon. I always view such certainty with suspicion because in my experience trout behaviour is full of inexplicable variations and baffling anomalies.

Just because a handful of trout in one pool are taking medium olives it does not mean that if a dark olive (for example, Greenwell's Glory) were to float incongruously down it would be disdainfully ignored. Trout are no more creatures of stereotyped appetite than humans are, and a varied diet is as exciting to them as it is to us. However, I accept that there are times when every trout in the river seems to be feeding on one particular species of fly and if you do not have with you an acceptable copy of it you may as well pack up and go home. The frustration of such moments can be alleviated, though, by doing something daft like putting on a huge haystack of a fly and defying the trout to take it. I have occasionally caught trout in August or September on a Mayfly.

Likewise, we can often obtain results with a wet fly or nymph when our dry fly is being pointedly spurned. In fact I am sure we often cover 'rising' trout with a dry fly when they are in reality nymphing. Sometimes it is easy to distinguish the humping and swirling of the nymphing trout but on hot afternoons in slack water a big trout can hunt nymphs with the serenity of a lazy surface-feeder. On such occasions, though a good hatch of small duns appears to be the fly they want, the only fly the fish will look at is a nymph. Nowadays if I cannot tempt a trout with a dry fly in some still reach of a river, instead of trying endless alternative patterns I put on a nymph and twitch it past his nose. There is something about the motion of a nymph which bewitches such trout into an impulsive attack, whereas a lifeless dry fly inspires only indifference. At these times we cannot be certain what the trout are eating, but the 'right' fly for us was a wet rather than a dry one.

WET FLY SELECTION

All my comments about fly choice so far in this chapter have obviously been about selecting dry flies. I think that wet fly selection presents less of a problem on rivers. Indeed, Major Oliver Kite suggests we only ever need one pattern of nymph: the Sawyer Pheasant Tail variety. Frank Sawyer himself only ever used five different types of nymph, and only two for river trout: the Pheasant Tail and Grey Goose, with a third, the Killer Bug, added for grayling. In the streams of the Midlands and the North, where I principally fish, the Pheasant Tail Nymph and Killer Bug are the only nymphs I ever need. Perhaps the explanation for this is that, before hatching, most ephemeroptera look very similar. As nymphs, aquatic flies are all olivey-brown creepy-crawlies, but as hatched duns and spinners they assert their individuality with different shapes, colours and sizes.

For traditional downstream and upstream wet fly fishing, half a dozen flies at most are all you need – a view endorsed by W.C. Stewart:

> We believe the angler who has a different fly for every day in the season will kill nearly as many trout as the angler who adheres to three or four varieties the whole season through; but he is proceeding upon an erroneous principle, and losing both labour and time.

Need I add that there are different types of fishermen and different types of challenge in fishing? There are those who, having spotted a good trout, will have him, even if it means spending an hour or more in the pursuit of just this one fish. (Sawyer tells how he spent an entire day over one trout.) The satisfaction and sense of achievement in catching a trout in this way is immense, and certainly demands as much skill as capturing several smaller, less cautious specimens.

Then there are the creel-fillers, anglers who like catching big numbers of trout in a day. Stewart was certainly one of these, not least because the sale of his trout was a livelihood to him. I incline more to the creel-filling mentality myself, and this admission may explain much of my angling philosophy. (The reasons for this approach are threefold, I believe. First, I do not fish as often as I would like, travelling long distances to remote locations, and once there I seek results. Secondly, the trout I fish for often run two or more to the pound (0.5 kg): one good chalkstream specimen is equivalent to eight or so of my little brownies! Thirdly, I enjoy cooking, and take a great deal of interest in my trout once I have brought them home.)

THE JOYS OF EXPERIMENTATION

It is all very well for W.C. Stewart to say that those who experiment with many flies are 'proceeding upon an erroneous principle, and losing both labour and time' as long as he is talking to would-be multi-trout slayers. But for leisurely chalkstream anglers out to bag an educated trout or two his is no advice at all. People fish for different reasons and to some a large part of fly fishing is the sheer fun of just messing about with flies. The sight of rows of multi-coloured patterns is one they cannot resist. For them the world of fur, feather and tinsel, with its many exotic and evocative names, is an end in itself. Writers of fishing books should be sensitive to the different needs of their readers. For those who merely potter about by the water, fly selection must be an amiable pastime, pleasantly free from the desperate struggle to find the killing pattern which afflicts more earnest anglers.

Nevertheless, Stewart's advice holds good for those whose quest is a good bag of fish at the end of the day, and as a ruthless catching machine myself I again quote him:

> In practice it has been proved beyond doubt, that a black, brown, red, and dun-coloured fly, used together, and varied in size according to circumstances will at any time kill as well, and even better, than the most elaborate collection arranged for every month in the year. If trout are at all inclined to rise, one or other of the above will be found inviting.

Coming from a man who believed that 12 lb (5.5 kg) of trout was what any decent angler should catch as a minimum on any day of the season, I think we can take this as sound advice. So much for wet fly. Let us return to the floating variety.

THE RATIONALE OF DRY FLY

If we accept that aquatic flies once hatched differ more markedly from one another than when in their nymphal stage, it follows that if we strive to copy these emerged insects our copies are going to be both more variegated and more numerous. Hence the extra difficulties the dry fly fisher faces when he approaches the stream. Since the time of F.M. Halford generations of dry fly anglers have come to believe that the essence of the art is to find the fly pattern that most closely corresponds to the natural insect on which the trout are feeding and then put this pattern to the test.

This approach might suit the rather rarified world of the southern chalkstream but I humbly submit that it is not the only way of proceeding with a dry fly. My approach, admittedly born of a different school, that of the rock-strewn northern rivers, is not painstakingly to find the correct copy but, as swiftly as possible, to induce the trout to take my fly, whether it is wet or dry. Oliver Kite coined the phrase the 'induced take' from Sawyer's ideas to describe the manner of inciting the trout to take a nymph. Similarly, I now coin the phrase the 'induced dry fly take'. Because this is an important idea, meriting a chapter of its own, I will take a short digression here before concluding my observations on selecting the right fly.

5

The Induced Dry Fly Take

'I can resist everything except temptation.'

Oscar Wilde

To recap a remark I made at the end of the last chapter: the central tenet of orthodox chalkstream dry fly fishing is to fish the rise with as perfect a representation of the natural fly as you can find in your fly box. In the United States of America, where they specialize in slick soubriquets, they have rather a good expression for this type of fishing: 'matching the hatch'. You are said to be a 'hatch-matcher' if you fish this way.

However, for years I have used a ploy which I have always referred to as 'shock tactics', as a successful alternative to the orthodox approach. It was not until relatively recently that I realized that the famous American dry fly fisherman Lee Wulff had coined a similar phrase for it, 20 years before I was born. His epithet, more poetic than mine, is 'peaches and cream'. The ploy is deliberately to offer trout something much larger, more juicy, more tempting than the actual flies in the hatch. Not so much 'matching the hatch' as 'doubling the grub'!

There is nothing startling or revolutionary in this idea and I make no claim to have developed it independently on this side of the Atlantic. Many rough-stream fishers use the method, I am sure, and other writers have mentioned it in their books. But the importance of this approach in the immediate context is that it forms the mainstay of the 'induced dry fly take'.

A SERIAL APPROACH TO PRESENTATION

The 'induced take' of Kite and Sawyer is a method of imparting life to the nymph underwater. The 'induced dry fly take' is not one step, but a series of different presentations one after another, any one of which might succeed. It is thus not so much a method as a methodology. The technique is also more of a philosophy than a startling new practical 'trick'.

There are plenty of opposites in fly fishing – age-old ones such as nymph v. dry fly, North v. South, fishing the rise v. fishing the water; and more modern ones such as knotless leaders v. knotted ones, still-water v. river fishing, kill v. catch-and-release, etc. likewise, the induced dry fly take is the very opposite of the orthodox, imitation-based take. The deception involved is in each case utterly different. The orthodox method of fishing the rise attempts to deceive by mimicking reality, the induced dry fly take sets out to deceive by shock, or surprise, or by arousing greed, jealousy, anger, tyranny, rapacity, bellicosity, aggression or simply curiosity.

The idea does not stop there, though. Merely floating a large fly down over a trout's head may not be enough. You might really have to make your point by dumping it right in front of him, or perhaps, to begin with, slightly to either side of him; or even on his tail, where although his eyes cannot see it, his neuromasts will sense the vibration, causing him instinctively to turn downstream and take it without deliberation.

THE INDUCED DRY FLY TAKE IN PRACTICE

A scenario to illustrate the induced dry fly take might be helpful here. You see a trout taking what appear to be, for argument's sake, red spinners. You try a Red Spinner (yes, 'matching the hatch'!) but it is rejected. But, instead of continuing further experiments to 'match the hatch' and running through endless patterns resembling red spinners, you switch tactics completely. You tie on a big dry fly. Which? A large Wickham's Fancy, dry Jock Scott, a Grey or Red Wulff – why not? – or some other substantial fancy fly. You float this down over the trout once or maybe twice in a sedate fashion, as in the textbooks. No good.

The next step. You must try a more vigorous presentation. At this stage you can change fly if you wish – after all the trout has already seen it once or twice. Either tie on another big fly, sufficiently different – for example, switch from a Grey Wulff to a big Wickham – or stick with the same pattern. You now have to decide where you are first going to plonk it down: to the trout's side, front or rear? Perhaps, to start with, a little to one side of him: not so near as to frighten him, not so far away as to be unnoticed – 3 ft (90 cm) in slowish water, 18 in (45 cm) or closer in ripple. Cast in such a way that the fly lands with a satisfying plump, but do not overdo it – *not yet.* Say you choose to drop your fly 2½ ft (80 cm) to the trout's left. You execute the manoeuvre with tasteful panache. Nothing. The trout turns slightly, but he does not come over for a closer look.

Reel in. Wait a little. Watch the trout. While you change fly hope that he takes another red spinner or two. If he does, this is an excellent sign, for it shows his suspicions are not yet aroused and he is still feeding. It is not a bad idea to let him rise to a natural fly between each of these operations, though this is not always practicable. (In an ideal world allow this to happen. Many fishing writers seem to inhabit a permanently ideal world. Reality is not often as it appears in books. In real life things can go wrong at every stage of the process, and usually do! Bear with this irritating success-story-so-far.)

THE REPLACEMENT FLY

The suggested fly now is a beetle-like pattern – a big, bushy Coch-y-bondhu, Kill Devil Spider, Alder or Eric's Beetle. There is no need to grease it, for it will probably fish best slightly awash. You can even lightly moisten the hackles in your mouth. It is still legitimately a *dry* fly fished this way, though after a few casts it might well become sunk. You are, however, gambling on the plan working first cast. There is a distinct difference, to which trout are most sensible, between the way a fluffed up, well-greased dry fly falls on the water and the way a slightly damp one does. Terrestrial insects, when they tumble from branches above, seldom fall on the water like a fluffed up, well-greased dry fly. This why you are going to employ the 'slightly damp' subterfuge. You want the trout to think that your Coch-y-bondhu is a fallen spider, bluebottle, hawthorn fly or luckless beetle.

You now have to choose: on his tail or on his nose? The danger of dropping it on his nose is that you might put him down, irrevocably. You pick the tail approach . . . and cast! Thwack! Down the Coch-y-bondhu comes in satisfying compliance with Newton's Laws just 6 in (15 cm) downstream of the fish. But what a scornful trout! Instead of turning savagely and snapping the irresistible object up, as so many of his less fortunate ancestors have done, he angrily wags his tail at you but otherwise does not flinch. But this is why he has grown to such a size: he is bright. You need to hit on a better trick than this.

SWITCHING TACTICS

So far your induced dry fly take has failed. Time to switch tactics: to abandon dry fly. Shock, horror – how unorthodox! Open your nymph box. Pick out either a Sawyer Pheasant Tail Nymph tied on a size 14 hook or a home-made Greenwell's Glory Nymph, weighted, and tied with a very pale yellow silk ribbed tawdrily with gold, on a size 12 hook. Let us say you choose the second. Knot the flash offering onto your line and cast a foot (30 cm) ahead of the trout. Twitch the nymph a moment or two after it has settled. No good! Ignored again. You should have listened to Sawyer and tried the Pheasant Tail! Another angry flick of the tail. The trout has got the wind up maybe? Certainly not! He has just taken another spinner. He is not only clever but impudent.

After momentarily ditching dry fly you return to the method. You have still got a few tricks up your sleeve. Besides, you still want to prove that this blasted induced dry fly take really does work.

THE *COUP DE GRÂCE*

An Alder. Not greased, slightly damp – no need to use your mouth, your fingers sweaty with tension and impatience are enough to do the necessary. On his nose, the so-and-so. The Alder lands 8 in (20 cm) in front of the trout's nose. You are trembling . . . he moves forward slightly, his pectorals spread, but he sinks back, not tempted. Blast!

But one last trick. A six-year-old memory is stirred: the old French farmer you saw on a Normandy stream bribing the trout to take his Mayfly by outrageously twitching it across the surface above their noses. *Pourquoi pas?*

You cast again: a foot (30 cm) in front of him. You twitch the fly blatantly. Too much! He has gone. Vanished to his holt deep down in the roots of that alder tree. Banished by an Alder into an alder.

Never despair. This entire encounter has taken only ten minutes. The hatch-matcher who fished this same pool three days ago spent an hour and a quarter fruitlessly flogging away at this same trout, during which time he experimented with 57 varieties of upwing imitations.

To look into the future though, this fish will be caught exactly a week to this day. You will be on the water again. On this occasion, however, another angler will beat you to this pool. You watch him for a while. He is covering 'your' trout. He is an excellent caster. A hatch-matcher, too. You proceed upstream. While this fisherman below you spends one hour casting for and catching the trout that eluded you last week, you cover six such fish, spending about ten minutes over each. Two you frighten, one you miss, three you catch.

COMPARING BAGS

You meet up with the other angler at dusk in the car park. He is very pleased. 'Your' trout, now in his creel, weighs 1 lb 4 oz (0.55 kg), an excellent North Country fish. It is the best trout of the day: your biggest is only 1 lb 1 oz (0.5 kg). He shows you his catch: three trout totalling 2 lb 13 oz (1.3 kg) – a very nice bag for a Yorkshire river this high up in the hills. You open your creel: six wild brown trout lie there . . . the limit. They weigh altogether 4 lb 15 oz (2.2 kg). What neither of you knows, because nobody was watching you both (except me in my imagination) is that together during the day you have cast at a total of 44 rising trout. The angler with the three fish attempted twelve of these risers, and you with the six trout tried for 32. His striking rate of takeable trout per attempt was higher than yours, the average weight of his fish – 15 oz (0.42 kg) as opposed to your 13 oz (0.37 kg) – was higher as well. You, on the other hand, caught twice the amount of takeable fish, as well as returning half a dozen undersized ones, while he needed to return only two. During the time he was deceiving, in a highly orthodox manner, three keepable trout with his dry flies, you induced six keepable trout to take your dry flies. I rest my case.

A FRESH PERSPECTIVE

Now all this is outrageous propaganda, and I admit it. I am also prepared to admit that all this could have been the other way round:

that the orthodox dry fly angler might well have outfished the fancy-fly 'inducer'. I am not trying to make out a case for the superiority of 'doubling the grub' over 'matching the hatch', though I agree it looks like it. I am simply inviting you to look at dry fly in a light which is perhaps new to you. Over the years much hysterical nonsense has been written about dry fly, both for and against, and writers continue to publish some pretty erroneous and emotive articles on the subject. All I wish to do is present some observations for you to mull over.

There are several important points to analyze that arise from my scenario illustrating the induced dry fly take above. First, at each step in the process of covering a rising trout you have several decisions to make. You are confronted by option after option. No one situation is ever entirely the same as another, so there are no hard-and-fast rules. Experience teaches you which choice to make at which time. Instead of going methodically through each of the steps I described, you might very well skip several, going immediately from the first sedate presentation I mentioned, to splashing a big Coch-y-bondhu right on the trout's nose. Indeed the orderly step-by-step approach was more of an illustration of a theory than an actual occurrence.

I have approached and caught (and put down) trout in this deliberate manner, but usually I get from A to B in a less ponderous way. One of the choices in this type of fishing is deciding what approaches to reject, a kind of Confucian tendency to argue from the negative. Many fishing books are very hot on telling you which tactics to adopt, but few advise the philosophy of judiciously deciding which to dispense with. Experienced fishermen weigh up these possibilities in a flash and as if by second nature they know what to do.

THE TROUT'S BODY LANGUAGE

It is not ridiculous to say that you can learn to interpret the body language of a trout. Subtle little signs, such as fin movement and the way a fish reacts to a fly presented well or badly, give you vital clues. Each of the trout's reactions tells you which step to ignore and which step to take next. The sex of a trout can be significant too. Female fish can be aggressive, but big male trout are even more so. If you can ascertain the sex of a trout lying in a clear pool, this will help in your tactics. Determining the sex of young trout at a distance is impossible, but with more mature specimens it is easier to spot the difference.

A large male trout will have an appreciably long, lupine head and noticeably big jaws. Such a fish is vulnerable to the strategic splash of a juicy Coch-y-bondhu in his vicinity. Again, if there are other smaller fish in the pool you can play on the male's arrogance and pride – he is bound to be a bully. If some fat insect falls from the branches above, a trout like this will want to get to it first, as much to show to the other fish that he is boss of the pool as to assuage his own hunger. Drop your fly between a big fish of this kind and his vassals and you will see what

I mean! Big male trout are even more aggressive late in the season, as the spawning urge increases. They will often exhibit this aggression to impress attractive hen fish and this too can benefit the watchful angler.

The majority of fishing books seem to ignore details of this sort. The sex, size, personality and river position of fish are seldom described. We receive copious information about flies and the kind of hatch at the time but nothing about the personality of the trout. (Skues and Sawyer and Ritz are notable exceptions.)

INTERPRETING RIVER POSITION

River position is particularly important. You can determine much about a trout's character by his position in the stream. Backwater trout are shy but greedy. They are curious, used to snapping up terrestrial strays, and are prepared to investigate anything. They often inhabit 'impossible' lies – those that are impossible to get at – but herein lies one of their chief weaknesses: only get a fly over them and they will attack it. Backwater fish are usually bullies too, defending territories against all comers, a weakness a fisherman can exploit; by waiting for a smaller fish to swim near and choosing this moment to present the fly.

Midstream trout are generally more choosy than lazy backwater bullies. These fish are very often beyond the reach of branches, and therefore less susceptible to terrestrial temptation. They tend to rely more on flies appearing in hatches and therefore feed at intervals. They are fitter than eddy-loving trout, for they have to battle against the midstream current to maintain their feeding position. They will travel less far to right or left to investigate food, preferring the river to bring the titbits down to them in steady supply. These trout are not easily tempted, are easily scared by drag, and form the main quarry of the hatch-matching fraternity.

PSYCHOLOGICAL TACTICS

Mere entomology and fly-tying technology are not enough in induced take dry fly fishing. Deception is not merely achieved by throwing a procession of beautifully tied, carefully chosen dry flies at fish after fish, but by out-thinking your quarry by 'psyching' him out.

The next important point raised in my earlier scenario is that of the casting involved. Standard received wisdom is that dry fly presentation is all about how deftly you can place the fly on the water. This is a key skill, but only one of several. The crafty dry fly fisherman must also be able to plonk a fly down on the water with varying degrees of force, be able to adjust this ability depending on the type of fly (for instance, big, small, greased, dampened) and also manage these operations in the different conditions typical on rivers, while allowing for wind, currents, trees, rocks and so on.

Finally, it is clear from my remarks that I am not the kind of fisherman prepared to devote several hours of my day to the catching of one individual fish. Indeed I hardly ever find this necessary, preferring always the short cut, but I admit mine is not the disposition for this approach. I like action when I go fishing. Besides, my views are not exactly without precedent. J.W. Hills, himself no mean orthodox chalkstream man, quotes the famous William Lunn as saying that in some circumstances 'it is better to change the fish than the fly'.

Actually, I do on occasion relish pitting my wits against a single trout for a long period, but I do know when I am beaten and will progress to another fish without feeling depressed. I regard Oliver Kite's, 'it is a shameful thing to be beaten by a trout' as nonsense. He obviously had a lower opinion of the noble *Salmo trutta* than I do. I would have died from shame seasons ago if I had ever listened to bosh like that!

KEEPING AN OPEN MIND

In many of the preceding paragraphs you may have discerned a tone which is critical of, even antipathetic to orthodox dry fly. I apologize if I have given this impression. I am not opposed to orthodoxy in dry fly or in any other branch of fly fishing. Orthodoxy maintains standards; it is the standard-bearer of excellence. But I am not averse to doing a little debunking now and again. I like singeing the tails of some of the more silly sacred cows in trout fishing. Rigid orthodoxy can allow some idiotic taboos to linger. The flexible fisherman will invariably get better baskets than the rigid, narrow-minded one. I often fish in an orthodox way myself. I sometimes 'match the hatch'. But I also mix it. My fishing is a blend of the orthodox and the heterodox, of the subtle and the crude, of the deft and the aggressive, of the sage and the rash, of the patient and the impatient, of the meticulously planned and the improvised.

MAKE YOUR FLY WORK

In the last chapter I was concerned about selecting the right fly, finding the appropriate pattern, but now I throw out a counter notion: making do with the fly you have. There will be days when neither imitative pattern nor fancy fly seems at first to work, and in that case you must *make* your fly work. Forget about the 'right' fly and make *any* pattern you choose *become* the right fly – by inducing the trout to take it.

Having just introduced the idea of egging a trout on to take your fly, almost challenging him to take it, before we go back to fly selection it seems appropriate to continue the digression a little further. If dry fly splits naturally into two divisions: orthodox and unorthodox, we could just as well refer to dry fly as imitation and dry fly as lure. Since the great majority of fishing books concentrate heavily on dry fly as imitation, discussion of the immensely important practice of dry fly as lure should occur at this convenient point.

6

Dry Fly as Lure

'A glint of sun has warmed the air,
The flies will soon hatch out,
To lure and tempt, from their deep lair,
The bonnie speckled trout.'
Wilfred Walter Morris

On a cheerless spring day some seasons ago I had reached my wits' end. Using traditional downstream and upstream wet fly, I had caught a few trout early on, but they were all too small to keep. Absolutely nothing was showing. The odd iron blue had hatched and skittered down the current, pointedly ignored by all fish. Distant rumbles of thunder seemed to be threatening me with a soaking – clearly it was not my day. That is until, in a moment of sheer desperation, I took off my wet fly team and tied on some light nylon with a bushy dry Wickham's Fancy on the point.

The effect this tactical switch had on the trout was galvanic. The dark, oily water, tumid with mid-week rain, seemed no longer a depressing and impenetrable mystery. Within a cast or two the best trout of the day, a big male with a kype, had fastened on to the Wickham and was duly landed. Fish after fish hurled themselves up at the big fly until I had caught a dozen. I kept only the best four, three of them good fish for the stream. The sun even came out in mid afternoon and my photograph of the catch shows a gleaming double brace on the bright grass. The storm passed me by too, so I avoided a wetting.

A REMEDY FOR DULL DAYS

The point of the story above is not just to show how an indifferent day became a very good one but to show the efficacy of the dry fly on dour and dismal days. Though I put together a basket on this day I hardly saw a trout rise unless it was to my Wickham. The fish had stomachs crammed with caddis larvae, yet earlier my deep-sunk Pheasant Tail Nymph had not attracted them in any quantity, which it usually does on such days. No, it was my bonny, fluffed-up Wickham, almost the sole floating fly to drift over them all day, which compulsively attracted the trout.

That day serves as an important illustration of my theory of the dry fly as lure. Incidentally, the experience has taught me on subsequent similar dull spring days to fish wry fly with a bushy dry fly on the top dropper (Wickham's Fancy, Rough Olive, Greenwell's Glory or Gold

Figure 10 *a*) and *b*) Aerial comparison of fields of vision of surface-feeding and deep-lying trout

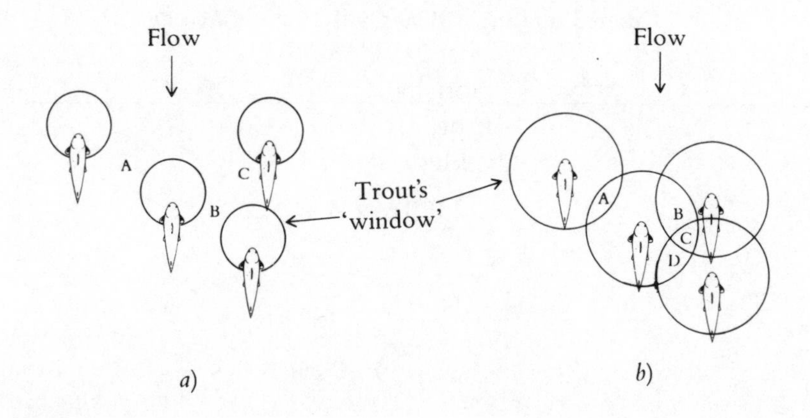

This bird's-eye view illustrates the difference in the field of vision between surface-feeding trout and deep-lying trout. In a) on a summer's day four trout lie near the surface feeding. A dry fly floated downstream to pass over areas A and B would be quite invisible to all four fish. Only a fly presented over area C would be visible to more than one trout during that cast. Four separate casts would have to be made to present a fly satisfactorily to all four trout. In b) on a chill spring day four trout occupy the same positions in the river but lie much deeper. Their fields of vision ('windows') are much wider. No single cast could cover all four trout, but a fly floated over area A would be visible to two of them. A fly floated down the line BCD would be visible to two trout, three trout and two trout respectively. In other words, two good casts could satisfactorily cover all four trout. More trout per cast would see the fly on the spring day, prompting in addition an element of competition among the fish.

Ribbed Hare's Ear, for instance), a mid-water ephemeral nymph copy on the next dropper (Snipe and Purple or Waterhen Bloa, for instance) and a Pheasant Tail Nymph or Killer Bug on the point to attract the caddis hunters and grubbers deep below.

Another point, and an important one, is that deep-lying trout have a wider field of vision than those lying near to the surface. This means that on cold spring days, when trout are deep down, a big, bushy dry fly, curiously, is often more visible to more trout on each cast than it would be on a summer's day. Hence on dour days your dry fly is in fact more visible to more trout (promoting an element of competition among them) and thus by the law of averages must attract a few fish to the surface to take it. See fig. 10.

Figure 10 *c)*

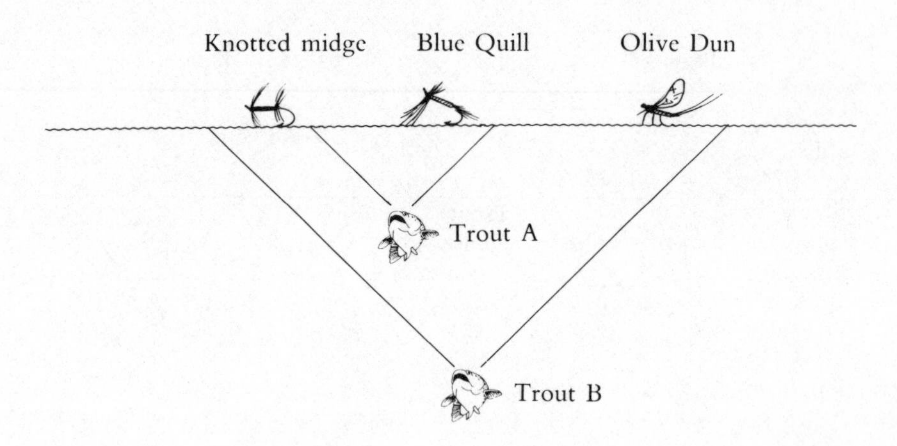

Cross-section illustrating the difference in the field of vision between a surface-feeding fish and a deep-lying fish. The surface-feeding trout at A can see only the Blue Quill: this is all his 'window' permits. The deeper-lying trout at B has a much increased field of vision. He can perceive all three flies. He therefore has the choice of which to take, but will have competition from the trout at A if he decides to go for the Blue Quill.

BASIC PRECEPTS OF WET FLY V. DRY FLY

Conventional angling wisdom about wet fly v. dry fly throws up several dicta, the three most rigid being:

(i) As trout's stomachs reveal mainly subaqueous material it is more profitable to fish with subaqueous flies as opposed to surface ones. (Skues originated this view.)

(ii) Deep-lying or deep-feeding trout are not easily tempted to the surface to take a fly so it is better – rather, imperative – to use a nymph to get down to them (Sawyer, Kite) or to ignore them completely and move on to a surface-feeder, if you can find one (Halford, Lunn, Bridgett).

(iii) Trout feeding on one particular type of fly or nymph are best tackled with – should *only* be tackled with – an imitative pattern (Halford, Skues 90 per cent of the time, the Purist School 100 per cent of it).

Many other writers have endorsed these precepts and generations of anglers have adhered to them.

To go off at an apparent tangent, imagine we were about to creep up a stream with a spinning rod, a jar full of worms and another of preserved minnows. Those who have ever used these two methods will vouch for the truth of the next few statements. A trout feeding exclusively on nymphs or surface duns/spinners will never refuse a well-presented worm or minnow. A deep-lying fish will often rise to upper water to grab a tumbling worm or minnow before it has sunk many inches. A surface-feeding fish will dive greedily to intercept a sinking worm or minnow beneath him. A sedate trout, immobile at his station, quietly sipping down duns, will suddenly, seemingly out of all character, dash sideways to seize a worm or minnow tossed there. Likewise, a baby frog, beetle, moth, wasp or grasshopper jerking about on the surface (attached to your hook) will invariably lure a trout to it, whether that trout is lying 1 ft (30 cm) or 4 ft (1.2 m) below.

In other words, a trout feeding exclusively on ephemeroptera can easily be induced to vary his diet and take a juicy worm, grasshopper or minnow skilfully presented in his vicinity. There exists no healthy trout anywhere which cannot be *lured* into taking an exceptionally provocative hors d'oeuvre or dessert.

AN EFFECTIVE SUBSTITUTE

What has all this got to do with fly fishing? A great deal. As a boy I spent endless long summer days creeping and crawling up burns and brooks observing the behaviour of trout at very close quarters. I have chucked my worm, grasshopper or minnow at scores and scores of trout. I have experimented with fish lying doggo and seemingly not on the feed and with ones choosily taking only one type of fly. I have also experimented with brown and rainbow trout, as well as grayling. The result is always startlingly the same: they take. There is a side to a trout, a combination of his curiosity, aggression, envy and greed, which can always be pandered to. Things like this are not said in modern books on dry fly fishing, but they need saying. A hatch-matching dry fly purist never learns about this earthy side of a trout's personality – perhaps he regards it as sordid – and it is an omission in his education. For, should you find a *substitute* for the worm or minnow lure, a legitimate *fly* lure, then you are able to play the same game as the wormer or spinner and *lure* the trout to his doom.

Reservoir and stillwater fishermen have tackled this aspect of trout behaviour with great ingenuity and created a mind-boggling array of lures; indeed the majority of stillwater flies are termed lures and the method of fishing them has become known as lure fishing. River angling has not needed such large or colourful attractors (we may smile at the thought of how an angler using a Tandem Traffic Lights or

Flashabou Pretty Dog would be received at the Houghton Club on the Test); but it has come up with some fancy flies of proven deadliness over the years. The majority of river flies, however, are patterns which attempt to imitate nature, and most river fishermen have become conditioned to their use.

It might seem that I am about to announce that we river fisherman require a similar array of exotic lures as the stillwater fishers have developed, but not so. The patterns we have already are adequate – it is the way they are often used that is not. Actually, just before I leave the subject of reservoir lures, there is no reason why this kind of wet fly lure should not work on rivers, especially in deep pools. The Bullhead imitation by Taff Price, or the Sculpin Muddler, seem to me to have distinct possibilities. Try them!

ADAPTIVE APPROACH

To return to dry fly as lure. My years of observing the predatory instincts of trout when fishing for them with worm and spinner in my youth have had a huge impact on my fly fishing philosophy. At this point I might just add that even as a boy fly fishing was always my first love, and especially dry fly – a method which for me has always had the strongest emotional pull of all the types of angling. What I have done, though, is harnessed all that I have discovered about trout personality in whatever conditions (for instance, whether holding a spinning or a fly rod in my hand) and adapted it to the technique of dry fly fishing.

There is nothing new or revolutionary about using a dry fly as an attractor, a flashy or bushy goad to incite interest. The addition of the word 'fancy' to a fishing fly immediately indicates that it is designed for just this meretricious purpose. The use of coloured tags, especially in the grayling range of flies, betokens naked ostentation as opposed to dowdy imitation. Nor is there anything new in the idea of speculatively using such a fly in order to bring some unseen fish up to it. Indeed the basis of North Country dry fly technique is fishing the water, searching pool after pool in the hope of luring a trout up to your offering. Nor is this idea the exclusive property of the North, for even the southern purists used the method on the right day. Take Halford:

> . . . some of the cleverest fishermen occasionally float a dry fly on spec over the best looking of such places if even they fail to see a sign of a rise, knowing that if a fish is there he must be in position, and ready to take advantage of any unexpected treat provided for him.

Certainly not fishing the rise! Elsewhere he says:

> Both trout and grayling will, in such a case, often rise at and fasten to a somewhat large fly if quite dry and cocked. I do not think a particular pattern is of very

> great importance; but for what it is worth, my own experience gives the preference in such a case to the Wickham.

A PERSPECTIVE ON THE IMPORTANCE OF A PATTERN

The statement 'I do not think a particular pattern is of very great importance' is quite some admission from the man who put both dry fly and detailed entomology on the angling map. Admittedly, in this second quotation he is talking of fishing in blustery conditions, but it does echo my contention that fly pattern is not the most important factor in dry fly fishing.

Skues too, a brilliant dry fly fisherman, it must not be forgotten, was not averse to fishing the water with a bushy fly. In a section he entitles 'An Abnormal Day' he admits to being bored because no fly could be seen on the river and no trout were feeding. So what did he do? He knotted on his favourite Landrail and Hare's-Ear Sedge and proceeded to fish upstream. The result?

> But by degrees, picking up here a trout and there a trout, the bag worked its way by 3.30 to the comfortable total of four brace, including the brace of grayling. And all the while not a dun or a sedge showed on the water.

Hardly an object-lesson to a purist!

Another chalkstream man, and champion of dry fly, G.A.B. Dewar, makes a case for non-purist tactics. He talks of days when 'the duns are usually ignored, and the difficulty of coaxing a good trout is great'. Here is the solution:

> It is best, perhaps, to try some small fancy fly if an imitation of the dun, may-fly or alder prove unavailing.

And he adds:

> The Wickham is a capital fly of the fancy order for dry-fly fishing.

That Wickham again! All of these references show that even traditional orthodox dry fly theory embraces the idea of the dry fly used as a lure. But the difference between my philosophy and that of these three august anglers is that dry fly as a lure was the exception for them, whereas for me it is the rule. The use of a fancy fly was for them an anomaly, almost something to apologize for. The same Skues who tells us of his abnormal day when he fished the water with a bushy fly can also give us evidence of incredible scruples. For instance, he has a troubled conscience about the Red Quill. He does not know what this fly represents or why trout take it. This clearly disturbs him greatly – so much so that he feels the fly is slightly reprehensible:

> I am left with the facts and no theory to account for them. For this reason I seldom use the Red Quill.

I have no such scruples. As a Northern fisherman I cannot afford them. Perhaps, for all that, I have a less enquiring mind than Skues. I frequently find that I do not understand things that I have witnessed on the river. For instance, I still have no idea why the Wickham's Fancy works so well for me when trout are smutting or during falls of black ant. This mystery, though, does not prevent me from using the Wickham at such times. In a way the mystery rather enhances the love I have for the fly. Most unSkuesean.

PRACTICAL APPLICATIONS

My philosophy of dry fly as lure, then, is not rational in the entomological, Skuesean view, but it is immensely practical. It has two different practical applications. The first is in fishing the water, where the idea is to fish with a fly sufficiently bulky and fluffy to lure up a trout or grayling from deep below. It will work on days when no surface fly is visible, when dry fly seems a lunatic approach. It will work when no fish are visible and all seems dour. You must use your imagination and fish over lies where you expect a take. You must be on your mettle, ready to strike at any moment. Rises are usually sudden and savage, but also infrequent. It is a true test of reactions.

The second application is in fishing the rise. With unchoosy fish it works and with very choosy ones too. It even works with bulging trout or 'tailing' fish by weedbeds. In fishing the rise it is not only the bulky size of the fly which matters but also the mode of presentation. The 'plonking down' technique (as opposed to the 'thistledown' one of the textbooks) often works, as does the skilful placement of the fly in such a spot that the trout must instantaneously make up his mind whether or not to take: my 'shock tactics' of Chapter 5. You give the trout no time to think, no opportunity for deliberation – you play on his instinct, not his intellect. The trick is to present the bushy fly in such a way that you make the trout feel that he would be a fool not to take it, that he would be missing out on a great opportunity. This is dry fly at its most alluring, as irresistible as a juicy worm.

A WORTHY PRECURSOR

I should like to provide further documentary evidence to strengthen my case, because, in my view, the value of these tactics cannot be overemphasized. I began the chapter by telling of my experience some years ago on a cold spring day. In the introduction to his marvellous *Diction-*

ary of Trout Flies A. Courtney Williams cites an identical occurrence. He says that there was 'cold, dull weather, with a nip of east in the wind' and 'not one trout was seen rising and there were no insects of any sort either on or near the water'. So, like me, he changed from fruitless wet fly to dry fly, saying:

> This was a policy born of desperation and was quite unjustified by the conditions which would scarcely have been less propitious for the use of a floater. Yet within half an hour, a brace and a half of sizable trout were in the creel and on the following days fair catches were recorded, all the fish being taken on either the Grey Duster or a Dogsbody.

Being the kind of enquiring angler he was, Courtney Williams performed an autopsy:

> An examination of the stomach contents of some of the trout taken, showed that they had been feeding exclusively on caddis larvae. Why then they should have risen to a fly on the surface and totally ignored a sunken one, appears to me to defy any logical explanation; but fishing is prone to such anomalies.

For me, what was once, to use Courtney Williams's words, a 'policy born of desperation' has become a regular and reliable way of catching trout. It is as if the anomaly has become the norm. I am sure Courtney Williams only quotes this experience because, like me, he used the event as a springboard for further 'anomalous' success. He certainly champions the dry fly throughout his fascinating introduction, believing it to be a more profitable method than wet fly on both swiftly flowing river and heavily bushed little brook, and observing that 'on fast rough waters, rather larger patterns than those generally recommended, may be used with advantage'. He clearly understood dry fly as lure.

A LUCKY FIND

My next reference to the technique came to me by a happy chance. On a recent short holiday I bought a book I had not seen before, *From Tyrone to the Test* by James Dickie, a first edition in faded buckram bearing no date, but 1940s at a guess. Back at my hotel, I realized just how timely my purchase had been, for my eye alighted on a chapter entitled 'Bumbles'. I soon saw that a heaven-sent reference had been given me right on cue. What follows is the fruit of my serendipity.

Mr Dickie was on holiday in Ireland when he witnessed a local angler, B——, reputed to catch large bags of trout, fishing in the following way:

> He stopped and cast, and the fly hit the water with such force that the disturbance could be seen from where we stood. I asked my friend what he thought of B____. 'Why,' he said, 'he can't fish at all.' 'Watch,' I said. 'This bird has a system of his own.'
>
> B____ worked on up, banging his fly on the water at intervals; he never dried it more than four times between casts; sometimes he fished a rising trout, at other times he apparently 'fished the stream', but he never stayed long in one spot.
>
> Opposite us, a large trout had been rising at regular intervals; he was over thirty yards away, under B____'s bank. B____ saw him rise, and the fly hit the water heavily somewhere near where the rise had been. There was a plunge, and the trout was on.

Dry fly as lure!

Mr Dickie went on to witness four more trout caught by the canny B____, all fish round the 1 lb (0.5 kg) mark. His curiosity aroused, Mr Dickie began to make enquiries about the type of fly B____ was using and discovered that a certain Joe Young, professional fisherman and fly-tier, was responsible. Not long after this discovery Young agreed to give Dickie a lesson in this style of trouting. Dickie caught three tiddlers, while:

> Young stood in one spot and caught five good trout, none of which were taking natural flies, but which came up and attacked (for that is the only word which describes the form of rise) the monstrosity on the end of his line.

And the fly? A few sage old heads will nod when I reveal it: the Claret Bumble. Young was very fussy about the dressing of it: apparently, only a winter-plucked Andalusian cock's hackle would do. The dressing: size 14 hook, body – bronze peacock herl, hackles – dark claret, cock's up the body, dark grouse at shoulder. This fly was for dark days and on bright ones he suggested a Worm Fly (hook: 12–16, peacock herl body, red hackle.) Butcher that I am, I would suggest these on size 10 hooks too!

From this point on Dickie became hooked on this approach to dry fly. He discovered that 'in a blazing sun and dead low water, trout would come up and take the "hairy worm"'. He describes how a rising fish which had spurned his tiny duns and spinners fell for the new approach:

> I sent him a size 1 (hook 14) hairy worm. It lit about a foot to one side of him and, as it touched the water, he had it.

Yes! The technique really does work! He adds, with the enthusiasm of the newly converted acolyte:

> I moved on upstream, killing enough trout, under unpromising conditions, to convince me that I had found a new form of fishing.

AN OBSESSION WITH IMITATION

Why is it that so few books mention this form of deadly dry fly? Possibly because the kind of crafty local angler such as B____ or Joe Young are not writers of fishing books. For years books on dry fly have been stuck in the 'replica rut', written by elegant men, with elegant theories, in elegant prose. Pronouncements such as Dewar's 'The dry fly fisherman must strive to hold the glass to Nature' have held sway for too long. Dry fly cries out for a new, more enlightened era. I humbly suggest that if a dry fly fisherman strives to *better* Nature both the size of his baskets and the quality of fish in them will improve.

Dickie exported this Irish knack and brought it home with him. He tried it on the Kennet and caught a 2 lb (0.9 kg) nymphing trout with a size 2 Worm Fly on his second cast. He tried it on the Test, describing how he 'firmly banged' a Young's no. 2 Claret Bumble down near a trout, which 'instantly rushed at it'. He tells us that this experiment was often repeated with success, and concludes:

> The moral appears to be this: one way of dealing with educated trout is not to give them the time to inspect the fly carefully; send them something attractive, which looks as if it were capable of escaping and they will either attack it at once or ignore it completely.

There it is, my own pet theory penned by another's hand! There is little that is new in fishing, and if we are prepared to explore a little we will discover the right books.

My next reference is Halford, again, because I cannot leave the subject of Bumbles without his mention, for he introduced these famous Derbyshire flies to the Test. He recommends the Orange Bumble for tricky nymphing trout downstream of weedbeds: fish 'picking up any little larvae, caddis, shrimps, snails or other molluscs drifting off the weed'. He suggests both the Gold Ribbed Hare's Ear and the Orange Bumble for this difficult task, musing:

> What the fish mistake the Hare's Ear or Bumble for is mere conjecture. The Hare's Ear possibly is taken for a dun just emerging from the nymph envelope, and the Bumble does certainly bear some faint resemblance to one of the orange tinted freshwater shrimps.

This is curiously impressionistic, and the phrase 'faint resemblance' oddly vague for such a purist. It is impossible not to conclude that Halford very well understood the theory of dry fly as lure.

My penultimate reference comes from a delightful little book published in 1949: *Thoughtful Practice with a Dry Fly* by Arthur Woolley, a minor classic in its way. His 'Bug', a large, parachute-tied Orange Tag, he designed for flicking into tree-covered lairs, eddies and backwaters. It is clearly designed to fool big trout prone to feeding on terrestrials which have unwillingly taken the plunge; a type of fishing he will not apologize for since it 'demands knowlege as well as skill'. He clearly understood dry fly as lure.

A THEORY ON TRIAL

My final reference comes from my own pen. A few years ago on the last day in June I was fishing the River Ure. It had been a great day with a tremendous fall of spinners, a real Lunn's Particular day. But, suddenly, as evening drew on the fish stopped taking my fly. It took me a while to realize that they had switched from sipping spent pale wateries to shovelling in the smuts. I have several tiny smuts of my own for use on these occasions but these offerings were all spurned. Even Wickham's Fancy failed, though it rarely does at such times. Perhaps I was not fishing well because I was weary after a long day. Still, I wanted to prove equal to this new challenge. But after a while, defeated, I decided to plod home. A heavy creel dug into my shoulder as I trod slowly back up the river.

Then I spied a titanic trout. Under a small alder a big fish was smutting with such glee that his head was breaking the surface twice a second. It was a display of frenzied feeding such as I have rarely seen. Trembling, I approached more closely. The question was: what fly? My little smuts and gnats had not worked so far. I picked out the biggest, bushiest Coch-y-bondhu in my box – certainly an outsized smut! With wobbly fingers I tied on this mammoth offering. I began to put out line, heart in mouth, for this was some fish.

He took first cast, pouching the huge fly without deliberation. I struck. For five minutes I never saw the fish. He dashed out of his lair down to the bottom of a deep run and sulked there, doggedly tugging like big brownies do. He was so glutted with smuts he could hardly do more than this. But he came to the net, 1¼ lb (0.6 kg) of spotted Yorkshire bronze, the best fish of the day by 5 oz (0.14 kg). Twenty-seven trout (not all kept) had fallen to my spent spinner imitation, but the twenty-eighth, and biggest, had fallen to a dry fly as lure.

CHOICE OF FLY

What is the best type of dry fly to use as a lure? I agree with Halford that it is not very important to select a particular pattern. All the flies mentioned so far in this chapter are excellent for the job. My personal favourites are Wickham's Fancy, Gold Ribbed Hare's Ear, Coch-y-bondhu and Blanchard's Abortion. To these I would add two dressings of my own invention, the Haystack Greenwell, a giant variant tied on a no. 8 or 10 hook, and the Hotspur (of this, more later) plus Courtney Williams's favourite, the Grey Duster, the Soldier Palmer, the Stone Fly and the Silver Sedge. Nor should the Wulff series be overlooked, as they were created for this very purpose.

My own special penchant is for the Grey Wulff, a superb fly. From across the Atlantic, the Bi-visibles and the Adams are also splendid flies. For grayling the various tag patterns are excellent – they take trout galore too. The list is endless. Perhaps a final mention for three patterns normally tied as wet flies which for me work as deadly dry flies. The dry Butcher, which Courtney Williams has also heard of and which Maurice Wiggin also praises, the dry Peter Ross, one of my father's favourites, and the dry Jock Scott.

ACCURATE CASTING

It is also clear from this chapter that rising trout are apt to lash almost instantaneously at a dry fly presented as a lure. I always aim to catch a trout first cast with whatever method I choose. With worm or minnow a trout will not demur: he will have it straight away or not at all. In my boyhood I got used to this rhythm. I learnt that if the first cast was clumsy or inaccurate it meant no fish. It is a principle which is engraved on my fisherman's psyche. Hence, many of the trout I spot and cast for I get first cast, or if not, within three. By the time I have made half a dozen casts unnecessarily it is almost time for me to move on. This may sound very restless and impatient, but in practice I find I rarely need more than a cast or two per trout before I have got him. My whole approach is geared to this mode of attack. Only great distance, drag or very exposed lies – and hence extreme nervousness in the fish – consistently defeat me.

The longest time I have ever played a freshwater fish for is one and a half hours. I was fishing the River Tyne with a 7-foot (2.1 m) trout rod when I hooked a 14 lb (6.5 kg) salmon. Ninety minutes later I beached her, a dogged hen fish, on the gravel. That kind of excitement I can bear (those runs she made still bring my heart to my mouth) but the idea of spending that length of time after one trout is an anathema to me. We are all victims of both our upbringing and our vices. My upbringing was with the worm; my chief vice is that I like to catch a trout first cast.

It is a private suspicion of mine that many of the trout I have read about which succumbed to writers' umpteenth beautifully presented imitations, would have been suckered first chuck by my splashy Wickham's Fancy!

7

Selecting the Right Fly
Part Two

'God in his wisdom made the fly
And then forgot to tell us why.'
Ogden Nash

Whether we are seeking to imitate Nature with a facsimile fly or to outdo her with a spectacularly fancy offering, some kind of selection must take place. This process might be highly scientific, highly theoretical, deviously cunning, merely whimsical or simply based on close observation and good guesswork. In the first part of my discussion of this subject I rather mischievously suggested that it is the fisherman and not the fish who must be taken most into consideration when a fly is being selected. There is an element of truth, and certainly common sense, in this assertion but it is too much of a simplification to be the complete picture.

I believe that an expert fisherman can make any fly the right fly. Charles Ritz says that 'the fundamental rule' in fly fishing is, 'the fisherman counts for 85 per cent and the fly for only 15 per cent'.

THE DANGERS OF DOGMATISM

And yet I still admit that there are days when fly selection counts for more than presentation. Such days may be rare but the fact that they exist at all proves that it is dangerous to be dogmatic about fly selection. Eric Horsfall Turner encapsulates this wisdom thus: 'the only fly-fishing conviction I have reached is that the wise fly-fisher should have no convictions', while Skues issues the wise warning, 'the trout is the most extraordinary creature at bringing to nought, not only theories, but definitely established principles'.

Having watched me start down this cautious track, you might well be wondering if I am about to sidestep saying anything more positive than this on the subject. I do have a few more positive things to say, but first I should like to examine the views of a few other authorities. As early as the nineteenth century, anglers were being warned against the mindless ritual of ceaselessly changing fly patterns, by no less a master of imitative fly selection than Halford:

> The modern school are far too much addicted to continual change of fly, often changing merely for the sake of changing.

A warning indeed. Such mindlessness is also attacked by the modern American writer, Art Lee, who comes down firmly in favour of the Ritz dictum that presentation is more important than fly pattern. Lee gives us his own golden rule: 'Thus, if readers glean anything from this volume, let it be that *no fly is "right" unless it's fished correctly*.'

And a very good golden rule this is too. The book is *Fishing Dry Flies for Trout on Rivers and Streams*, published in 1983, and it has some interesting material in it.

William B. Currie, uses a simple system when he fishes dry fly. Like me, he angles mainly in rocky Northern rivers, and admits:

> I am not bred in the school of entomological imitators who change their fly to match a change in temperature which darkens the olives' wings. I know most of my rough stream flies and I have half-a-dozen flies in my box which represent them well.

Currie's selection, which allows for variation in size (mainly 12 and 14) and sparseness of dressing, is: Greenwell Spider, Black Spider, Tup's Indispensable (parachute style), winged Greenwell's Glory, winged Dark Olive and a Badger Spider. What strikes me about this selection is that it is more imitation-based than attractor-based. It is conservative but sporting – as his smallish hooks attest. I favour the odd flashy fly in my collection (I am fatally attracted to tinsel!) and I am not averse to brutal great size 8 and 10 hooks, like my American cousins. Still, William Currie is one of Britain's premier anglers and I commend his selection (and his books).

A STREAMLINED SELECTION

Harry Plunket-Greene, the great chalkstream fisherman, showed that even in Hampshire, deep in the heart of exact–imitation country, an angler can get by with a handful of flies. He says:

> It is surprising how few you need. I only want half a dozen, in the following order – iron-blue, red quill, pale watery dun, ginger quill, olive quill and hare's ear.

Oliver Kite, another Hampshire angler says:

> In practice, not more than a dozen dry-fly patterns are needed during the course of a full chalk-stream season.

He adds that he himself uses only ten varieties of dry fly. As for wet flies, Kite says that only one is necessary – the Pheasant Tail Nymph. Frank Sawyer, the angler who invented the modern dressing of this fly, advocated just two or three wet fly patterns for river fishing. All these men were great fishers, so their opinions are worth hearing.

Another writer, alas now somewhat neglected – quite unfairly for he is a man to heed – Arthur Woolley, suggests a similar short list of flies. He argues that you cannot hope to carry a representation of every variety of fly. But he sagely remarks that it is unnecessary to bother even trying to do so. Woolley calls his list of seven 'an irreducible minimum'. They are: Red Quill, Gold Ribbed Hare's Ear, Lock's Fancy (Pale Watery imitation), Black Gnat, Iron Blue Dun, Little Red Sedge and his 'Bug' (an Orange Tag tied with a parachute-type hackle – a creation of his for luring cruising fish). Of all the many short lists I have come across this is definitely one of the canniest, in my opinion, and worthy of careful consideration.

Charles Ritz writes very interestingly on this subject, not least because he mentions the differing tastes of many of his fishing friends. What I find fascinating about this is how divergent is the fly choice of these friends. He tells a story against himself. On the USA's River Beaverkill one evening he caught nothing while three companions 'all had considerable success with different flies'. It is also clear that many of Ritz's friends had extremely brief lists of flies. He quotes the case of Simonet, 'the best fisherman I know', who fished quite happily with only two flies: a grey spider with a yellow body and ginger-brown spider with a red body.

THE ONE-FLY ANGLER

To take reduction to its logical conclusion, it should be possible to fish exclusively with one pattern. I remember many years ago reading in *The Field* an article in which the author revealed the results of an experiment he had carried out that season. He had fished the entire season on a chalkstream with just one fly, Kite's Imperial, if my memory serves me correctly. The result? His baskets had apparently not suffered at all. His conclusion? That the one-fly approach works.

I sincerely hope that this writer went back to his former ways in subsequent seasons. It was not an experiment I could have kept up – I would have become bored very quickly. Once a trout fisherman becomes separated from the necessity to observe nature minutely, and is fishing mechanically, he is surely missing much of the charm of the sport.

John Roberts, in his splendid *New Illustrated Dictionary of Trout Flies*, published in 1986, tells us that the celebrated North Country angler, Arthur Oglesby, once used the dry fly John Storey for an entire season 'to the exclusion of all other patterns'. Apparently, he caught slightly above his average seasonal haul of fish.

TO EACH HIS OWN CONCLUSION

I suppose such experiments do lead to some interesting conclusions, but which one are we to set any store by? That a good fisherman can make do with just one fly? That good fishing, not good flies, is the key to catching trout? That trout are stupid creatures because you can catch them on any old pattern, no matter what they are feeding on? That the practice of often changing flies is a pointless one? That you can save yourself a great deal of money (and pocket space) by only ever carrying one pattern of fly. That some anglers are incredibly boring, unadventurous and unimaginative in limiting themselves to merely one pattern of fly?

I presume we each select the conclusion that provides us with the ammunition we need to make our case. However, to rely on merely one fly, I believe, runs counter to what trout fishing is all about: ceaseless enquiry into Nature. Monomania in fly selection is surely a stultifying habit. Indeed Courtney Williams warns against just this practice.

> I must freely concede that it is not a difficult task to take a large number of fish on a small number of patterns, but I feel that by imposing a limit of this nature upon himself, the fly-fisher must rob himself of a great amount of pleasure. For that reason, I am always a little sorry for the 'one-fly' man because he must lose some sport and a great deal of interest and fun.

I agree with Courtney Williams. My position is really a compromise between the modern school of compulsive fly-changers that Halford criticizes and the rigidity of the one-fly fraternity. Though I have a tried and trusty core of favourites, about a dozen altogether, I use more flies than this in a season, although not necessarily in one day. Like Arthur Woolley, I could boil my selection right down and with this I would be entirely confident about fishing all season. For details of these flies, plus others I favour, see the next chapter.

THE IMPORTANCE OF MOBILITY

I generally carry four fly boxes with me. One is a big sixteen-compartment aluminium Wheatley box and contains hundreds of dry flies of many patterns; another is a small aluminium box holding mainly olive-imitation dry flies; the third is a medium-sized clear-plastic box enclosing most of my flashy, attractor dry flies. The fourth box is a small plastic one full of nymphs. I also have other boxes, which I carry only on special occasions: my mayfly box and a box full of river and lake wet flies. Some anglers carry fewer fly boxes than I do, many carry more – and bigger ones. Even my biggest boxes slip easily into a jacket pocket, unlike the huge wooden variety which so many modern anglers favour. Like Wemmick in *Great Expectations* I like my property to be portable, since for my kind of trouting mobility is the golden rule.

We all have favourite flies, and the reasons we like them so much can be most arbitrary. Perhaps the best expedient is that of success, though even our favourites let us down at times. I admit that many of my own favourites are inherited, and reflect my father's and grandfather's taste. There is also fashion in flies: certain patterns fade into obscurity to be occasionally resurrected, or, more sadly, to be entirely forgotten. For instance, who nowadays still uses the Tod Fly? Yet the creator of it, one of Scotland's greatest-ever anglers, highly recommended it earlier this century. The Chambers, one of my father's favourite flies, is in no dictionary of mine, nor can I find any reference anywhere to one of my special favourites – Blanchard's Abortion. Maybe its name militates against it, especially in Catholic circles!

I too am subject to fashions in flies. For years Greenwell's Glory was my favourite dry pattern but in recent seasons I have come to prefer the Gold Ribbed Hare's Ear, and this is the fly I now knot onto the end of my line more than any other. And the Silver Sedge came back into my favour last season.

FAITH IN YOUR FLY

Confidence in your fly is important too. Many an author has stressed this, Eric Horsfall Turner among them: 'F.M. Halford, despite his insistence on the ultimate importance of imitation, was a very practical angler. He observed that confidence in a fly helped the fly-fisher to success.'

Maurice Wiggin states how crucial this kind of confidence is, suggesting that there is some sort of mystical connection between an angler and his fly when he has faith in it:

> You must have confidence in your fly. Why this is so, I have no idea. But every experienced angler knows it to be true. It would be too far-fetched to suggest that somehow your confidence is transmitted to your artificial fly. But that is what *seems* to happen.

Henry Williamson mentions this same thing, in his short story 'Trout'. Here the advice appears all the more sage because it is a grandfather's:

> Your grandfather used to say, I remember, that to fish with the fly you believe in is nine-tenths of the way to persuading a fish to believe in it also.

This confidence works whether you have selected an imitative fly or a flashy one. When using an imitation the trick is to try to get the trout to take your fly for granted, so that among a string of real ones yours will go undetected as a phoney. Like us, trout take things for granted – just as well, because we would never catch any otherwise!

The trick is to put your imitation over a trout in such a way that he suspects nothing. Once his suspicions are aroused and he looks critically at your fly, you are lost. The difference between the expert and the ordinary fisherman is that the expert's confidence and skill allow him to present his fly in such a way that its general appearance arouses no suspicion, whereas the ordinary angler lacks this crucial knack.

A CONFIDENT APPROACH

Likewise, the expert will still have confidence in his fly if he tries a bold stroke whereby he proposes to make his fly stick out like a sore thumb. His use of a gaudy fly, or the employment of a deliberately splashy presentation are each an assertive switch of tactics, not some apologetic last straw. In other words, whether you seek to deceive a fish by avoiding arousing his suspicions or by openly stimulating his interest, the subterfuge will always be the more successful if executed with confidence.

Thoughtfulness helps, adaptability too, and also imagination. J.W. Hills has some particularly good advice in this regard. He suggests this tactic for the educated trout: 'In fact, the more trout are fished for and the cleverer they become, the more inclined are they to refuse the copy and take the variety.'

It is the application of just this sort of intelligent idea that keeps the wily angler one step ahead of his less thoughtful peers.

To sum up, there is no doubt in my mind that good fishing – skilful presentation – obviates the necessity for accurate or exact fly imitation, and also sidesteps the need for entomological knowledge. Yet I feel that putting some thought into fly selection, based on a grounding in entomology, greatly enhances the enjoyment of trout fishing. Perhaps it is all a game and it does not really matter which fly we use. If we find a fly which works we often delight in assuming that only this one works, and that we alone have been intelligent enough to discover it. If this way of thinking brings pleasure, who am I to question it?

8

Flies
My Selection

'Each to his choice, and I rejoice the lot has fallen to me.'

Rudyard Kipling

As a result of writing the last chapter I decided to analyze my own fly-selection process over a number of randomly chosen seasons. I thought half a dozen seasons would be enough to give an accurate picture. I chose 1965 as the year to start because it was the second year that I had kept detailed records, and the one in which as a fifteen-year-old I really began to bloom as a fly fisherman, tying many of my own flies and catching trout on them. The last three seasons I chose are more recent, and show my current habits.

In my records I tend to mention only those fly patterns with which I succeeded in catching fish, so I probably used a few more in practice than are counted here. The results are shown in the table that follows:

Year	*Wet flies*	*Dry flies*	*Total*
1965	4	10	14
1966	6	14	20
1970	4	9	13
1982	10	13	23
1985	10	19	29
1988	8	17	25
Average:	7	14	20

The picture is quite a consistent one. I seem to use around half a dozen wet flies per season, around 15 dry flies, and about 20 patterns in all. This table shows me to be rather conservative in my fly selection. I have become slightly more adventurous in recent seasons but still rely on less than 30 patterns per year.

My count included all trout fishing – stillwater and rivers – so my selection seems even more limited when this fact is borne in mind. Also, the table does not show the following piece of information: that the majority of trout I catch fall to an even smaller selection of flies than those totalled here. In reality I rely on about three or four wet flies and about half a dozen dry flies for 80–90 per cent of my fishing.

CHANGING HABITS

This core of workaday flies on which I chiefly rely has changed slightly over the years. For instance, in my teens I used the Tup's Indispensable and Ginger Quill more than I do today; likewise in my teens I was oblivious to the powers of the Pheasant Tail Nymph and Killer Bug – two flies I would not be without today. There are a few patterns, however, which have remained constant to my taste. The Greenwell's Glory and Wickham's Fancy are dry flies common to all six seasons, while a Black Gnat and a Sedge of some variety or other get a mention five times. The Partridge and Orange is a wet fly I have used on five out of six of these seasons. In my records for 1984 I find that my three usual favourite flies were: Greenwell's Glory, Wickham's Fancy and Gold Ribbed Hare's Ear. If I had to be silly enough to limit myself to only three dry flies then I think those patterns would be my choice, though I would want to add a fourth to be really content: something dark – an Alder, Black Gnat or Coch-y-bondhu.

A CORE SELECTION

I will now play the game that many other writers have played in the past and draw up a list of my indispensable favourite flies, or to use Arthur Woolley's phrase, my 'irreducible minimum.' He boiled his dry flies down to seven favourites; I can go one better and make do with six. Add three wet flies and I have nine flies to deal with almost every situation, whether fishing dry, wet or nymph. The list reads: dry flies – Gold Ribbed Hare's Ear, Greenwell's Glory, Wickham's Fancy, Alder, Blanchard's Abortion and Grey Duster; wet flies – Killer Bug, Pheasant Tail Nymph and Partridge and Orange. The Alder I include as a utility fly to be fished either wet or dry. This selection also covers, although in a basic way, all the colours and tones the fisherman needs as he imitates Nature. Ideally, however, I would want a few more than this to be comfortable, so I now draw up a slightly more comprehensive list of 15 flies: five wet and ten dry. Those patterns above the dotted line are my 'irreducible minimum'.

	Wet flies		*Dry flies*
1	Killer Bug	1	Gold Ribbed Hare's Ear
2	Pheasant Tail Nymph	2	Greenwell's Glory
3	Partridge & Orange	3	Wickham's Fancy
4	Snipe & Purple	4	Alder
5	Black & Peacock Spider	5	Blanchard's Abortion
		6	Grey Duster
		7	Black Gnat
		8	Silver Sedge
		9	Soldier Palmer
		10	Grey Wulff

This list is very condensed and omits several important patterns, such as wet Waterhen Bloa, Mallard and Claret, March Brown, Greenwell Nymph, Black Pennell and famous dry patterns such as Tup's Indispensable, Lunn's Particular, Ginger Quill, John Storey, Coch-y-bondhu, Badgers and a Mayfly – the Summer Duck or Straddle Bug. Alternatively, the Grey Wulff would double as a Mayfly.

The only change to the list I would contemplate would be for limestone or chalkstream fishing. For such waters I would exchange the Blanchard's Abortion for a Lunn's Particular or a lightly dressed Tup's Indispensable.

For my rough-stream fishing the Grey Wulff, Blanchard's Abortion and Soldier Palmer are included because they will float on the most turbulent and frothy of runs. They are also good Bustard alternatives for night fishing.

HOOK SIZES

As for hook sizes, I would like most of these flies tied on both 12 and 14 hooks. A few Alders, Dusters and Black Gnats on size 16 and 18 would be very handy, as would a few Wulffs and Wickhams on size 10 hooks. Winged or hackled patterns? I am not too fussy, though in general I prefer my Hare's Ears and Wickhams to be winged. A Spider Greenwell will do for most of my rain-fed river fishing. I would like my Black Gnats tied as spiders too, with a plain black cock hackle and some twists of red silk along with the black silk on the body.

In my view there is no necessity, especially on northern and western waters, to carry masses of olives, quills and other ephemerid copies. Upwing flies seem to have a stranglehold on the imagination of many trout-fishing writers. Perhaps in days gone by there was a justification for this. In the Golden Age of Angling, before farmers had polluted the environment with artificial fertilizers and pesticides, there was probably much richer upwinged feed for trout in most rivers in the country.

While upwing flies are still very important to fly fishermen, especially in limestone and chalkstreams and on big rain-fed rivers with rich fly life, there are many smaller rivers where ephemerids are something of a rarity. In high summer on many of the upland rivers and streams that I fish, especially wooded ones, terrestrial insects account for at least half of all the food that the trout consume. Terrestrials and Diptera make up a good 90 per cent of their diet. On such waters there is no need to be pernickety about what sort of olive to fish. Similarly, on some rich waters, where upwing flies do hatch out regularly, trout can often be found feeding on midge pupae, gnats or terrestrial strays.

OPPORTUNISTIC FEEDERS

Hence, the need for the fisherman to have some Black Gnats, Knotted Midges or herl-bodied flies handy. An Alder or Coch-y-bondhu is good for most situations. In general there is no need to be too precise in your terrestrial copies because trout feeding on such manna are none too choosy. There is also an irony about all this: time after time I have found that trout feeding on Diptera prefer the ephemerid copy to the realistic–looking gnat. The only explanation I can offer is that trout are even more opportunistic than we realize and find juicy morsels hard to resist. Top of all ephemerid dressings for its value as an attractor, in my experience, is the Gold Ribbed Hare's Ear, which seems to have some extra magic about it.

The value of fishing twin dry fly can hardly be overestimated in this context either. The combination of size 14 Gold Ribbed Hare's Ear on the point and size 16 Alder on the dropper is deadly, because any fish from the most opportunistic to the most fastidious feeder can fall for its attractions.

There are no hard-and-fast rules about fly selection in trout fishing. Indeed there are many ironies, puzzles and perplexities in the sport. Your fly will succeed as well as my fly, or vice versa, or sometimes neither will do. Any of the flies on this list could work for any trout at any time.

My short list is comprised of patterns which have worked best for me day in, day out, season in, season out, for more than 20 years. I can do no better than recommend those flies which have caught the most trout for me. My selection 20 years ago, though containing some of these patterns, would no doubt have been marginally different. If I am still lucky enough to be fishing two decades hence, my selection might well be slightly different.

9

A Question of Light

'Enwrought with golden and silver light,
The blue and the dim and the dark cloths
Of night and light and the half-light.'
W.B. Yeats

For years it troubled me why in a stream of rising trout an angler could induce fish, all obviously feeding on one pattern of hatching fly, to take a variety of different patterns of artificial. Sometimes change is forced on an angler: he may break in a trout and lose the only 'killing' pattern in his possession, or the fly might become unravelled or mangled or thoroughly waterlogged as a result of its success. This might happen to a succession of dry flies, and the angler becomes increasingly astonished at the sheer variety of the fly patterns which are acceptable to the trout.

Similarly, it troubled me why fish which have doggedly spurned all attempts to snare them with one particular fly, suddenly and irrationally it seems, snatch confidently at it. We have all had the experience of this. We say to ourselves: 'I'll just make one more cast with this fly and then try another pattern,' when, lo and behold, on that very last attempt the trout suddenly takes. Why?

This is not a case of 'hammering' – George la Branche's technique of endlessly covering a fish with a fly until out of weariness or submission he takes it – a technique, incidentally, which I have never had the patience to employ. I merely refer to the presentation of a dry fly some ten or a dozen times to a fish you have seen rise. You feel you must change pattern because the trout has had plenty of opportunity to inspect it, when to your surprise he changes his mind and seizes it. Why this sudden change of mind?

So, too, we must have had occasions when a fly floated over a trout either directly above him or to one side of him, is ignored, but as soon as we plonk the very same fly on the trout's other side it is taken guilessly. Charles Ritz tells a wonderful story of a trout caught this way, a fish which upon examination proved to have only one eye and had therefore spurned flies on its blind side. But the explanation for many similar occurrences is not always as unusual: it is, I suspect, more often just a question of light.

EFFECT OF LIGHT

For years these were conundrums I could not solve. I am not saying that I now have a definite solution but I do have what I believe to be a sensible hypothesis which will do until some other angler comes up with a better theory. My hypothesis is that a trout's perceptions of a fly can be radically altered, muted or blunted by light. Changing a fly is just one way that a fisherman can alter a trout's perception of the offering laid before him. The thoughtful angler can sometimes alter a trout's perception of the same fly by employing one or two little ruses. This requires that he use his imagination to picture what the trout is seeing, rather than simply relying on what he himself sees. Frank Sawyer's remark, 'the view of the fish must have primary consideration', cannot be overestimated. But first let me illustrate my hypothesis in human terms.

Imagine two people, one sitting at each end of a rectangular room on a bright summer's day. A window is at one end of the room and one of the people sits with his back to this window looking into the room. At the other end of the room there is no window, merely a wall. The other person sits here, his back to the wall, looking towards the window. At this moment a third person enters the scene, through a door halfway down the room at a point equidistant from the two seated people. What do those two sitters see? Not the same thing. The person seated at the bright end of the room with his back to the window sees the third party with the clarity of even light coming over his shoulder. He sees every feature of the entrant: height, build, hair colour, age, physiognomy, clothes, and so on. The person at the other end of the room sees something very different. He sees a tall shape silhouetted against the glare of the bright window. For a moment his eyes struggle to fix detail as his pupils contract in the dazzling light. He may not be able to determine the hair colour, age, mode of dress, or even the sex of the newcomer.

AN EXPERIMENT IN PERCEPTION

When angles of light differ from one observer to another enormous differences of perception result. You can perform a similar experiment for yourself. Sit sideways to a source of bright light. Put up each hand at arm's length: one against the light, one bathed in it. Observe how each hand is a different colour: one dark, one pale. Now do this holding identical patterns of fly between finger and thumb. Next try holding a dark fly in front of a whitish background and then in front of a dark background. Do the same with a pale fly. Notice how light and background alter your perception of colour.

These are no doubt crude attempts to explain a very complicated matter, but the inescapable conclusion is that light plays tricks on us all, human or beast, bird or fish. Even in the same stream, pool or run a trout will see the odd fly coming down with a perception different from that of his immediate neighbours. If this fly is a natural one it hardly concerns us, but if it is an artificial it concerns us greatly. Perhaps our Gold Ribbed Hare's Ear has been ignored for half a dozen casts by this fish, then on the seventh he takes it. If there is any truth in my hypothesis, then maybe the reason the Hare's Ear was taken the seventh time of presentation was that for some reason it looked more inviting than on the first six casts *because a trick of the light made it seem so.*

A hundred and one different factors could account for this. A change of light, for instance a sudden blotting cloud or a sudden brilliant break in the clouds, could alter a fish's perception of a fly. The reflection of light off a pale underwater stone could distort the view in one zone of a trout's 'window', explaining his madness in taking a fly all his peers have refused. Equally, a ripple of water could do the trick, or the waving of a distracting piece of weed, or glare from an old bottle on the bank, or merely the fact that the angler has changed his position and thus altered the presentation of his nylon cast and the angle from which the fly floats over the fish.

A SPECIALIST FEEDER

Before I go any further with my theory and become too dogmatic about its accuracy, I must admit that I am only groping in the dark. It is all guesswork. We do not really know what the water surface looks like to a trout. What is certain, though, is that the trout is a very specialized predator and he specializes, among other things, in raking the water surface with his eyes in search of possible food. He has evolved over millions of years (a much older race than *Homo sapiens)* and it is both impertinent and imprudent to make concrete assumptions about what exactly a trout sees when he looks up at an artificial fly. As Skues points out:

> His eye is adapted to the medium in which it works, and it is at least conceivable that it is so constructed as to enable him to overcome the difficulty of appreciating colour with the light behind it.

So it is only speculation on my part when I put forward these ideas about the possible factors that alter a trout's perception of a fly.

Over the years various experiments have been performed in an attempt to discover what an artificial fly must look like to a trout. Skues performed several tests but admits that they were rather amateurish and established little, concluding that 'others, more fortunately situated and better equipped' might one day 'follow up and verify or disprove' his ideas. Ingeniously, Eric Horsfall Turner photographed artificial flies from below water. He built his own tank, and tried to simulate differing conditions of daylight, using an electric fan to create ripples. Praiseworthy though all these experiments are, none of them in any way really comes anywhere near reproducing the realities of surface conditions on a river. I have yet to read of an experiment conducted actually out in midriver, especially in ripply or turbulent areas of water. In the trout's real underwater world, current, counter-current, swirl, ripple, turbulence, colouration due to sediment in suspension, weed, gravel and rock, plus sky, sun and cloud, all influence fishy vision. Few wild trout ever see flies in such serene and civilized conditions as those detailed in these experiments.

UNEQUAL VISION

It is reasonable to assume that in any river there will be competition for the best 'lies' and that some trout will have to make do with less desirable feeding stations than their bigger and stronger brethren. It is reasonable to assume further that some trout must lie in stations where their windows do not have an even clarity. Maybe a stick or ripple on the water surface, or turbulence welling up from below, or a bright sky above a dark bank, or an overhanging branch, or reflected glare from a nearby rock, will result in part of a trout's window being blurred slightly – like a motorist driving with a windscreen partially fugged up on a damp day. Maybe – though how can the pursuing angler perceive such subtleties from 15–20 yards (14–18 m) away? – it will only be when an artificial is floated through the blurred or dazzling section of a choosy trout's window that the fly will have a chance of being taken.

So what can a fisherman do to exploit these apparently blurred or fuzzy areas in a trout's window? Well, though he will not know where exactly these areas are, he can cover all the options. In other words, he must make sure that he searches out every zone of a trout's window before either changing fly or moving to another fish. See fig. 11.

AN EARLY LESSON

As a lad I was scrupulously taught to fish ripply North Country water by my father (who to this day remains the best dry fly fisherman I have ever seen) and I learnt early that there was no point in moving upstream and abandoning a rising fish until that fish had been properly covered. I well remember his quiet voice from behind my left shoulder saying: 'And now a cast just to the left of that little ripple on the trout's right.' How often such a cast was rewarded!

I have often experienced the same thing since those days, but in reverse, with beginners or less experienced friends. While I watch them cover a trout and see them about to progress to another fish, I have advised just one more cast slightly to the left or right. It is surprising how often this cast, if it can be performed, succeeds. In some cases, if such a cast is beyond him, I sometimes take the rod from the beginner and, having watched him present the fly 15 times to the trout with no reward, catch the fish on my first attempt.

Figure 11

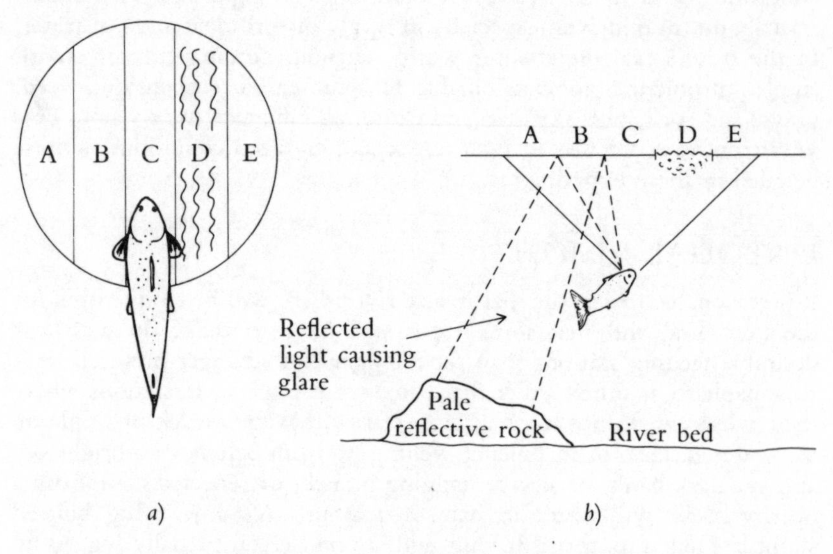

a) Bird's-eye view of the zones of a trout's 'window'. Zone D is ripply water and could possibly be exploited by the fisherman.

b) Zones of a trout's 'window' in cross-section. Zone D, the ripply area, is visible to the fisherman, but what he cannot know is that a pale rock on the river bed is creating an area of glare on the underside of the water surface; and therefore in the B Zone the trout might more easily succumb to an artificial fly.

Different beginners react differently to such a performance: those already pleased with their own skill put it down to my outrageous luck, others less sure of themselves regard it as some magical ability I possess. In reality, it is neither. When you have fished for a long time you become able to read water well. Every time you see a rising trout, or come to a place where you believe a trout to be, you have an instinctive, in-built perception of when you have properly covered the fish. You take your own judgement for granted, without thought, but in fact what you have done is very logically and methodically put your fly over every zone of the trout's, or supposed trout's, window.

In fig. 11 a fisherman who does not cover zone D is careless because the ripple (caused maybe by a stone or stick upstream) should have been exploited by his fly. Likewise, though he cannot know that zone B is subject to underwater glare and therefore a blurred area for the trout, he should have covered his options and still floated his fly down over that zone. He who fishes most thoroughly catches the most fish, is an axiom I stand by.

ESSENTIAL SKILL

The ability to know when a trout, particularly one rising in streamy water, has been covered properly is one of the premier skills of the first-rate fly fisher. It is the combination of good eyesight, good sense of water orientation, ability to 'mark' a fish, ability to gauge distances both minute and long, and a fair degree of hand-eye coordination.

The whole operation is complicated by the fact that it may not be possible for a fisherman in one stationary position to cover all of a trout's window properly. For instance, he may have to move to avoid drag. More subtly, he might move position in order to present less of the nylon to the trout. This option is certainly one that the alert fisherman should always bear in mind, for it is an especially useful tactic on bright days. The position of the sun in relation to your intended approach is also a major consideration on very bright days. Sawyer advises that you choose the bank from which you can fish into the sun in order to avoid scaring fish with your line. Of course, you do not always have the choice of bank: you simply might not have permission to fish both. Again, either topography or thick vegetation may prevent such choice.

Many of the heavily wooded little rivers that I fish have lengthy sections fishable only from midstream in waders, so sometimes neither

Figure 12 Avoiding frightening a fish

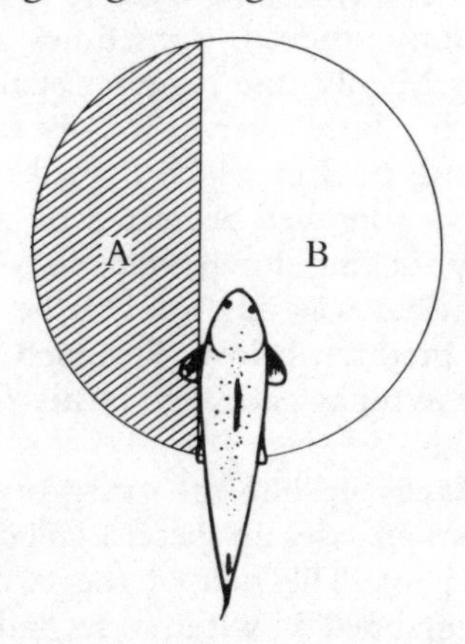

This is a common problem which arises from the extent of the trout's field of vision.

The fisherman can cover Zone B adequately from his present position, but to cover the shaded Zone A properly, he must alter his casting position and therefore his angle of approach. If he does not do so he might frighten the trout either with a dragging fly or with a visible fly line and leader.

bank is possible. However, a compensation of such streams is that the full glare of the sun is often masked by branches. Therefore, even if you lack complete freedom of choice, you can still alter your angle of approach slightly by moving a yard or two, and this small adjustment could be enough. See fig. 12.

This tactic cannot be overestimated and can be far more profitable than merely willy-nilly changing of fly pattern. No fly, however well tied, is any use at all if its presentation is flawed.

UNSOPHISTICATED PREY

All that I have just said implies that trout are frightfully tricky to catch, but in fact I am only talking about those choosy, problem specimens which evade all but the most thoughtful of approaches. Some trout are far less fussy. Sometimes you have only to plonk your fly – any old pattern will do – down anywhere in the trout's window and he will snap it up without a qualm.

One of the alluring endearments of small trout streams that are not much fished is that their inhabitants are all too often joyously unsophisticated. Free-rising fish eagerly gobble up anything that falls on the water, your fly included. In mayfly time this lack of caution can be still more pronounced, to the extent of your not even needing to drop the fly in a trout's window. In slowish water neuromasts along a trout's lateral line will register the vibration of a big fly hitting the surface with a smack, and a fish will often come over to investigate, seizing your offering without scrutiny. Indeed, sometimes you will find several trout rushing for your Mayfly, the biggest usually getting there first.

I remember just such a little river in mayfly time some years ago. I came to a big, deep, still pool in which I spied three feeding trout. At the head of the pool, in a lie well protected by overhanging branches, one trout was greedily sucking down every mayfly that filtered downstream. Indeed, so efficient was this fish that he had cut off all surface supply of duns to his brethren below. Resigned to this, the two other feeders had settled for nymphs and were busily feeding at the depth of about 5 ft (1.5 m).

I tried to get my Mayfly up into the overgrown neck of the pool to attract the very ostentatious riser up there. I failed. But I let my fly drift on slowly down the pool. The first of the two deep feeders rushed spectacularly up and grabbed it without second thoughts. I fastened into him and played him out. My very next cast came down over the other deep lier. He had it with a similar gusto. Two good trout in two casts and neither called for any complicated calculation about window zones. It all goes to show what a wonderfully easy business trout fishing can be on occasion.

CLEAR VISION

More generally, however, trout feeding in the stiller, smoother parts of rivers are more difficult to deceive than those inhabiting the more tumbling, rushing reaches (though not necessarily more difficult to catch). This is because they have both clarity and time on their side. There will usually be no blurs in their windows, and in the clear slow-flowing water they have time to scrutinize any artificial offering; time to be both choosy and snooty. Sometimes they will even follow a fly downstream only to ignore it with even greater disdain. One of the features of big Don trout is that they will turn and shadow your fly downstream for a yard or two in placid places. They do not always spurn it, often taking like a porpoise, with an exciting great downstream head-and-tail roll.

Usually, though, in slow parts of the river the angler will have less resort to the tactics described in this chapter, needing to rely more on changing fly and achieving deception by sheer imitation of the real. (However, I admit I will quickly abandon dry fly in such places if I am having no luck, resorting to a twitched nymph instead.)

I remember once spying a big trout in a moorland river in Yorkshire. He was lying in a stillish pool and I put the fly which had been doing all the damage so far for me that day (a hackled Wickham on a size 14 hook) right through his window. He was not at all interested. I switched immediately to a nymph and tickled his nose with that. Somehow I contrived to frighten him, with rod shadow, fly line or my own silhouette I know not. At any rate, he moved rapidly up into the head of the pool where there was a ripply stream. Despite the strong water, because of its clarity and a trick of the light I could quite plainly see the big trout – a hovering dark shape. Indeed, I even saw him barge another sizeable fish out of his way as he took pride of place in his new lie – he was obviously lord of the pool. I waited for a while then decided that this was an opportune moment for lunch.

A SECOND TRY

While I ate I watched the show. The big fish stayed up in the stream at the head of the pool, from time to time moving sideways or up and down. He was clearly feeding, though under water, for he had not yet broken the surface. I smoked a cigar, still watching, planning my next move. The nymph again? Perhaps not, because something about my last cast had frightened him. Big trout have long memories – that is why they get so big. Not worth the risk, I concluded. Why not the Wickham again? It was the fly of the day. In the ripply water it might appear more attractive than it did on the placid surface downstream 20 minutes ago.

I finished my cigar, knotted the Wickham back on my line and crawled into position. I began to put out line, hoping that the streamy water would lull the trout into a false sense of security. I need not have been apprehensive because the big fellow took the Wickham confidently on the first cast. I hooked him and, after he had put on a display of aerobatics and predictable power, I landed much the best fish of the day.

This throws up various questions, the most interesting of which is: why did the trout take the Wickham the second time? My conclusion is that he took because the ripply water either disguised the artificiality of my fly or hid the nylon from his critical view, or both. At any rate, it confirms my long-held opinion, rather an obvious one, that trout in ripply or running water are more easily deceived with a dry fly than those in smooth, slack-flowing stretches.

It is conceivable that different fly patterns are acceptable in the different zones of a trout's window. Referring again to fig. 11, in a hypothetical example we might find a fish feeding on pale duns which will only be susceptible to a pretty good pale dun copy (Tup's Indispensable, Lock's Fancy, Poult Bloa, Little Marryat, Goddard's Last Hope, etc.) floated down over his nose (zone C) but at the extremities of his window he might fall for a fly which he *thinks* is a pale dun. To his right, in nice even light, he will probably require a pattern fairly closely resembling a pale dun, but the ripple will enable us to get away with something as impressionistic as a Gold Ribbed Hare's Ear, Grey Duster or Ginger Quill. On his left, where there is some glare on the water, almost any fly of the right shape – the colour is unimportant – will do: anything from a Wickham's Fancy to a John Storey, even a Coch-y-bondhu.

This is, I repeat, only a hypothetical case. It is perhaps too neat to be true, but it illustrates my theory. My argument in this chapter is only a hypothesis, an attempt to explain why trout in the same river on the same day fall for different flies. It is a theory that will only stand until it is proven to be incorrect.

THE ATTRACTIONS OF TURBULENT LIES

Before I come to the concluding part of the chapter, let me clear up a few loose ends. I implied earlier that trout in turbulent lies might have been driven there from easier positions by stronger fish, but this is by no means always the case. Some particularly active trout take up turbulent positions where much surface food is brought down to them in a kind of drowned mulch and all they have to do is sieve up the debris. Others occupy turbulent lies because sub-surface food, larvae and molluscs, are funnelled into that locality. Incidentally, though such a fish might be nymphing, he could prove susceptible to an attractive surface offering.

While it is normally advisable to fish into the sun to hide both your shadow and the shadow of your line from trout, it may sometimes profit you to cast with the sun behind you. Provided your figure and your waving rod are not seen by the trout, this situation may have the following advantage. As he looks up towards your fly he is looking into the sun and will be a little dazzled. In such a situation the impression your fly makes might be attractive enough to prompt the fish to take. The very same pattern presented in the opposite zone of his window would be scornfully rejected. This is a variation worth trying when all else fails.

In some areas of his window a trout's vision is binocular, in others monocular. Right in front of him all is seen in binocular clarity, but to the extreme right and left he sees in monocular fashion. A fly falling in the periphery of a trout's monocular vision might just trigger his feeding impulse, and he will turn to take it without binocular scrutiny.

DIFFERENT WAYS OF SEEING

A fisherman sees his dry fly against the predominantly dark background of the water. Trout see dry flies against the predominantly light background of the sky (unless there is a branch or bridge overhead). Surely this must produce differences of perception? Something which looks ginger to an angler could look anything from pale olive to black for the fish. Perhaps this explains the success of mid-brown flies such as the Pheasant Tail, Ginger Quill, Dogsbody, Gold Ribbed Hare's Ear and Wickham's Fancy when ephemerids ('olives') are being taken by the trout? Brown and ginger are colours which work on any day in any light. Pale flies, in my experience, work best in bright, open water. Almost all my really big trout taken in rough, open water away from trees have fallen to large pale flies.

Obversely, dark flies are best under trees, certainly better than pale ones. A good proportion of my best bosky backwater fish have made their last mouthful a Black Gnat, Beetle or Coch-y-bondhu. Brown flies are equally effective under either branch or open sky. Light and background certainly have something to do with these responses.

A fisherman should not feel cheated if when he finds olives hatching he can only attract the trout with a fly which to him looks quite un-olive-like, such as a Coachman, John Storey or Wickham. How sad that all his home-made olive imitations have been spurned! No failure is implied. A fly in splendid isolation in your vice might look the very image of a medium olive, but on the water on some days it will not look realistic to the trout. The reason why the famous old patterns of fly have become famous is that, often for reasons unknown, they consistently prove fatally appealing to trout. The whole business of the attractiveness of flies is gloriously complex. Even the most scientific anglers are far from completely understanding the trout's perception. We might get closer to this understanding one day, but at present we are still stumbling in the twilight. So we should not feel depressed if we do not understand *why* the trout are taking our fly. Rather, we should feel lucky that they are taking *any* fly of ours!

To conclude, I think that too many anglers judge their fly patterns by what they themselves can see stationary in their palms. They simply fail to imagine the differing perceptions of rising trout in a ripply, reflective, mobile, constantly flickering, flecking environment. It is a dappled, dancing, opaque, diaphanous, rainbow world. Light flits, flutters and twinkles. Shadow and sunlight vie in a turbulent battle – one minute tenebrous, another minute brilliant. Into this turmoil we cast our flies.

The fisherman can, as we have seen, try a few tricks to equalize the struggle if the trout seem to be getting the better of him. In summary, he can:

(i) exploit any ripple, glare or shadow he perceives in the vicinity of the trout;
(ii) make sure he covers thoroughly all zones in a trout's window;
(iii) try altering his angle of approach, which includes using the sun to his advantage.

It is the ripply, reflective world described somewhat euphuistically above that accounts for so-called anomalies, when trout take unexpected patterns of artificial. At such times it is not so much science and entomology that must come to our rescue, but perseverance and imagination.

10

The Wickham's Fancy Puzzle

'How I wonder what you are.'
The Star, Jane Taylor

There are some famous and successful trout flies which suceed day in, day out throughout the season, and have succeeded season in, season out since they were invented. Some of these have an understandable success – for example Lunn's Particular, an excellent imitation of a spent pale watery spinner. Others, however, have an appeal to trout which is something of a mystery to fishermen. Many of these flies bear their inventor's name plus the appendage 'fancy', as if to announce that they are less an actual representation of a natural fly than the mere artistic whim of their creators. Trout like bright and bushy flies. The explanation for this is not always clear, but terrestrial morsels like grasshoppers, bees, crane flies, greenbottles and moths, all bright creatures, are on occasion greedily accepted.

Some years ago while lunching beside a little river I witnessed an interesting event. A moth, unluckily awoken from its slumbers and completely dazzled by the brilliant sunlight, came fluttering blindly across the pool. Utterly disorientated, it plunged onto the water where it vibrated helplessly. Its very desperation to free itself was its undoing, like the splashing swimmer whose flailing arms and legs attract the attention of a hungry shark. Somewhere down in the pool, neuromasts along a trout's flank registered the poor moth's struggle for survival. As soon as trouty eyes locked on to their target the insect's fate was sealed. I waited without breathing, expecting something spectacular. I did not wait long. Within three or four seconds the moth was gone in a flurry of ecstatic foam. Back down in the depths a happy trout was chewing on his unexpected hors d'oeuvre.

A TACTICAL SUCCESS

After I had eaten, I knotted to my leader a big bushy fly, three times bigger than the one I had succeeded with so far that day, and put it on the spot where the moth had met its demise. It was a horrid cast beneath some tangled low branches but I had two strokes of luck – one good, one ill. The good luck was that my nylon caught over the tip of a branch, making my fly dibble and dap upon the surface most attractively. The ill luck was that when the trout took, which he did with delight, the same branch impeded a clean strike so I missed the fish. Still, I had proved my tactics to be correct. The important part of the experiment had worked: my bushy fly had fooled the trout.

Now, I realize that our use of bushy eponymous flies is not often linked to such a spectacular event as this, and that more often than not we simply fish up a run with a fancy pattern and cannot be certain what the trout mistake it for. I also concede that for the thinking angler there is an element of dissatisfaction about the success of fancy patterns, though not, I hope, a dissatisfaction which detracts from the pleasure of angling. I hope, in several paragraphs' time, to give these discerning fishermen a few crumbs of consolation.

A dry fly, unlike a nymph, wet fly or reservoir lure, is a static object: it is not fished in jerks or twitches or hops (at least not usually) and so it must attract fish solely by its shape, size and combination of colours. It certainly does seem that some fancy dry flies do trigger the trout's feeding impulse better than others. There is a nucleus of celebrated dry fly patterns, none of which is a close representation of an actual fly but each of which is a renowned killer. I am thinking of proven deadly patterns such as, in alphabetical order: Baigent's Brown, Dogsbody, Gold Ribbed Hare's Ear, Grey Duster, John Storey, Orange Bumble, Red Quill, Red Tag, and Wickham's Fancy.

The excellence of each of these famous flies has been championed by some of the greatest angling brains of their day. Hence Rollo extolled and wrote at length about the Baigent's Brown; Courtney Williams underlined his preference for the Grey Duster; Halford thought so highly of the Bumbles, the Orange in particular, that he introduced them to the Test (from Derbyshire); while generations of North Country anglers have sworn by the John Storey, including such distinguished practitioners as Arthur Oglesby, Donald Overfield and John Roberts.

Two flies on this list, Gold Ribbed Hare's Ear and Red Quill, bemused G.E.M. Skues, precisely because he was not sure what either of these flies represented or why their appeal was so marked to the trout. It is quite clear that though he used both patterns he was vaguely uneasy about doing so: their success was a puzzle to him.

Two flies on this list are pre-eminent among the affections of great writers. The Wickham's Fancy and Gold Ribbed Hare's Ear are more often mentioned as superb trout attractors than any other fly that I have come across in print. Quite independently, I have come to the same conclusion. If you had asked me at 15 and again at 30 what was my favourite fancy or attractor dry fly, I know what my answer would have been. If you ask me again at 45, I am pretty sure my answer will be the same: the Wickham's Fancy. The reason I like the fly so much is that it catches me so many fish; likewise, the Gold Ribbed Hare's Ear, which is generally the first fly I knot to my cast at the beginning of any day. Add a Greenwell's Glory to these two and here is my Great Trinity of Flies, the last three I would abandon.

THE WONDERFUL WICKHAM'S

But the Wickham's Fancy has to be the most curious killer of the three. Greenwell's Glory is an excellent dark olive copy; this is established. The Gold Ribbed Hare's Ear, while not a precise imitation has a very strong resemblance to several members of the Ephemeroptera. It looks very like an olive on the water. Though perhaps best as a copy of a medium olive, it can certainly pass as both a dark olive and a pale watery. Slight variations in its body colour create even greater versatility. Skues, though puzzled by it, was forced to acknowledge its brilliance, remarking that the man 'who first conceived its possibilities' was a 'genius'.

But the Wickham's Fancy is something else. It does not really look like any aquatic fly. Perhaps its closest resemblance is to a member of the sedge family. Among terrestrials it will certainly pass as a moth. So, as an evening fly it is superb, doubling as a sedge or a moth. This is but one of its uses. For some reason trout taking olives will also fall for a Wickham, especially in streamy water. It has been pointed out that the gold body looks green when it floats on water. I have certainly found that the fly works wonderfully well on very bright days in open water, a time when the gold of the body will be at its most reflective. But it is also equally effective in sombre and shady places.

For another inexplicable reason the Wickham's Fancy is also renowned as a fly which will take smutting trout. On the rivers of the North York Moors in late summer there can be prolific falls of black ants. When the ant is up I know no better killer than the Wickham. Why this is so I have no idea.

A MULTI-PURPOSE PATTERN

This fly will also lure a nymphing or tailing trout to the top on occasions. It acts as an excellent attractor on cold spring days, likewise in the hot dog days of August it pulls trout up to it in streamy places. It is a splendid end of season stand-by, a marvellous September fly. It is very bushy and unsinkable, floating better than most flies, and is one of the premier flies for rough water. Curiously, however, it will also account for trout in very still water, not prolifically perhaps, but it is remarkable how many fish come slashing up at the great ginger monstrosity as it sits there like an alien on the calm surface. It is a very 'visible' fly for fishermen, always buoyant and of a colour which has strange properties: it stands out on bright water, where it looks dark, and on dark water, where it looks pale. I also find it a splendid fly to use when fishing twin dry fly or wry fly. In these situations its power to attract trout when other flies fail can be most apparent.

Truly, the Wickham's Fancy is an amazingly versatile fly. Its versatility has no equal – it is the ultimate utility dry fly. If the man who invented the Gold Ribbed Hare's Ear was a genius, the inventor of the

Wickham's Fancy is an ever greater one. (There is some question as to *which* Wickham did invent the fly: Dr T.C. Wickham, a friend of G.E.M. Skues, or one Captain John Wickham? Others too have been put forward as the originator. Donald Overfield makes a case for one George Holland, while Courtney Williams puts forward the name of George Currell. What is less in doubt is that the fly originates from the Winchester region and was first tied in the 1880s.)

This fly is very useful in differing sizes. I like to have dressings of it in my box from size 10 to 16. In every size it has its purpose: winged or hackled, I do not mind which, though I probably have a slight preference for the winged version, especially on size 12 and 14 hooks. Like rubber waders, plastic floating fly lines and nylon for leaders, the Wickham's Fancy is one of angling's utterly indispensable accoutrements. I would rather have invented it than have written *Hamlet*, have been the first to swim the Channel or the first to walk on the Moon!

MYSTERIOUS ATTRACTION

Now, I think we have a right to ask *why* some fancy flies are so successful. Could there be some hitherto hidden reason why flies such as the Gold Ribbed Hare's Ear and Wickham's Fancy are so popular with trout? I have listed all the exceptional merits of the Wickham's from the fisherman's point of view but come no closer to accounting for its attractiveness. Could there be a reason, one not advanced before to explain the fly's success?

If my hypothesis in the last chapter was the slightest bit shaky, then my present hypothesis is even shakier. Here it is. Could the reason for the Wickham's success be that it closely resembles an *extinct* fly? An extinct fly, moreover, that was of such appeal and deliciousness to trout that they hunted it into extinction, either that or watched it vanish forever under the glaciers of the Pleistocene ice? Was it a fly so popular with trout and so much part of their diet and their evolution that its recognition became part of every trout's instinct and that deep inside each trout brain is still this image of the ultimate food – even juicier than the mayfly or more succulent than the blue-winged olive?

Could it be that, though extinct, so inextricably part of trout's history for eons was this fly that any echo of it instantly triggers prehistoric memory deep in a trout's cerebrum? Could the Wickham indeed be the replica of some vanished aquatic fly, a fly which no literate human ever saw because it disappeared before or during the Great Ice Age? Or perhaps it was even older, flourishing in the Miocene before the advent of *Homo sapiens?* The history of the trout is long and ancient. Humans have a puny history in comparison: salmonids have ninety million-odd years start over us! A fly which disappeared a million years ago, just as we were beginning, might have flourished for several million years as the trout's favourite dish. Such a heritage could not easily be expunged.

AN EXTINCT ORDER

A vanished order of red flies! It is an exciting thought. An order in which there were other Wickham type species. It would explain the susceptibility of trout and grayling to the colour red. An order of which Wickham, Orange Bumble, Red Quill and Red Tag are reminiscent. We have all heard of flies in amber and perhaps seen examples in books or museums. Certainly there were some exotic insects in days gone by. It would be an irony if when Skues and other chalkstream purists of old rejected the Wickham's Fancy as merely a 'lure' they were in fact spurning the finest imitation of the most popular fly on which trout ever fed, albeit if its invention was haphazard and its inventor knew not that he had created a mere fancy but had stumbled on a superb copy! The most outrageous example of serendipity in angling history! Equivalent to Archimedes' bath or Newton's apple!

Too far-fetched? Perhaps, but then perhaps not. Nature's irresistible laws hold fast and throw up some surprises, especially to the urbane. Trout fishing is not like golf or cricket where the laws are all man-made. Beside a trout stream the angler has only some influence – Nature has the rest.

A trout is an opportunistic predator. He is superbly well evolved. Despite nitrates on the land which cause his rivers to clog with weed, fertilizers on the fields which reduce his aquatic food, industrial and agricultural pollution and acid rain which thin his ranks, he survives. If a fly he likes disappears from his environment he makes do with others. Those of his brethren who cannot make this compromise, do not survive. The fittest and cleverest trout adapt quickly to their new lifestyles. Some trout in the big English man-made lakes do not waste their time eating minuscule chironomids in the sultry heat of dour August days but have, like pike, learnt to hunt shoals of freshly spawned coarse fish. Hence the modern branch of fly fishing termed lure fishing.

ADAPT OR DIE

If the law that Darwin discovered is to be obeyed by all successful species then aquatic flies too must adapt to their environment. If they become too attractive to trout they could be eaten into extinction: their quest must ever be to strive to become unappetizing to trout. Perhaps some aquatic flies have learnt to emigrate from water in order to survive? The Alder is a fly which, in its adult form, has learnt to keep well clear of salmonid jaws. Perhaps for an attractive fly species to survive it has to protect itself by sheer numbers, and perhaps once such a species begins to dwindle in size its fate is sealed because trout's teeth will do the rest. Possibly this explains why the dwindling Yellow Sally continues to survive: because it has made itself repulsive to all but the most undernourished trout? (I watched it hatch steadily over two days recently and never saw one of its number taken by a fish.) Certainly the March Brown is a fly which is now more or less extinct on many of the northern rivers where it once flourished. The great hatches of this fly that I have witnessed in recent years on the Aberdeenshire Don I have not seen on the Eden since I was a boy, and in Yorkshire never in any quantity.

I am depressed to admit that the Dark Olive seems to be on the wane in some of the northern rivers I have fished all my life. The Iron Blue as well seems to be under threat in the North, alas. (Plunket-Greene would turn in his grave beside the Bourne if he knew – it was his favourite fly, indeed the 'only fly' for him.) All upwing flies have been savaged countrywide by modern farming methods.

Do you suppose that when the last ephemerid has gone, choked to death in a mixture of pig slurry and industrial effluent, that trout will refuse to take a Greenwell's Glory? I doubt it! How long will it take trout to delete their memory of the order Ephemeroptera? The difference will be that when ephemerids disappear they will be documented as extinct, like the Dodo. If my hypothesis is correct then the race of Red Wickhams has not been documented, which also means that my hypothesis will never be proved.

NATURE'S IMPRESS

So change occurs. Evolution is synonymous with change. But alongside the change the vestiges of old behaviour still flourish. Nature's impress is so severe that her survival traits are not easily erased: old habits die hard and robotic instinct lingers curiously on. The domestic dog turns round and round three times on your carpet in front of the gas fire, flattening down grass on the Miocene Savannah, an echo from 20 million years ago, before he sleeps. Other evolutionary ghosts still eerily haunt his subconscious, for when you take him out on a walk he still marks his scent on a concrete territory he will never defend.

When humans sit at the dinner table they turn from side to side to converse civilly as they eat. Put a human in the wild, ask him to eat alone, and the video recording made of him shows his looking from right to left, not in conversation but with the instinct of a wild creature to protect its food. Out of his inherited past a ghostly remembrance of sabre-tooth tigers and troglodyte competitors comes to his needless rescue: things that went bump in the night a million years before the first Hammer horror film.

To conclude: my hypothesis is that for reason or reasons unknown a variety of red or ginger aquatic fly became extinct sometime in the last few million years, but the Wickham's Fancy so much reminds a trout of this vanished delicacy that his automatic response is to take the artificial with glee.

Typical small river.

Casting can be tricky when the banks are this overgrown.

asti pstream on a small hi

Fishing dry fly on the River Rye, Yorkshire

Stalking a trout beneath overhanging branches. In such places side casting is necessary.

Playing a wild trout on a larger river.

Where wild brownies rise!

A typical Northern rocky river: Scotland's River Deveron.

A beautiful brown trout and a grayling from the River Ure: both over the 1lb mark.

A good wild trout takes line on the River Eamont.

The author with his day's catch.

The author aged eight with his first trout!

11

Nymph Fishing
Some Minor Tactics

'The best fish swim near the bottom.'
Proverb

Nowadays, as I fish carefully upstream with a dry fly, when I come to a still, smooth pool I will often switch immediately to a nymph if I see any fish moving there. Late on in the evening I would not make such a switch, nor would I do so during mayfly time, nor during a good hatch of fly on a windy day when the river surface was ruffled. But on a calm bright day I would almost certainly change to a nymph. Why? Because trout in slack-flowing parts of the river are far more pernickety about the dry flies that you present them than trout in streamy places. Besides, half the time it is your nylon, however fine that puts them off. With a nymph, however, you have three distinct advantages: (i) your nylon no longer matters because being sub-surface it is not so visible to trout; (ii) the pattern of fly matters much less, especially if it is a Sawyer nymph; and (iii) you can impart some life into your fly, making it additionally attractive to the fish.

SIMPLE SOLUTIONS

It is true that a well-selected, well-presented dry fly can lure up a nymphing trout, but the obverse is also true. A trout taking duns or smuts or sedges will take a nymph, especially a well-presented, nicely animated one. On hot afternoons, in the stiller pools, cruising river fish are often smutting or taking midge pupae. Finding a good smut copy is not always easy. There are now some ingenious smut imitations using modern synthetic materials (which I will not list, because they will already be out of date by the time this book is on your shelf) and while these hi-tech solutions no doubt work there are, as usual, several perfectly effective low-tech solutions to the problem. I have always found that a lightly dressed Black and Peacock Spider (size 16 or 18) works for me, so I rarely use any other pattern. A Goddard Smut works, and so does Pritt's simple trick of winding an ostrich herl on to a size 15 hook – no hackle, no wing! (If you want to read about this try Courtney Williams under 'Black Gnat' – cheaper than buying the original works of T.E. Pritt, for which you have to pay hundreds of pounds.) A variation on this theme which works for me is a peacock herl, ribbed with silver wire, on size 16 or 18 hook, again with no hackle or wing.

Midge pupae imitations include standard Buzzer patterns as well as Goddard's ingenious Suspender Hatching Midge. I have found that a small lightly dressed wet fly (such as Snipe and Purple or a Spider pattern) will work provided it does not sink too deep. I also find that smuts and midge pupae are best fished with wry fly. By employing a dry fly as a marker on the point, any tiny wet fly (especially with no hackle) can be comfortably fished on a short dropper. This way I can take smutting fish at 30 yards (27 m) or more (even in the gloom under trees) by the simple expedient of using the dry fly marker on the point to register the take.

TACTICS FOR SMUTTING TROUT

On many of the little upland rivers of the North, which I spend so much of my time fishing, smutting trout will take a midge pupa copy (Buzzer or Suspender Nymph). John Goddard has also written that he has found the same thing to be true on chalkstreams of the South. It is rare that I find one fly to the exclusion of all others in the stomachs of free-rising rain-fed river trout. Usually, smuts (Simulium) and midges (Chironomids) are there all mixed up side by side, along with all sorts of other grub, such as the odd olive and terrestrial insects. So several different patterns of small fly are worth experimenting with in high summer for these lazy, surface-sieving feeders.

Wry fly is a good tactic to employ because with a buoying dry fly on the point you can keep your wet fly/nymph nice and high in the water, just like a hatching midge or reed smut. A Black and Peacock Spider works so well for me that I seldom use any other pattern at such times.

Another ruse is to use a midge copy (Goddard Suspender) and a smut copy (Pritt's Black Gnat) on droppers of the same cast with a Black Gnat dry fly on the point. You can offer a trout three different flies one after another without once delving into your fly box. Very effective!

The good old Pheasant Tail Nymph and Killer Bug, especially given a jerk or two, often work as well. Many years ago I began to experiment with the technique of imparting more life to a nymph than the subtle induced-take method. Indeed, before I had ever read Sawyer or Kite on the subject I had already used this method, albeit clumsily: in my ignorance I had known no better. The technique was really born from my upbringing as a downstream wet fly fisher in the North. My father taught me to 'work' my wet flies when fishing slow-flowing parts of the river – flats and pool tails – because it proves irresistible to the trout. This is not lure-stripping, but merely a jerking figure-of-eight retrieve, the speed of which is varied according to conditions and the trout's whim.

'ANIMATED NYMPH'

When I began nymphing, being self-taught in the method (my father was not a nympher and I had not yet read Sawyer) I made many mistakes, but I did find that on some days a jerked, twitched or 'animated' nymph certainly attracted the fish. Thus I developed a style of fishing which in my fishing log books I began to record as 'animated nymph'. Generally, I found the method worked best on flat parts of the river, especially with rising trout that I could actually see. The kind of trout which had for years spurned my dry flies, unless at dusk, now fell to my animated nymph. I developed a special nymph for the job too, a heavily weighted, very pale dressing of a Greenwell's Glory: pale yellow silk ribbed with bright flat gold wire, rabbit-fur thorax and a turn of dark hackle clipped down short. I also learnt to twitch, jerk or animate my nymph not with my left hand on the line, but with little jerks of my rod tip, a series of tiny arcs. During the process the rod is slowly raised to the vertical, then I cast again. Takes are detected either by eyesight, or, if fishing quite quickly, by touch.

There is nothing new in fishing, though. A book I bought recently, *Small-River Fly Fishing* by James Evans (published 1972), describes exactly the same technique and the author even selected a soubriquet, which I, completely unwittingly, have echoed. His phrase is 'agitated nymph', which is more poetic than mine. Like me, Evans is not a chalkstream man, but an upland little-river angler. His stamping ground is the Welsh Borders, and mine the North York Moors, which means we must have a great deal in common. He describes his agitated nymph as a series of induced takes, which is most apt. By the sounds of things he uses his agitated nymph in rough water as well as slow, which marks him out as a fisherman of prodigious skill. Nowadays I tend to use wry fly, with nymph on the point, when fishing rough water: it makes things so much easier. The dry fly, acting like a buoy, bounces up and down on the streamy surface and imparts attractive bobbing, jerking life to the nymph below.

SAVING THE DAY

But on smooth water animated or agitated nymph is a trick worth using. I remember one hot day on the upper Ure when I took a good basket on a flat beneath some big trees. Various locals were out and doing no good. One old boy I got chatting with was astonished to see that I had done so well. He had caught nothing and was all for packing up. I introduced him to animated nymph. Within a dozen casts he had a good fish, much to his delight. No sooner had I turned and walked 30 yards (27 m) up the bank than he hooked another. He called out; I returned to him, and netted out a fish quite over the 1 lb (0.5 kg) mark. His pleasure was well worth witnessing. Admittedly, he was an experienced angler, competent to learn a new technique, but animated nymph is quickly learned and worth trying. Beware of moving the nymph too quickly; all you will then succeed in doing is getting trout to follow and bump at your fly but not take it.

Hooking trout this way is slightly more difficult than with the classical style but it is worth risking if normal tactics are not working. I find there are days when trout respond especially eagerly to an animated nymph and others when it is hardly worth employing. I remember two consecutive evenings I fished on the Manifold some years ago in June. The trout were choosy. Dry fly did not work for me, nor did static nymph, but as soon as I began to jink my nymph about the fish went mad. Just fishing in flat pool tails, I worked my way upstream and collected a great basket each evening: every fish took the nymph when, and only when, it was animated.

More recently, I was fishing a little Lincolnshire chalkstream which I visit from time to time because of the size and quality of its trout, when I came to a deep, elbow-shaped pool in the crook of which was a thick bed of weed. Something told me that there was a fish down at the foot of this bed. I cast softly over the weed, extended my rod to its full extent, and let my line sink. I had a weighted Black Chenille Nymph on my leader and when I judged it was deep enough, I jerked it back up to the surface in a series of animated hops. Just as it reached the top a great bronze shape came from below and took it 6 in (15 cm) from the surface. An exciting moment. After a frantic struggle I netted a splendid brown trout of 1 lb 13 oz (0.8 kg).

I was sure that farther along the weedbed I had seen a sub-surface disturbance. Vegetation did not allow me to make the same sort of cast, so I made a long cast along the bank to the spot I fancied. I let the nymph sink, then brought it up to the surface on a long, diagonal sweep. On about the third jink I saw a titanic shape dart out from the weed and snatch the nymph with a vicious jerk. I had hooked a biggun all right! He would try to get back into the safety of his weedbed, so I had no choice but to hold him. My luck and the hook held though, and I netted out a superb cock brown trout of 2 lb 10 oz (1.2 kg). I do not know if I would have caught that fine brace without recourse to animated nymph.

AN ESTABLISHED PRACTICE

I suspect that agitated or animated nymph is really only an extension of upstream wet fly, and I bet that many a crafty Border, North Country and Western Peninsula fisher has employed the trick over the generations, as they have wry fly. Generally speaking, I think we in the North and West have a fear of being out of contact with our flies and do fish them more quickly than our southern and south-eastern brethren. Gentle and subtle though animated nymph is, I think in Skues' day it would have constituted a 'dragging' fly and therefore been considered ungentlemanly. Free from the rigidity of such effete dogmatism, I suspect northern and western fishermen have developed more tricks to defeat trout than our chalkstream counterparts, where rules have always been writ in capital letters.

Nymph, whether static, induced or animated, is deadly on flat water, though. Indeed, if I have a bone to pick with Sawyer it is that he has helped to make nymph fishing too easy. His ideas were so good, and so well expressed, that has made a tricky form of fishing into a most accessible one. I feel a bit the same about wry fly, which absurdly simplifies the exceptionally difficult art of upstream wet fly and nymphing in rapid water. But still, we must develop. There are days when nymphing on smooth water is very easy, when all you have to do is put the fly near a trout and he will take it instantly.

In mid June 1989 I had two days on a small Yorkshire river at a time of year when I normally expect to fish most of the time with a dry fly. But not a bit of it. It was a warm and dry month in the North, and the weekend I picked was particularly hot and bright. The river was low. On day one I had an early fish or two on dry fly before the sun got up, then I switched to nymph. The trout were smutting, yet for some reason I found the Killer Bug to be the best fly, and it lived up to its name. I had only to plop the Bug near each fish I spotted (not difficult in the clear water) and he took. It really was absurdly easy, almost like shelling peas. I began to look for trout in difficult places, ignoring those in easy ones. I never needed to animate my fly. The odd inducement was necessary, but more often than not the trout took the Bug soon after it landed.

Finally, on the afternoon of the second day I switched to dry fly and found it much harder work. I rose fewer trout than I had done with the nymph and missed far more. Neither was a full day because I had tickets for York Festival performances in the evenings, but I caught 34 trout over the weekend and 21 fell to the nymph. That I had any at all on dry fly was testimony to my dogged determination to get a few that way. Both were nymphing days, as I recorded in my log book: occasions on which 'the careful nymph fisherman would be rewarded with opportunity after opportunity to practise classic takes'.

DRY FLY AND NYMPH COMPARED

This experience gives rise to the perennial controversy: which is more difficult, dry fly or nymph? Actually, in recent times popular thinking seems to have come down in favour of nymph being the more difficult method. Skues, Sawyer and Kite, quite an august trio of angling wisdom, rate dry fly as easier than nymph, but then, to misquote slightly Mandy Rice-Davies' notorious words: 'They would, wouldn't they?' As practitioners and popularizers of the nymph method you would expect them to sing its praises. But let me make it clear: nymphing is a technique which deserves to have its praises sung, though it is also true that in this life you can make yourself believe what you want to believe.

Frankly, I do not think there are absolutes in fishing. To say that nymphing is more difficult than dry fly is as absurd as saying that goalkeeping is more difficult than bowling. Each great exponent of his art is admirable and it is silly, in my view, to play one discipline off against another. What you can do more fairly, however, is make some considered generalizations about certain aspects of these disciplines. I think you can safely say that a great football striker will shine more when he plays in a great team or when the opposition is less distinguished. Likewise a great batsman can usually be expected to capitalize on an excellent pitch or on weak bowling. But there will always be anomalies in sport: for example, the great goalkeeper will have more chance of displaying his amazing skills to the crowd when he is faced with a strong team than when he plays against a weak one. In fishing, the angler who catches the most fish is not necessarily the best one. Another angler might have caught fewer fish but more difficult specimens.

Nevertheless, I am prepared to make some generalizations about dry fly and nymph. First, I must admit a prejudice: I prefer dry fly fishing to nymphing. It is purely an aesthetic thing – nothing to do with degrees of difficulty. But I do conclude this, that nymph fishing in clear, smooth water on rivers, where the trout are visible to the angler, is an easier way to catch trout than fishing with a dry fly in very rough or turbulent water. I should add that nymphing is more difficult in such places too. Detecting the take in rapid and turbulent water, even seeing your dry fly at all, can be fiendishly difficult. Indeed some anglers cannot ever attain such a skill because their eyesight is not good enough.

TIMING

I also believe that the dry fly strike is more complex than the nymph strike. In nymph fishing you can hardly be too quick on the strike: invariably, if you err you have been too slow, whereas in dry fly you can be either too quick or too slow. Learning to mix these differing tempos of strike is not easy and requires great discipline. The situation is complicated because you cannot always be sure what you are doing wrong, whether you are being too quick or too slow, With nymph you never have this doubt. I still miss more fish on dry fly than I do on nymph, and I have been a dry fly fisher longer than a nymph fisher. Late-evening dry fly is a craft not often mentioned. Some anglers are brilliant at it while others never learn it. The late-evening nymph fisher must cease his work well before the dry fly man, who can fish on much later into the dusk. This crepuscular skill is simply one a nympher need never bother himself with.

Maurice Wiggin goes so far as to say that dry fly is 'by far the easiest method of taking fish'. He says it is easier than worming and 'even easier than intelligent spinning'. This is a very sloppy argument. I presume that intelligent Snap or Tiddly-Winks is more difficult than idiotic chess, though I am sure Gary Kasparov could soon put the matter in perspective. Wiggin continues: 'In dry-fly fishing you see the fish take your fly and your hooking problem is solved for you.'

Absurd! In fast water first you have to *see* your fly, let alone strike correctly! But, in a way I sympathize with Wiggin's aims here. He is trying to demystify dry fly for the beginner, trying to help the tyro not to be daunted by the method. He goes over the top, and dangerously so – perhaps even into the realms of falsehood – but I can at least appreciate his intentions.

TWIN ARTS

Nowadays, it is not dry fly which people talk about in hushed tones but the wiles of the upstream nymph expert. I am not implying that I think it is about time the pendulum swung back in favour of the old dry fly shibboleth. I would just like both the dry fly master and the nymph maestro to be recognized as the great experts they are. Sawyer said of nymph fishing: 'It is not an art to be acquired in a season, or for that matter in a dozen seasons.'

In order to become an artist in dry fly fishing the same is undoubtedly true, though I ought to add, for the sake of the initiate, that with some grit and determination you should become moderately competent at both within a couple of seasons. I will let Skues, who despite his understandable bias towards nymph was the wisest of anglers, have the final word: 'There is no question of wet versus dry fly. Each in its place and used according to knowledge is surely the way of wisdom.'

This is what I find as I fish gently upstream – I switch from method to method according to conditions. In the slower pools I have already advocated the use of a nymph. Dry fly in such places requires experimentation with fly pattern and possibly the introduction of a very fine tippet on your leader (1½ lb/0.7 kg breaking strain, for example) all of which can be a frustrating waste of time. Why not adopt the nymph if the fish will take it?

THE NYMPH'S ADVANTAGES

There are other spots too where the nymph will usually work better than a dry fly. First, any place where your dry fly drags badly. Such spots are often little bays where big trout lie protected by a fast current between you and them. In nymph fishing drag is far less of a problem than with dry fly. A weighted Bug or Beetle lobbed across into such a bay will often capture you a beauty. All backwaters, eddies, swirls and whirls are worth exploiting in this way.

Secondly, the foamy backwater cries out for your nymph. Scum and foam prohibits use of a dry fly: only a nymph, and one well weighted, will work for you. For years such foamy corners of the river were beyond my penetration with a fly (I knew all about the efficacy of a worm or minnow in such holes though!) mainly because the North Country wet flies with which I had grown up were not heavy enough to cut through the scum. I wasted countless opportunities over the years until I was introduced to the weighted nymph in reservoir fishing.

I remember one particular foamy backwater on a rocky Yorkshire river which had eluded me often. On one occasion I approached it from down river to see, yet again, a big fish at work in it, nibbling away at the insects caught in the scum. I well remember the trout's response when my fly, for the first time ever plopped right through the scum, because it was a weighted nymph. The trout weighed an honest pound (0.5 kg). It is a trick I have often since repeated. (In this same backwater during the notoriously hot dry summer of 1990 on a torpid day, when no fish were moving, I picked up my only trout of the day with this tactic. A fine wild brownie of 1 lb 9 oz (0.7 kg).) If I had only read Sawyer on the subject first I would have cut many corners in my angling education, but as it is I had to reason out the solution for myself. Still, there is a sense of satisfaction in having quite independently come to a successful conclusion in some troublesome angling problem.

OTHER PROMISING AREAS

Thirdly, there are always scoured-out recesses and pots beneath waterfalls and weirs where no dry fly has ever penetrated. A weighted nymph dropped under such turbulent overdrops, be they ever so small, will sometimes result in you netting out a trout – and quite often a good big one too. Fourthly, deep pools which have depths never plumbed by the dry fly angler are always worth exploring with a leaded nymph. It is always a good idea to work your fly up to the surface in twitches, hops and jigs. If your river is stocked with rainbow trout this tactic could prove a real winner. A deep nymph may well yield you a grayling or two as well, and again one of them could be a biggun.

This is one of the joys of a carefully placed and fished weighted nymph: it could bring you the best fish of the day. Backwater fly-traps, eddies, deep pots and otherwise inaccessible holes are often the haven of really sizeable trout or grayling. Sawyer has commented on the usefulness of nymphs in luring out of the river big, oversize trout which would never have fallen to a dry fly. He writes with the concern of a keeper, knowing full well the damage to other trout which these wily old monsters can wreak.

It is interesting to compare Sawyer's advice with that of Halford, who advises us to pass by difficult trout, warning that the fisherman who does not do so 'is far more likely to add to the already far advanced education of the fish than to the contents of his bag'.

SAWYER'S LEGACY

Unfortunately for Halford, he did not know about Sawyer-type nymphing because it was yet to be invented. This, in my view, is one of Sawyer's great legacies to the world of angling. We need no longer take Halford's advice on this matter because Sawyer has given us the method to catch such big 'uncatchable' trout. Since the great keeper has shared his secrets with us we can indeed add to the contents of our bag rather than passing difficult specimens by.

I am profoundly grateful to Sawyer because without him I would never have caught my biggest-ever trout, which fell to a nymph. I was fishing a little Midlands river one bright spring morning when in a deep hole under my bank I spotted the fish of my dreams. I presented him with a size 12 Pheasant Tail Nymph. It took me several casts to get the fly to swim just right past this titan, for he turned at it at least twice before finally taking. He was so huge that my little landing net collapsed under his giant weight. When I tried to extract the hook from his great snout the metal sheared in two, so much stress had it been under during the fight. He was a fine cock brown trout of 4 lb 7 oz (2 kg) and, at 21 in (53 cm), a fish which had overwintered superbly. I will be lucky if I ever see his like again, for I am not used to catching trout of anything like this size. I doubt such a leviathan would have been lured up to a dry fly. As it was, I had read Sawyer and so was able to use a nymph . . . to my lasting satisfaction!

As a dry fly fisher by first inclination, the kind of nymphing I prefer is the occasional chuck into the sort of place I have been describing above. A hot day with big fish out and about on the opportunistic feed under trees, in swims and back eddies, is my favourite scenario. Wherever my dry fly cannot penetrate, pop, in goes my nymph. It is surprising how often, as I plod home into the setting sun after a brilliant dry fly day, that my best fish, lying like a lord in my creel, fell to a nymph.

Three final points. That wizard with a nymph, Oliver Kite, who could catch grayling on a nymph blindfold, and who said that he felt out of practice if he went three days without fishing (where does that put us poor amateurs who have to make do with three or four days a month if we are lucky?) has given us the 'presumed' take. The advice is that, when fishing a nymph over a trout, if we receive no indication that he has taken, we may as well strike anyway, on the presumption that the trout has taken. Advice too good to ignore.

DIFFICULTY IN DETECTING A TAKE

It is sometimes very difficult, even impossible, to perceive the take of a trout to a nymph when you are fishing a very long line. The sort of places I am thinking of are still, flat parts of the river where trout are moving right across on the far side, perhaps under trees or beneath a high bank, and where an extremely long cast is necessary. With such a long line out, too, you must strike quickly; otherwise you will miss the fish. The method I use is wry fly. Here, of course, the dry fly on the dropper is used only in a passive role, as a marker. It is much easier to keep sight of a bushy dry fly at 30 yards (27 m); particularly in the obscurity under branches, than it is your leader or fly line. Takes are quite easily registered. It is a trick which really does work. I have had four trout already this season by employing this tactic and all have been 1 lb (0.5 kg) or better.

For years now I have been salvaging old flies by converting them to nymphs. Any old fly will do. Rather than throwing an unravelled pattern away (or stripping it for re-tying), merely wind some copper wire over the body. Dry flies with nice bushy bodies are excellent for this. I call these conversions 'Copper Nymphs' – they have taken many a trout for me. The big four-and-a-half-pounder (2 kg) I have just written about took a shabby old Pheasant Tail Nymph which I had smartened up in just this manner.

Nymph fishing is a subtle and fascinating art. Once you know how to do it, it can be a simple way of picking up fish. You should certainly expect to catch about half of your trout you see *on the first cast*. If not, your technique needs some examination, though on some days even the expert will struggle: such is the challenge of trouting. Since Sawyer, nymphing has become a more accessible skill. No river fisherman can say that his angling armoury is complete without a few weighted nymphs in his fly box and the ability to use them effectively.

12

Imaginative Downstream Wet Fly

'Climbing up to a place
Where stone is dark under froth,
And the down-turn of the wrist
When flies drop on the stream.'
W.B. Yeats

Of all branches of fly fishing traditional downstream wet fly is, paradoxically, both the easiest and the most difficult to describe. The basics of the art are easy to describe and are the easiest for the beginner to learn, yet the more intricate and subtle skills of the technique are very difficult, even perhaps impossible, to put down on paper. This type of wet fly fishing relies more on 'touch' and less on eyesight than any other branch of fly fishing; indeed it probably has more in common with worm fishing than with dry fly or nymphing. The angler must use his imagination in order to 'see' where his sunken flies are in the river. It is a very tactile, subtle, delicate art. When fishing upstream wet fly a short line is almost a necessity and the angler knows almost exactly where his flies are. With a long line out in deepish water it is not so clear exactly where your downstream wet fly team is. To a beginner such knowledge is impossible; to the expert it can be astonishingly precise.

A SPRINGTIME TECHNIQUE

I am not going to attempt to get to grips with the most intricate wiles of downstream wet fly in this chapter, for two reasons. First, one chapter could hardly do the subject justice; second, I do not possess the authority, knowledge or expertise to write at length about it. For me, downstream wet fly is essentially a springtime technique, and more particularly an April one. I rarely fish much in March on rivers and by May I find wry fly and dry fly are coming more and more into their own. Basically, I am an upstream fisherman – whether with fly, worm or minnow – and it is here that any expertise that I possess lies. But I am glad that I have some smattering of downstream wet fly knowledge and I find that this knowledge spills out beyond spring, and beyond mere trout fishing. I do use the technique from time to time later in the season, and I have found that the skills dinned into me by my father when I was a boy have been of great practical use to me when tackling migratory fish, especially sea trout.

I can, however, throw out a few suggestions which may be of interest. Earlier I said that 'working' your flies was often necessary when fishing this style. Sometimes the slower your flies fish the better, and at other times they have better results if jinked or worked. The moods of trout will vary and the fisherman must adjust accordingly. Size of fly matters too. Trout will take a big, dragging lure, but not often and never big fish. For traditional downstream wet fly technique it is best to use small flies and sparsely dressed, with the exception of the top dropper, which can be a more bushy pattern.

A MOORLAND EXCURSION

A few years ago in the spring I met some anglers just as we were all packing up. The day had been stormy, the water high and rushing – though clear enough to be quite fishable with fly. The river was one of the typical moorland headwaters in which I specialize, where trout run small but where also an angler can bag the odd fish, trout or grayling, of 1 lb (0.5 kg) or more. The three fishermen were a little disgruntled about their day's sport. They assumed I had fared just as badly and were clearly somewhat surprised to learn that I had filled a limit creel. One of them was bluntly sceptical and clearly thought I was lying. I asked them what size fly they had been using, remarking that pattern was almost immaterial but size was very important. I looked at their casts and said that I thought they had been fishing too big.

'But I thought with such a big water we had to use bigger flies so that the trout would see them!' one of them remarked.

A QUESTION OF SIZE

I shook my head and showed them my flies. I had a size 14 on the point and only conceded a size 12 on the top dropper. My two bottom flies were very sparsely dressed too, especially the Snipe and Purple on the point. A Partridge and Orange was on the middle dropper with a March Brown Nymph of bulkier construction on the bob. Compared to their size 8 and 10 monstrosities, my cast seemed very sporting; more importantly, though, it contained far better imitations of the kind of nymphs on which wild river trout feed. The sceptic, obvious disbelief still writ large on his features, asked to see my catch. I showed them the six wild brownies, up to ¾ lb (0.3 kg), and only then did his doubt begin to fade and the realization start to grow that there was an element of truth in my tale.

The superb eyesight of trout is a phenomenon which many trout fishermen still do not take into enough consideration. These three anglers were guilty of judging the conditions through human not trout eyes. It is amazing how trout can see such tiny flies in turbulent or cloudy water and at night as well. Though I will successfully employ big, bushy patterns when dry fly fishing, I have found that a similar policy is not rewarded in downstream wet fly, and for this reason I rarely go above size 12 hooks in daylight with this method.

THE DEPTH FACTOR

Depth too is important. On days when trout are lying deep a sinking line is necessary. Weighted nymphs help you gain depth, the Killer Bug being a marvellous point fly. One of the advantages of downstream wet fly is that it enables you to use a long line quite safely and with this you can gain considerable depth.

It is surprising to see some fishermen's methods of attaining depth. A couple of years ago I was watching someone nymphing on the Kennet when I noticed that his fly made quite a splash as it landed. I asked if I might see his cast. He agreed readily. He seemed a pretty pukka sort of chap, wearing best Royal Berkshire gear, but his fly was hardly pukka. His 'nymph' was at least 1½ in (4 cm) in length – more like a reservoir lure. Nipped on to his leader right up by this monstrous offering were four huge leads. The whole arrangement sank like a plummet. Halford and Skues would turn in their graves if they knew to what crude depths chalkstream flies have now sunk! Rough and ready though we might be in the North, I have never seen a river angler up here stoop to such preposterous philistinism! Such tactics are not necessary – a well-fished wet fly can be made to sink deep without such clumsiness. With downstream wet fly you have several tricks to attain depth. Sheer length of line is one, another is to pay out a great deal of line, let it hang in the current then bring it suddenly upstream and let it go again: the cast sinks rapidly as the line drifts downstream. A simpler method is to pay out great loops of line direct from the reel, like long trotting, though the danger is that a trout which takes early in this type of cast will be likely to go undetected.

SURFACE TECHNIQUE

At the opposite end of the spectrum, up on the surface, you can incite trout to take by using the dropper flies attractively, especially the one on the bob: dapping and bobbing the dropper flies on the surface. A rod slightly longer than your usual one might be useful for such tactics, especially in bleak early spring when there are no leaves on the trees to snag your flies. Backwaters and eddies are worth exploiting with a dibbled bob fly. Last spring I had a good trout this way. I came to a place where the river narrowed and turned. Across river from me was a lazy, swirling backwater past which the main thrust of the current roared. I noticed a few olives trapped in this slowly circling eddy. Because the small river narrowed I was just able to reach across the current to the backwater with my rod extended at arm's length. A convenient rock on my side gave me extra distance. I let my point fly act as an anchor or drogue while I dapped, dibbled and bobbed my dropper flies about in the surface film of the eddy.

A lively fish came up and took on this first cast. A conventionally fished wet fly in such a place would not have met with success. After a moment or two in the eddy the flies would have been dragged out and away downstream as the main current pulled at the line lying across it. Only by using my height and reach was I able to negate the effects of the strong current between me and the backwater.

The alert downstream wet fly fisher will always be looking for ways to make his flies fish naturally and attractively. The power of the current will ruin any thoughtless cast. I remember many years ago on the upper Ribble in spring coming to a pool where I could see trout nymphing out in the middle of the river. The fish were moving in an apex of slack water between two strong currents. To try to cover these fish from either bank would have been folly because the strong current protecting each flank of the apex would have created the most vicious drag. But the river was swollen with spring rain and the wading looked dangerous. Nevertheless, I chanced it, being young and fearless. I got there all right and in 20 minutes took five splendid trout from the hang between the currents. Had I fished from the bank I doubt I would have had a single fish from that place. Never was a greater lie spoken than that downstream wet fly is just a chuck-and-chance-it business. The thinking fisherman turns it into an art.

LONG-TROTTING

I have already touched on the idea of long-trotting a wet fly. Sometimes you will come across a trout which is moving in a place quite inaccessible to an orthodox upstream or downstream cast. Such spots are often deep, tree-lined stretches of the river. Trout which inhabit such reaches are often more than willing to take an artificial fly because they are so rarely attacked by anglers that they are comparatively unsuspecting. They are often sizeable fish too, and well worth catching. Only contrive to put your fly over trout like this and they will have it.

A long-trot is a good idea. Go upstream of the fish till you find a gap in the trees. Pay out line till your fly has passed beyond the trout. Work the fly back in a series of little jinks and he will often take it. This is a good tactic in high summer. One point to bear in mind: fish for such a trout from the same side on which he is lying. Hold your rod out at right angles across the water and pay out line down the opposite side of the stream, so that the fish does not see your line being trotted down over his head. When you have sufficient line out, bring your rod tip downstream and allow the current to guide your fly right over the trout's nose so that the first glimpse he gets is of an attractive jinking nymph just upstream of him.

This same tactic works in spring too. I remember a cold April day up on the moors when I had done absolutely nothing. There was a big water running, no fly showing, and I was almost chilled to the bone. One of my favourite pools was unfishable in a conventional way because of the height of water. But I decided that I would long-trot it. Gingerly, I waded out as far as I could into the cold deep water and began to pay out line. I needed about 30 yards (27 m) or so of line out in order to fish the pool correctly. I began to jink the flies in deep, with my rod tip right down by the surface to gain extra depth (another useful little ruse) when, bang, a good 'un took. In this manner I had two splendid fish in two casts from this spot, and avoided a blank day in consequence.

Bridges and tunnels under roads are spots which can yield trout on long-trotted wet fly. Many is the trout I have slyly wangled out of such places. For a bet I once caught a trout this way down a pipe that ran under a farm track. My astonished friends could hardly believe their eyes. Who dares wins in fishing. It is all a question of imagination. If you were a trout you would like the security of the seemingly impregnable holt that a tunnel provides, where you were safe from the heron's strafing bill. Safe from most fishermen too. I freely admit that my scrambling boyhood with worm and minnow has had a huge impact on my fly fishing. I am grateful to this early education for it has given an extra dimension to my knowledge of trout.

USING THE CURRENT

One final long-trotting trick. You can use a powerful current to take your fly down into a spot which you cannot reach by casting. Imagine a backwater or flat cheek of a stream which you cannot reach with a cast because of a high bank or trees, but as luck has it a fast current runs right down the pool to this spot. Pay out line into this current and at the critical moment swing your rod tip to one side and draw your line out of the current. If you have judged it correctly your flies will fish nicely through the backwater or the cheek, possibly yielding you a trout. Such a capture would be an artful one, a triumph beyond the imagination of many fishermen. It is worth pointing out that these manoeuvres with long lines are chancy operations and many will turn out to be noble failures. You will often miss trout this way, or fail to hook them securely. But, unlike in dry fly fishing, in downstream wet fly trout sometimes hook themselves, so Chance can be both ally and enemy.

There are occasions when downstream wet fly beats either a dry fly or nymph. In the evening, if you are frustrated and cannot find the right fly, why not abandon dry fly and put on a wet fly cast? Fish down the big pool tails and work your flies as it gets dark. Such tactics could pip the dry fly man. When evening sedges are hatching, downstream wet fly in the pool tails can also be most effective. At certain times some find the grannom, a daytime sedge, the very devil to imitate with dry fly. Wet fly will account for trout in grannom time, though. Last spring I hit the grannom on the River Rye and I imitated the emerging sedges with my bob fly on the surface. The trout took it like tigers. Friends who persisted with dry fly caught nothing.

EARLY-MORNING TACTICS

Sometimes on cool summer mornings it profits the angler to fish with a wet fly before the action hots up. On such mornings the river can look very dour. Choose a long, nicely moving pool where you have room to get your flies working and try to fish them pretty deep. Though no trout might be showing, you might discover that deep down they are quite prepared to take. Another occasion when wet fly can score is on a low river which is dour in summer heat. No fish may be showing but try a wet fly down the runs and in all the pieces of broken water. In these conditions you might not catch many but they could be good ones. Big fish often lie in rapid runs during heat waves in order to get oxygen and avoid irritation from lice. They might not have the energy to come up for a dry fly but they will not be able to resist a Killer Bug or Black and Peacock Spider waving past their noses.

Fierce downstream winds in summer are also a factor in choosing wet fly. Why try and be a hero and flog fruitlessly into a strong wind with a dry fly when you could fish quite comfortably with downstream wet fly?

Recently I found myself by a low river on a hot, bright summer's day with a strong, gusting downstream wind. After a difficult and fruitless half-hour's dry fly fishing, I switched to downstream wet fly. I caught five fish in an hour. Later I switched back to dry fly and caught nothing. Downstream wet fly scored hands down over dry fly on this occasion.

For summer fishing I recommend something black on your cast: a Black and Peacock Spider or Coch-y-bondhu, for example, tied quite small: size 14 at the biggest. Killer Bug on the point is also recommended – size 12, no bigger.

DOWNSTREAM METHOD FOR GRAYLING

I remember another occasion on the Rye, years ago, when I was fifteen, fishing on the Duncombe Park stretch in the days when my grandfather was a member of the Ryedale Angling Club; the club which, incidentally, had the celebrated John Storey as its keeper last century. I came to a spot where a shoal of grayling were avidly rising. Owing to the peculiar nature of the place, access was difficult and I had to make a long cast over a harsh current. I rose fish but could not hook them. So, rather than mess about further, I waded back to the bank, put on a wet fly cast, then crawled to the head of the pool. Here I had a grandstand view of the grayling as they sailed up to the surface to take flies. I saw their giant, spotty dorsal fins quite clearly in the pellucid, sunlit water. I deftly flicked out my wet flies and had a brace in no time: ample proof of the efficacy of the downstream method.

There is one other occasion when a downstream wet fly might beat a dry fly and that is on a very wet day. I have fished dry fly on some very wet days and had marvellous sport – indeed two of my best-ever dry fly days were very wet. However, constant drizzle is one thing, so is gentle rain interspersed with the odd heavy squall, but a hard, steady, relentless downpour is another. The first two a dry fly man can put up with, but the third is almost impossible. You cannot keep your fingers dry, so each new dry fly becomes a sodden lump before you can even grease it. Your dry fly box clogs with damp and soon becomes a wet fly box. Why fight Nature? On such days wet fly, whether upstream or downstream, is best and sport can often be good.

HEAVY WATERS AND SPATES

Finally, on big, heavy waters or spates a wet fly can sometimes work a trout or two for you. Dry fly, it must be said, can often work in coloured water too, but you must pinpoint your fish carefully with this method. With wet fly you can search out likely places more quickly because the motion you give to your flies can be sensed by the trout before they are actually seen. I recall a memorable day on the Ure with my uncle. As we drove over the moors in pelting rain our mood was sombre. We had looked forward to this day together but feared the worst. As my log book records: 'we suspected that we might find a swollen, unfishable torrent.' As it turned out, the river was certainly up and coloured but not yet a roaring flood. We put our rods up and walked doubtfully to the water. Before we had a chance to make a first cast the rain began to come down in ramrods. We sheltered under a tree, shivering in a miserable silence apart from the drilling of the pitiless rain. The squall lasted half an hour. Then suddenly it stopped. All went silent apart from the distant roar of the river and the drips from the trees. Nature seemed to be holding her breath. The cold front had passed. Though the sun had not come out it was palpably warmer. My uncle and I began to fish and were cheered by an early fish apiece; no great shakes for size, but a good breakfast. After a while we decided to go downstream to some slacker pools because the river was rising and getting more turbulent where we were.

As we walked downstream through the lush vegetation of the tall riparian woods, shafts of sunshine broke through and everything began to glisten and steam. It was early June and we were surrounded by great swathes of red campion, and mare's tail, interspersed with brilliant yellow splashes of leopard's bane, creamy clusters of sanicle, and the contrasting blue of forget-me-not and bugle. The day was improving.

SUCCESS IN CLOUDY WATER

The water was clouding up but I found a superbly inviting backwater where, in the gently circling current, two or three fish were opportunistically sipping down trapped morsels. It was a big backwater, 8–10 yards (7–9 m) across. I gently twitched my wet fly through it and took a fine brace here before further rain and a rapidly rising river brought our day's activities to an end. My worked wet flies (Pale Watery Nymph was the successful pattern) ensured that these cruising fish were attracted despite the thickening water. Dry fly would have been very hit and miss. What threatened to be a disappointing and fruitless day had brought some unexpected nuggets. My uncle had a brace in a quiet spot similar to mine, so, what with a leash apiece of wild Yorkshire brown trout up to 1 lb (0.5 kg), and a walk through a riot of wild flowers to remember, it had turned out to be a marvellous day: one which might well have deterred most fishermen.

This is all I intend saying about my approach to downstream wet fly. There are undoubtedly many other tricks you can call on: wiles such as 'backing up' which a Scots salmon ghillie taught me years ago. This is a ploy by which on a slack pool you walk downstream while your line is still in the water, thus getting your fly to fish in the opposite direction up the far bank. This trick should work for trout too, though I have never tried it for *Salmo trutta*. Another ploy is to vary your length of line as you fish down a pool. Make a short cast and fish all the water close to you with the bob flies, then, from the same spot, make a long cast to fish deeper. Keep up this routine all down the pool: short cast, long cast, short cast, long cast, and so on.

Another trick is to fish a pool down twice. Fish it down once with a medium length line while standing on the bank, searching just your half of the river. Then walk back up the pool, wade out to midstream, and fish down the far side of the river. This way you not only avoid frightening trout along your own bank with clumsy wading on the first journey down the pool, but you end up fishing the whole pool more thoroughly. No doubt there are many other stratagems of which I am ignorant.

BACK TO THE ROOTS

I am a dry fly man by inclination, and after April only rarely use downstream wet fly, but I do find the technique a useful one at odd moments throughout the season, and the fisherman who spurns it, on whatever grounds, does so to his own detriment. One of the intense satisfactions I get from employing this method is that it is one of the most ancient branches of fly fishing, far more venerable than the kind of modern dry fly we practise today with our machine-made floating lines and hi-tech equipment. There is something primitive and urgent about the tug of a trout on my wet fly, giving me an excitement quite different from the more visual art of upstream angling.

As I fish quietly down some North Country river I can imagine that I am covering water which generations of my predecessors have covered in just such a way; I feel part of a noble tradition. Even the names of the flies I use seem to have a historical feel to them as they display the materials traditional to their construction: Partridge and Orange, Snipe and Purple, Waterhen Bloa, Teal and Silver, Mallard and Claret, Woodcock and Yellow, Grouse and Green, Dotterel Spider, Hare's Ear.

I have a friend who is rigidly dry-fly-oriented and he rang me in early April for some information on a place I had told him about. He announced that he was going to use dry fly there. I advised him to use wet fly – at least until a hatch appeared. He stuck to his guns. Within 24 hours he was back on the telephone, asking about the sort of tackle he should use for downstream wet fly.

13

The Evening Rise

'The murmurous haunt of flies on summer eves.'

John Keats

We were fishing at a little stillwater stockery earlier this season: not many trout were showing and those that were we could not interest. All we had to show for our efforts was a 6 oz (0.2 kg) roach, returned. My friend, a far less experienced fisherman, suddenly remarked: 'This is the typical evening rise for me!'

There was little I could say to console him. What use tales of my past glories at dusk? Better not to mention a trout of 2¼ lb (1 kg) on a dry fly in a Scots river when I was only fourteen; nor one of 1 lb 15 oz (0.9 kg) taken on a Pale Watery, the tenth fish of a basket weighing 10 lb (4.5 kg); nor a monster of 2 lb 11 oz (1.2 kg) which fell to a Buzzer; nor an evening catch of 26 trout on a tiny Yorkshire beck only a season or two before.

The evening rise can so often be like the beautiful flirt, the politician, or the lottery ticket: promising much but delivering nothing. J.W. Hills says: 'It is an unsatisfactory thing, this evening rise. You get fish, certainly, but you seldom get as many as you feel you ought.'

His chapter devoted to the subject in his brilliant book *A Summer on the Test* is perhaps the best ever written about the evening rise. His biggest-ever trout, taken at dusk, weighed 4 lb 9 oz (2.1 kg), but he is under no illusions about this so-called magic hour for anglers: 'The trout, too, during an evening rise are always difficult and often exasperating.'

A CAPRICIOUS TIME

Frustrating though the evening rise may seem to a beginner, he needs only to experience one successful and rewarding dusk encounter and he will be forever hooked on the charms of evening fishing. Experienced fishermen are well acquainted with the disappointments of fishing in the gloaming but they have long memories and know that at any moment their bad luck could change. Sporadic, unproductive, fickle and capricious though the evening rise can be, it can also be the saving of a bad day or the crowning glory of an excellent one. One of the most exciting things about the evening rise is its anticipation. We can never be sure beforehand whether it will be good or mediocre, easy or difficult, or even if there will be one at all.

If there is an evening rise the burning question is: what is the correct fly pattern? Perhaps more print has been expended on this one question than any other issue in trout fishing. I am not going to add my hesitant voice to the pandemonium. I have no secret dressing up my sleeve, no technical observations to make about mole fur or special silk dye or a particular hue of hackle from Andulusian cocks reared exclusively on paella soaked in ferret's blood. But what I can offer are a few practical suggestions, some tactical alternatives.

If trout are smutting you might well have a problem. You could try some tiny representations on size 20 hooks, but if these do not work then you could try a bold stroke. 'Double the grub' and put on a big Coch-y-bondhu. Wickham's Fancy, too, will sometimes work. If none of these ploys does any good then a nymph might be worth trying, animated or static. Failing this, move to a streamy or ripply place where you can see fish moving. Put on a fly which will be visible, say a Coch-y-bondhu on a size 12 hook, and fish this up carefully, covering all the run. I will be surprised if this tactic does not secure you a brace.

CHANGING FISHING POSITION

If trout are feeding on Ephemeroptera you are more in luck, though finding the right fly at first could be tricky. Do your best to imitate the dun or spinner the fish are taking and if you find no response then, rather than waste vital minutes of the dying light trying to find an acceptable pattern, stick with a fly which looks roughly similar to your eyes and go to a more ripply, brisk stretch of the river. Here you might find trout are more easily gulled by your imitation. In the evening rise you are always operating against the clock so you really do not have time for endless experiment with fly patterns. Sooner or later it is better to change your place than your fly.

Twin dry fly really comes into its own in this situation. You have the choice of whether you change both flies together (if neither is acceptable), thus speeding up your search for the 'right' fly, or using a bushy fly on the point as an attractor and the dropper for your experimenting. Either way, you have twice the chance of interesting a fish that you have with orthodox solo dry fly. Using three dry flies is not a bad idea either, giving you even more chance of hitting on the killing pattern. You have to have good eyes to keep sight of all three flies as the light thickens, so this trick does have its drawbacks. My father uses the ruse in spring during the midday olive hatches, which are often short-lived, dubbing the technique 'The Gang of Three'. Wry fly is also a valuable tactic in the evening – the method with the nymph on the dropper.

TWIN DRY FLY IN THE EVENING

When employing twin dry fly in the evening I usually put a really visible fly on the point as the light begins to die. A big Wickham, Red

Sedge, Grey Wulff or Jock Scott are all valuable allies for this task. (I have developed my own fly for the purpose, the Hotspur, more of which in Chapter 19.) This way I can use the large point fly as my marker but still continue to fish successfully with a smaller fly on the dropper. As darkness falls the big fly can pass as a sedge or moth and I can switch to downstream wet fly, twitching my flies across the water surface . . . deadly!

I cannot overemphasize the importance of moving from flat or smooth stretches of the river to more rapid runs if you are finding the trout difficult to rise. In these streamy runs not only is your fly going to receive less scrutiny but your nylon leader will be impossible to see. Nylon, I believe, can be a very real problem for the evening fisherman. The even grey light can, surprisingly, make nylon more visible to trout than it is in bright, sunny light. We have all experienced those grey, overcast days when trout seem jittery and easily spooked. This is possibly because the unchanging, reliable light renders everything crystal-clear in their world and anything from the angler's nylon to his carelessly moving shadow is highly visible to all fish.

When the sun is shining there are so many reflections and glimmers in the sunny, sparkling underwater world that nylon can go utterly undetected. But in the calm of evening it is completely different. Gone is the brilliant interplay of sun and shadow. The wind has died down. Birds have gone to roost. Above the water nothing shines, no feathers flap, no branches sway. Nylon perhaps sticks out like the proverbial sore thumb. This is only a theory, but it does explain why trout in one pool will reject a fly and in one just upstream take it eagerly. A question of light.

A QUESTION OF LIGHT

I remember a strange occurrence on the Eden some years ago. I was fishing a flat and my fly, a Blue Quill, had no appeal to the trout at all. I moved upstream and tried my luck above. Again no good. I returned to the original spot to find that my fly – the same one – was now more acceptable and I filled a creel. The same natural fly (pale watery) was still being taken but it was now just a little darker. I think it was merely a case of my nylon being visible to the trout on my first visit to the pool and invisible on my return.

I think the policy of sticking to the runs and ignoring the flats and smooth pool tails, at least until dark, is a gamble that usually pays off. Your fly does not have to be a brilliant facsimile and your nylon is conveniently disguised. You eliminate in this way many of the snags which hinder the smooth-water fisherman. One of the deadliest evening fishermen that I have ever observed used to fish this way. Like Jack Nicklaus in golf, or Steve Davis in snooker, this chap played the percentages game – and was just as wonderful to watch. He only fished in streams and broken water and was an absolute artist in his precision, control and guile. He was a Frenchman: a head shorter than me but immensely broad, tanned and muscular – a Mediterranean type with grizzled hair and Roman forehead.

I lived in France for about three years and got to know the French fishing scene quite well. I found serious French fishers in general to be as fashion-conscious by the river as anywhere else. Everything about them was neat, new and in good order – prim, well-pressed and expensive. How they used to laugh at me with my makeshift net, battered old Sharpe's 9-foot (2.7 m), three-piece cane rod and trousers tucked into my socks (my waders and most of my tackle remained in England). To them I was *le jeune anglais avec la vieille canne* and I admit I must have cut an odd figure along the banks of the Charentonne where I mainly fished. They all had short, light carbon wands, automatic reels and immaculate fishing vests, in which their spotless tackle nestled at the ready. They were courteous and good-humoured, interested to engage me in conversation and offer information freely. They held British anglers and angling in high esteem, which I found rather touching. They were competitive, knowledgeable and fished well. One of them sometimes used to give me lifts from Paris (where I lived) to Normandy (where I fished). They were good company and I remember them with affection.

AN INSPIRED APPROACH

But the chap I mentioned earlier was different. For a start he was quite unconcerned about his appearance, possessing absolutely no French chic. No smart fishing vest for him – simply an open–necked shirt, baggy shorts and plimsolls. Slung round his neck was an ancient osier creel and a huge net with long wooden handle. His rod was very long, 10 ft (3 m) at least. He used to fish only the last hour of the day, and his technique was unlike any other that I have ever seen. He fished directly across stream from him with a very short line. He often used to progress downstream rather than upstream, though it was by then too dark for the trout to see him. I think he did this only when necessary in order to exploit whatever light still existed. He could fish extremely rapid water in very poor light; indeed I marvelled how he could see his fly. I think perhaps he just watched a patch of water where he knew his fly to be, distance estimated accurately because of his very short line. I think that perhaps he struck whenever he saw any disturbance near his line, rather than actually eyeing the fly for every inch of its path. It was a technique all his own and deadly effective too.

When he hooked a fish he got its head up quickly through the power of his big rod and with a deft motion of his left hand slung his net out over the water, submerged it, and drew the trout into its capacious meshes. Fish of 1 lb (0.5 kg) would be on the bank in 30 seconds. It was an extraordinarily efficient method: quick, no nonsense, ruthless. He was French after all, and fishing for the pot. I bet he was as impressive in the kitchen as he was by the river. Of all the many fishermen I have watched over the years he is the best dusk dry fly fisher I have ever seen: he had his own method and was brilliant at it.

He was not the slightest bit interested in swapping stories or enquiring about my philosophy or methods. He was there to get on with it and a fraternity of anglers did not exist for him. I suppose he was so competent at his job that he felt he did not need extra information. He had that quiet assurance of the man who knows he is really good at what he does. Sometimes I would struggle all day beneath a hot French sky and pick up only a couple of fish or so, to which I might add one or two more in the evening rise, then this chap would turn up just before dusk and in one hour catch more than I had caught in twelve!

PACING YOUR FISHING

This raises an important point: you must pace yourself in fishing. In my younger days I would often flog all day and become too weary to be at my best by the time the evening rise occurred. There is much to be said for coming fresh to the river to tackle the evening rise. If you are faced with a complete day on the water in summer then it is not a bad idea to take a break about tea time. Have a rest in the shade, or a quiet nap, or take afternoon tea at a local hotel. You will feel much refreshed if you do so and will be in much better shape to concentrate on the evening rise than the angler who has flogged on heroically all day.

There are some fishermen who have little interest in the evening rise: Kite, for example, said it had limited appeal for him. Yet anyone with curiosity and imagination must find the phenomenon one of the great sights of nature. One of England's greatest-ever anglers, G.E.M. Skues, was clearly fascinated by it and his writings on the subject make riveting reading. For some fishermen, evenings are the only time they can get away from work or family commitments, so those in this category have to learn to profit from their crepuscular opportunities.

AN IDYLL

How wonderful it is to go down to the river after a day's work, or after demanding children have been put to bed. If there has been sun, it is now burnt away; if there has been wind, it has now blown itself out; if there has been rain, the last drop has fallen, leaving a beautiful clean sky full of crystal light. The angler catches the scent of meadowsweet as his waders swish through the damp grass. A late heron flaps lazily away into the pink evening horizon, and an early bat flits greedily through a cloud of great red spinners. The evening is deliciously cool and quiet. The church clock strikes eight as he approaches the river. By the time the last peal has faded away he notices that the roar of the weir pool upriver is already louder.

The water comes into view. He stands motionless and looks upstream. His eyes adjust to the light reflected off the water. A few fish are already rising in one of his favourite spots. Great red spinners, eh? Why not try one? He flicks through his fly box. A Red Quill looks about right. He knots it on and creeps down over the moss-covered stones. An owl hoots as he begins to lengthen line, enjoying the feel of the rod flexing in his impatient hand. His evening sport is just beginning. . . .

IN REALITY

This is all rather idyllic. In reality things are not always like this, though all of us have experienced the splendid cool and calm of a summer's evening after either a hot or stormy day. Sometimes when we get to the water it is cold or dour. A raking wind scours downstream and makes our eyes water. Or it might be warm and calm but the river is dead, and not a fish can be seen. What do we do? We get fishing for a start! In such a situation I would put on a bushy kind of fly, a Wickham or Red Wulff perhaps, and fish up the sides of the river.

Many of the little moorland rivers I fish do not often have a concerted evening rise. Fish rise here and there and can be picked up as I fish quietly up pool by pool. Sometimes all seems dead yet the trout will take. On evenings like this I find the big fish often take. They lie invisible at the edges of the stream in quite shallow water: in little bays, under trees, by big stones. Probably they are waiting for moths or sedges, or even ovipositing spinners to come down. They will pouch a fly quite sedately, without any fuss, and on striking you suddenly realize that you are fast into a thumping good fish. So, dour-looking evenings do not always render you dour sport. The important thing is to keep your fly, a nice sized one, on the water, searching out all bays and shady nooks. If this tactic fails I would then try a team of wet flies across the bigger pools and down pool tails.

Another point worth making is that though a river seems completely dead in mid evening it may suddenly burst into life at dusk proper. I have seen anglers get discouraged, pack up and miss some excellent sport later on. I might add that I have often left the water and wondered, as I was driving home, if the trout were now rising madly in the very spot that I had vacated.

But to return to where I began: the evening rise at its most capricious and irritating. All around you trout are sipping down flies. The surface of the river is pocked with their impertinent noses, while every now and then there is the portly thwack of a trout which has leapt clear of the water in his glee. You can see that the fish are rising to a small grey dun but no artificial fly that you can find, however similar to the natural in your eyes, is remotely acceptable. You, an angler of a dozen years' hard-won experience, are being made to look utterly incompetent. What on earth can you do?

APPLIED PSYCHOLOGY

Luckily for the small-stream fisher, such experiences are rare. Little-brook trout have fewer scruples than their broad-river cousins, but many medium-sized rivers accustomed to big hatches can frustrate the angler in this way. We need to apply a little bit of psychology to the situation. As I said earlier in the book, trout display different personality traits according to their size, sex and feeding position. The mid-stream feeders who select their food away from overhanging tussock or branch are the really choosy blighters. They are the demure spinsters of the river, sipping down the spinners genteelly. It is better to leave these fastidious fish and go for less subtle quarry, the villains of the river.

All big trout are thugs. Look for backwaters. In such places there is never a constant stream of hatching duns, rather a willy-nilly assemblage of all kinds of insects which have been sucked into these swirling traps: a soup of mixed ingredients – duns, spinners, smuts and terrestrials all stirred up together. Trout which live in such places are used to a mixed diet. Try dropping a big fly into such spots and you might find that you pick up a good bag, while anglers who stay with the choosy risers get comparatively few. Fish under trees, overhanging banks and round all little promontories – anywhere you can imagine terrestrial insects, moths especially, at this time of day, dropping to their doom.

FISHING HEADS OF POOLS

As light dims and thickens, shady places can no longer be fished with dry fly, since you cannot keep sight of your fly, however large. Find some flat open water and look for a big or very confident fish which is feeding. Try to drop your bushy fly between him and his nearest neighbour. Ten to one he will take it. Another ploy is to select fish at the heads of pools. Trout lying here have first pick of anything swept down from above. Play on their dog in a manger instinct. Float a nice juicy fly down over them to convey the message: 'Well, if you don't take it, the chaps below you will have it!' Psychology.

One of the prime skills of the expert fly fisher is that he knows which fish to attack when. He recognizes the time–wasters and ignores them to concentrate on easier prey. He will not be beguiled by a pool of seductively rising fish if he perceives that they are being choosy (or merely seeing his nylon). He knows that light is fading fast and so moves to a stretch where conditions work for rather than against him.

During the evening rise you have no time to mess about. Your enemy is the fleeing daylight. Do not get bogged down in a tricky place. Move to a run or some tree-lined stretch while there is time to fish them. Return to the flats or pool tails later and, by facing West, use what is left of the light to fish these spots – you will now find the trout far less choosy. Then, as night falls, pack up, or stay on with the brigand band of Bustard fishermen. The night is yet young – shall we join them?

14

Night Fishing

'I must become a borrower of the night
For a dark hour or twain.'

Macbeth

'Angle in the dark, when others dream.'

Thomas Barker

Just as the owls are beginning to screech and daylight flees into the cloak of dark you reel in, for your day's sport is at an end. But in what is left of the strangled light you see an old man with a long greenheart rod approach the river. He is accompanied by two acolytes, his teenage grandsons. You decide to watch, or to be more precise, to listen. You have read about fishing the Bustard but never seen it practised. You offer the old boy a cigarette, which he accepts, and by the flame of your lighter examine his cast. You see two huge, bushy flies: a brown pattern, size 8 hook. These are Bustards or moths. You also notice the thickness of the nylon, not less than 7 lb (3 kg) b.s. No messing with this method!

You listen as the three anglers quietly begin their night's work. The two lads, agile as monkeys, scramble down the bank without once stumbling. The old man is also as sure-footed as a goat and wades out into the big pool tail with less noise than you managed half an hour ago. There is the regular swish of their lines, quite audible above the clatter of the run downstream of this big pool. Before you have finished your cigarette there is a sudden loud splashing.

'Got one, Grandad!'

'Good. Don't rush it!'

Nobody helps the boy: brother and grandfather keep fishing. All is quiet. Then comes the final commotion before a fish is netted.

'About a pound!' the lad announces happily.

You wince slightly. Your best fish after ten hours in the daylight might be just 14 oz (0.4 kg). Before long you have borrowed a Bustard and have started yourself. You manage a brace, the best fish 1 lb 1 oz (0.5 kg). The other three get 17 between them, the best 1 lb 13 oz (0.8 kg). A new convert to Bustard fishing has been made.

MIXED RESPONSES TO NIGHT FISHING

I can understand some fishermen's prejudice against night fishing for brown trout. How much of this is based on either a simple dislike of the dark or the assumption that by using the cover of night the angler is in some way 'not playing the game', I do not know. Certainly, being alone in the dark on some remote river is not everyone's idea of a picnic. Humans are not nocturnal mammals and there is an innate fear of night in us. For some anglers, though, there is quite the opposite feeling: a lonely night on the river is an exhilarating experience. The stars overhead, if the night is clear, are an inspiration, and the chuckle and prattle of the current over the gravel is a beautiful accompaniment to the sport, filling the dark with magical sound. The nocturnal sea-trout fisher lives for such moments. If it is fair to fish for sea trout at night then surely it is not unsporting to try for brown trout in the dark? Trout with red spots are great night feeders just like their silvery cousins, and many a good brownie has ended up in my creel during a night spent in pursuit of his sea-going relatives.

While the night-time Bustard fisherman might seem like a smuggler or brigand, he is in fact a trout fisherman of consummate skill, a practitioner who has developed an uncanny and subtle craft. Hearing and touch take over from sight. He feels the fish take on most occasions but sometimes he will strike by sound. A big, sucky take out there in the dark as soon as your fly lands on the water usually merits an instant strike. It is very similar to sea-trout fishing in the dark. The angler chooses flat tails of big pools and wades out softly if the river is a big one, or stays on the bank by smaller waters. Casting out across or slightly downstream, the angler works his flies somewhat faster than the sea-trout man. A quick, jerked retrieve is best, providing good imitation of the scooting action of emerging sedges or stranded, flapping moths.

The Brown Bustard is possibly the best dressing of all the Bustards. Here it is:

Body: Light tawny brown chenille
Hackle: Buff or reddish
Wings: Feather from the wing of a brown owl
Hook: 8–12

It is not necessary to use Bustards, however. These are simply the flies used on the River Eden where this practice of night fishing is ancient and has become celebrated. There is a wonderful description of it in *Fishing in Eden* (published 1922) by William Nelson, which contains the best chapter ever written on fishing for brown trout at night. See also a very good chapter in *Holiday Trout Fishing* (1943) by H.S. Joyce. For a more modern perspective, read Chapter 8 of Dr Malcolm Greenhalgh's *Trout Fishing in Rivers* (1987) which is very interesting on the strike-by–sound technique.

FLY SELECTION

Almost any big wet fly (or dry fly!) will do. I have found an Invicta a very deadly pattern for the job, and so is an Ackroyd. A big wet

Greenwell or Wickham are also excellent flies. Muddler Minnows, too, are perfect for the job. Any pattern will do but it must be sizeable: 10 at the smallest, but 8 is a good compromise. I recommend sturdy nylon: tackle is not easily checked in the dark. Strong nylon is less prone to tangles than delicate line and you are also well prepared if a big brownie, or surprise sea trout takes hold. Six pounds (2.7 kg) b.s. is the lightest you should fish, while 8 lb (3.6 kg) is recommended for beginners at the art. Beginners should also not use a dropper on their cast. I myself rarely use more than two big wet flies in the dark.

I have found big slow pools, especially their tails, excellent spots to locate trout in the dark. One other kind of place is also worth trying in my experience and that is a corner pool. Here trout tend to lie on the outer side of the bend where the water is deepest. It also goes without saying that it is essential to try stretches where you have no trees within range of your back cast.

My view of night fishing for brown trout is that it is a very useful additional skill for the fly fisherman to acquire. I do not prefer it to daytime fishing, but I do enjoy it very much, finding it a very exciting way of catching trout. I have often gone out in the middle of the night to fish for sea trout but never done so for brownies. All my night fishing for brown trout has involved staying on the river as night falls and fishing for an hour or two in the dark.

I have found night fishing a welcome way to add some needed fish to the creel. It has been my saviour on quite a number of occasions. On hot, sticky, bothersome days trout will often remain dour until dark, when a sudden change of mood makes them catchable. The angler who gives up, fishless, at this point is denying himself a brace for breakfast. If you have toiled all day beneath a hot sun in an unequal struggle with the fish and you have a chance at the day's end of turning the tables, then I think you are fully justified in seizing your chance. It may only take you half an hour or so in the dark, for trout often come very quickly to your fly at night.

MARATHON SESSION

I well remember a marathon day I had on a Staffordshire river when I was 20. I had been fishing for about 15 hours and all I had to show for my efforts was a brace just on the size limit. It had been a long, hot day full of disasters. But at dusk it clicked. I had a splendid brace on a big wet fly in the dark. It had taken me 15 hours to get my first brace and 15 minutes to get the second!

On another occasion I had taken a friend to fish with me on the Ribble, telling him what a superb river it was beforehand. As things turned out it was a brute of a day: very hot, very bright, with a raking downstream wind. By dusk we had had three trout between us and that was all. In addition I had fallen in and also caught a chub getting on for 2 lb (0.9 kg), which I had taken for a huge trout until disappointment dawned. Then, after dark, as we walked back downstream to my car I thought I heard a few fish feeding in a big junction pool as we passed. I proposed a few casts here. I knotted a big wet fly to the point of our casts and we began to fish.

It was not the easiest of places, since a high bank behind us hampered easy casting. My friend, who had never fished this way before, was utterly confused and soon gave up, having produced a horrid bird's nest. I had three fine trout in barely quarter of an hour, however, and had salvaged a nugget from the day. This is typical of good night fishing after a hot day and I have cheered myself up in this way many a time. It can be a frustrating business (as my friend on this occasion found) until you have picked up the knack of fishing in the dark. But it is a skill worth acquiring and can be quickly learnt. I was fortunate because my father taught me the technique when I was a boy and by the time I was in my early teens he had also shown me how to catch sea trout in the dark. The two skills are definitely related and the knowledge of one makes it much easier to master the other.

A POACHER'S TALE

The following story of night fishing shows me in a dishonest light but I trust you will forgive my piracy and put it down to youthful high spirits. Years ago I was fishing in France and, trudging back to my car in the dark, I came to a private garden which came right down to the river bank. Now, I knew that in this garden the proprietor had recently built himself a pond which he had stocked with trout. There was a party going on indoors and nobody was going to take any notice of me. I wanted but one extra fish to accommodate every guest at a dinner party I was throwing the next day (an Englishman cooking for French people!) so a mischievous thought came to me. It was the work of a few seconds to step over the fence, cross a few yards of turf, and throw my flies onto this private pool. I hooked a fish almost immediately and soon a stocked rainbow lay in my creel among the wild brown trout from the river. Here I really was a brigand with a Bustard.

My final tale (and I could tell many more) really concerns sea trout, but I cannot resist relating it, particularly since it has some brown trout connections. The principal character of this story is a Bighead, a species of fisherman we have all met at some time or another. On this particular occasion my father and I had decided to fish a tributary of the Welsh Teifi, the beautiful little Cothi. We turned up in the afternoon to recce the river in daylight, with the intention of fishing after dark for sewen. Different anglers have different ways of casing the joint for sea trout. Some walk up and down the bank with Polaroids looking for holding pools, others, such as my father, fish down the runs with wet fly, while I prefer to fish upstream with a dry fly. I have caught a good few sewen, phinnock and sea trout on dry fly. The method also allows me to fish for brown trout at the same time.

On this particular afternoon I caught a good number of small wild brown trout, all of which I returned, and I also rose and missed what I took to be a reasonably sized sewen in a small run between my bank and an island in the river. This was a lovely spot. The island was only a quarter of the way across the river and on the far side of it was a broad, shelving pool – most inviting, and perhaps the obvious place to fish. However, something had attracted me to the narrow little run on the near side of the island. Halfway down this run was a deep bubbling pot and it took my fancy. It was here I missed what I suspected was a sewen.

THE VOICE OF EXPERIENCE

My father and I had dinner at the hotel which had the fishing and here we met the Bighead. In fact, he was well-meaning and kindly but in a patronizing and self-important way. Whatever you had done, he had gone one better. He was full of stories about fish of great size, each related fortissimo so that all bystanders could bathe in his brilliance.

After dinner he attached himself to us and we all three strolled down to the river together with our rods. He was full of advice about the best spots for my father and me to fish, about the best flies to use, and so forth. He was, I suppose, about a dozen years younger than my father and a dozen years older than me but he treated us both with the same condescending ebullience: that he was a far less experienced angler than my father seemed never to occur to him.

When we reached the river it was still light enough to see clearly and I announced my plan to fish the near side of the island. Our uninvited guide ridiculed my intention. 'No point in fishing there, it's not a holding pool,' he said, 'I have fished here for years, so I should know.'

A short, very deafening silence followed this remark. If our tame expert expected his authority to go unchallenged then he had underrated his company. 'Nevertheless, I'm still going to fish it,' I replied doggedly.

Before long, my father, who I suspect had very gamely taken it upon himself to draw this nuisance's fire, went upstream with the man and I was left blissfully alone. At last I could listen to the Voice of Nature and not that of Assumed Authority. The light was rapidly fading. I sat on the bank to await nightfall. A sandpiper called shrilly from upstream, perhaps disturbed by incessant human tongue-wagging up there. I watched and, sure enough, he came skimming downstream calling *tee-wee-wee* as he came. With a superb display of braking on the wing he slammed to a halt, alighting on a big stone at the southern tip of the island. He perched there for 30 seconds or so, bobbing his head, then took off with another shrill cry and vanished downstream. Two bats began to work round the island and in the woods above the Cothi an owl shrieked. I checked my cast: Alexandra on the point, Ackroyd on the dropper, both size 6 or 8 if memory serves.

THE INTUITIVE APPROACH

When it was truly dark I stood up and walked to the head of the insignificant little run about which I had such a gut feeling. I only needed the shortest of lines. I began to fish carefully down the small channel. When I reached the deep little pot midway down I had a take, a savage one more typical of a brown trout than a migratory trout. But it was a sewen all right. I played him out and netted a lovely, lithe, fresh fish. It was a very dark night but his silver flank almost glowed. I laid him on the bank and fished the rest of the channel down, missing a fish at the tail. I walked slowly back to the head of the island, glancing with pride at the splash of silver on the black grass as I passed.

I fished the channel down again. When I came to the deep hole halfway along the island I had another extremely positive take. I had hooked another sewen, a stronger fish. I was trembling with excitement. If ever a hunch had paid off, this decision to fish in the narrow channel behind an island had! One sewen was good, but two was superb! I played the second fish with trepidation. But he came inexorably to the net – it was my night.

I sat down beside the two bars of gleaming silver on the bank. My heart was pounding. Clearly, the swirly pot where I had missed the good fish on dry fly in the afternoon, and now hooked two sewen, was a holding pool. I walked back to the head of the run. Third time lucky? I fished gently downstream. In the magical place I did indeed get another take – the most savage yet – and found myself fast into the biggest fish of the night. Splash! Thump! At this point I heard voices, or should I say the Voice. My father and the loudmouth were on their way back downstream. The sewen jumped again.

'Into a fish, Nick?' came the Voice through the dark. 'Good lad ... Don't rush it.' Then, after a pause: 'Let me net it.'

He did net the fish, the biggest so far.

'Oh, so you got one there did you! No point in fishing there any more. Only a question of an odd fish, and that a lucky one,' announced the Expert. I carried my sewen to the spot where the other two lay.

'Gosh! Is that your third from this place? Well I never! Talk about beginner's luck!' said the Voice, and in the same breath: 'Here, let me show you how to unhook a sea trout in the dark.'

At 16 I was certainly no expert, but neither was I anything like a beginner, and as for luck, there was no point in me explaining why I had chosen the run: our unwanted guide was no listener. As it turned out, he had the greatest difficulty unhooking the sea trout, even blaming me for striking too hard and driving the hook in too deep. I was glad that it was dark so that I could not meet my father's eye.

All of which proves that if you get a hunch, then stick with it: certainly never let yourself be diverted. All three fish took the Ackroyd, by the way; a fly I have found excellent when fishing at night for both brown trout and sea trout.

15

Dry Fly
The Strike and the Sixth Sense

'Strike at him as hard as you can and as often as you can, and keep moving on.'
Ulysses S. Grant

I like to catch more trout per season on dry fly than with any other method. My best-ever seasonal haul on dry fly was in 1983, when out of the 415 trout I caught that year, 266 fell to the floater. These were all wild fish individually stalked and earned. In my teens I caught more trout on worm and spinner than with any other method, even though my preference for dry fly was already established. This was because I was so keen to catch trout that I took whatever fishing I could get, mainly in neglected, overgrown streams where fly casting was limited to the odd pool. After a typical afternoon's work on a stream of this type I would often end up with a dozen fish – a brace caught on dry fly, the other ten on upstream worm.

My father, a busy doctor, used to take me to some celebrated dry fly waters in those days, but not often enough for my liking. So, despite my staple diet of upstream worm and minnow in the tangled woods, by the time I was fifteen dry fly was my favourite form of fishing. It has remained so ever since. Why? I think it is really just aesthetic, a question of personal taste and nothing more. I would never claim that dry fly is the best method or even the most challenging; it is simply the method I prefer.

THE BEAUTY OF NATURE

Aquatic flies in their adult form are such beautiful things: so delicate and so colourful. The sight of a hatch of duns or spinners bouncing down atop the current in fluttering drifts is one of the most exciting things that I can experience in the wild. And as a for a trout coming up to take a dun with the almost exaggerated slowness which a really confident fish exhibits, my pulse never fails to quicken when I see that. A head-and-tail rise is one of the great sights of Nature – something you need not be an expert or specialist to witness, unlike the subtle underwater blink of a trout taking a nymph, which is a phenomenon obvious only to the initiated.

To see my own fly come bobbing down on the back of the current with the possibility that it will be engulfed at any moment by a big bronze head is the zenith of trout fishing for me. Trout feeding beneath the surface often do so quite invisibly, whereas the vigorous splashing of hungry trout in spring as they rise to grab dark olives or March Browns is a joyous and visible affirmation of a life-form continuing to flourish and survive. Dry fly is a spectator sport.

The flash of a trout underwater as it takes my nymph is also most exciting but in a different way: an impalpable, altogether less showy phenomenon. Nymphs are not such interesting creatures to look at as duns and spinners, in my opinion. They are brown, earwiggish things which at a casual glance all look the same, no matter what species. Their artificial copies are also less aesthetically pleasing than the copies of their adult forms. With a Sawyer Pheasant Tail Nymph you have a copy which will work for you every day the season through. From nymphing there is absent that whole ritual of fly selection which lends such an extra dimension of fascination to dry fly fishing. What is more, your nymphs do a disappearing act when you cast them, whereas your dry flies remain aloft, perkily on display.

Just as I prefer wading in a river to merely scrambling about on its dry banks, so I enjoy the extra physical casting effort that dry fly necessitates with its endless flexuous false casting. Fishing is a form of exercise for me. I like giving my rod some 'stick', making it work to its limit. It is a physical sensation I enjoy, the most important physical part of the sport. False casting is like breathing, second nature to me. When wading, I like the contact I get with the water. I *feel* the river: it is a sinuous, plastic entity and I am part of it. I am invading the trout's world, albeit in a very ungainly, clumsy way. I stand on a rocky bed which has been scoured for millions of years by a ceaseless, pellucid, moving serpent of water. My dry fly rod is a ceaseless switch, as restless and as mobile a thing as the river itself.

When a trout mounts to the surface to take my fly he is invading my element in the same way that I am invading his when I wade. It is an act of faith: he breaks from his own element and enters mine to seize a creature from the world of air. It is the shattering of the mirror between two elements that most attracts me to dry fly fishing.

An aesthetic thing entirely. Nymphing arouses the craftsman in me, dry fly arouses the poet.

TWO WORLDS

Skues, Sawyer and Kite, in contending that nymph fishing was more difficult than dry fly, were clearly referring to the kind of dry fly practised on sedate southern chalkstreams – streams where water levels remain constant, duns come downstream with unerring regularity, and where the edges of the river are carefully manicured and preened for fishermen. How different from dry fly in the uplands of the North and on the windswept moorlands of the Western Peninsulas! Here water levels can go up and down like a yo-yo and, with varying degrees of opacity. Fly life can fluctuate alarmingly too, and the borders of the water can be tangled, uncleared, rough, wild and revealing no evidence of the hand of Man. Here dry fly is a superb challenge and an entirely different art from the more civilized, relaxed business of the cultivated southern chalkstream.

Not that I am trying to make out that the North's rough-and-tumble type of dry fly is necessarily more difficult than chalkstream dry fly. For a start, in rivers where trout run really wild the 'educated trout' is not a factor. One of the features of well-visited rivers, and chalkstreams especially, is the wary, educated trout. These fish pose their own unique challenge. But I resist the charge that dry fly is subject to less subtlety and variation than nymphing. When Skues, in the same breath as he talked of the 'subtle fascination' of nymph fishing, also accused the successful hooking of trout on dry fly as having a 'sameness and comparative obviousness and monotony of achievement' about it, I know he had his canal-like stretch of the Itchen in mind and not the crumbly, foaming runs of the Don, Tyne, Eden, Eamont or Ure. There is never anything monotonous about dry fly on rivers of this category!

A CONTENTIOUS VIEWPOINT

Ironically, though, the most vociferous (and amusing) put-down of dry fly fishing that I have ever come across is not by a chalkstream nympher with an axe to grind but in a booklet entitled *How to Catch Trout* published in Edinburgh in 1888 by 'Three Anglers' – presumably Scotsmen and therefore Northern, rain-fed river fishers, men who ought to have known better. This sententious triumvirate maintains that dry fly is 'of all ways of catching trout the most "cushie"; for it is most used throughout the pleasantest season of the year' and that: 'It is also decidedly less hard work than wet fly-fishing, and does not, we think, call for so close an acquaintance with the haunts and habits of trout.'

I doubt Halford would have endorsed this last statement, nor, I suspect, would a contemporary dry fly entomologist such as John Goddard. As for hard work, I have a Scots acquaintance, a ghillie and great wet fly advocate, who laughs at me and my ceaseless false casting when I am dry fly fishing.

'There ye stand, thrashin' away, Nicky, with ye flees more often in the air than on the water! I conserve my energy and keep my line in the water. Och, wet flee's the job, man!' he says to me with relish.

The three Scottish anglers are not finished, however, their *pièce de résistance* is to come. Their conclusion on dry fly fishing is: 'All this appeals to the nature of the mature elderly angler, as our own personal experience shows, who inclines to give up the more strenuous method for the easier if less scientific one.'

Anyone who came up a small Yorkshire river with me for a day would soon find out whether dry fly was 'strenuous' or not! And as for the 'mature elderly angler', alas, many lose the sharp eyesight necessary for dry fly, preferring the more easily registered tug of trout on their downstream wet flies. I well remember fishing with my grandfather, a great dry fly man in his prime, and having to tell him that his fly was caught on the opposite bank. He shook his head stubbornly and went through the charade of watching his fly come downstream only to find himself well and truly snagged in the vegetation as he lifted his line off for the next cast. I felt for him: it is not pleasant to see the powers of a great sportsman on the wane.

ROUGH-STREAM DRY FLY

It could be argued that rough-stream dry fly is the most demanding type of dry fly there is, as Courtney Williams observes:

> active little trout of the fast rivers are amazingly quick. Unlike the fat and lazy fish which, inhabiting the gently flowing streams, generally rise to the fly in a deliberate manner, they are inclined to dash at the lure and will often seize and eject it again before the fisherman has even thought of striking.

He continues in the next paragraph:

> But on any swift river, trout are generally prone to pluck at a dry fly in a most disconcerting manner and unless the angler's brain and wrist work in unison, more trout will be missed than hooked.

Certainly on many of the small, rushing rivers that I fish you need to have a sharp eye and a quick wrist to keep up with the fish if you want any trout in your creel. Yet even on these rapid rivers there will be times when a more deliberate strike is needed. No river, however turbulent, is devoid of slack water: big deep pools, elbow bends, flats and calm pool tails. Trout which rise in these locations, especially if sizeable, require a slower strike than those found in runs and tumbles.

The dry fly fisherman must adjust his strike accordingly and this is no easily acquired skill. The necessity for the rain–fed river dry fly fisherman to vary the speed of his strike from pool to pool – anything from lightning quick to deliberately slow – is one of the greatest demands made on him. It is also a skill which is hardly ever touched on in fishing books. On the contrary, many writers in a very blasé manner mention the dry fly strike as if it is a uniform process, subject to no variation whatsoever. The beginner looking for solace will therefore seldom find it in the pages of fishing books. Wanting to know what he is doing wrong with a dry fly, wondering why he is not hooking fish, he will not find much suitable corrective advice.

There is another category of angler who might also be seeking expert opinion on this matter and that is the individual who is returning to fishing after an absence from the sport. Such a fisherman is bound to be out of touch after a long lay-off and the dry fly strike will take time to re-acquire. I speak from experience here for about ten years ago I was in this exact position myself. Between 1974 and 1978 I was continuously abroad and though I did fish during these years I hardly ever wielded a fly rod. When I returned to England after this prolonged absence I was extremely rusty, sadly so, and at the time it caused me to do some soul-searching. I picked up the wet fly and nymph strike in no time, because I still possessed the ability to react quickly, but the dry fly strike eluded me. It took me half a season to recover it. I was striking too quickly and could not find the discipline required to delay in gently flowing water.

RELEARNING SKILLS

My sojourn in England was short-lived, for off on my travels I went again, though this time I did have access to trout streams. I invested in a lovely glass rod and this compounded my problems because it was stiff and transmitted my orders to it very quickly. It was not until 1983, when back in England permanently, that I really rediscovered my magic touch. I began to use an old spongy split-cane 8-foot (2.4 m) Cummins I had inherited from my grandfather. What problems I could have obviated if I had only experimented with this rod in the summer of 1978! I now use a 7½-foot (2.3 m) Airsprite cane rod, made by Fosters of Ashbourne, when fishing small streams where I regularly have to switch my strike from lightning fast to slow. I find cane more forgiving on the strike when using a very short line; carbon is much more savage and extreme delicacy is needed to avoid breaking in fish.

For bigger rivers I use either a 9-foot (2.7 m) Shakespeare Sigma Graphite carbon rod or an 8½-foot (2.6 m) Sharpe's impregnated cane rod. The old Cummins is a bit of a museum piece and I rarely use it nowadays, but I am very grateful for the favour it did me. I have completely regained my touch now, no matter what rod I use, but I will never forget the tangle I got into after that four-year lay-off.

It is my opinion that there are three reasons why fishermen systematically miss trout on dry fly. First, beginners miss trout consistently because they strike too slowly. They do not read the signs on the water quickly enough and are unprepared when trout take their flies. Second, those who use too long a line when fishing will miss the majority of the fish they rise. I cannot stress enough the importance of using as short a line as possible when dry fly fishing, especially in water with any current to it. Third, everyone else missing fish consistently will be striking too quickly.

Fishermen who come into this last category are those who have got out of practice, those who are in a bad mood or whose nerves are frayed for one reason or another, and those beginners who have realized that they are striking too slowly and have overcompensated. Most tyros go through this agonizing process of at first striking too slowly and then too fast until they learn the middle path. Frustrating! But nothing worthwhile is ever learnt in a hurry. Once the apprenticeship is served the rewards begin to accrue.

IMMEDIATE STRIKE

This is a problem that never confronts the nymph fisher, who never wonders how quickly to strike. Once he suspects that a trout has taken his nymph he has only one duty: to strike immediately. There is never the prospect of the strategic delay which the dry fly man has to learn to cultivate. In nymph fishing the main problem is detecting the take in the first place. Once it has been detected the only error possible is to delay. It is significant to me that on my return from those years overseas the nymph strike presented no difficulty whatsoever, and that it was the slightly delayed dry fly strike which troubled me. I am in no doubt that the discipline of the delayed strike truly takes a long time to master, especially on swift-flowing streams where an angler is never allowed to get into a regular dry fly strike rhythm.

Years ago I knew an old retired doctor (Dr Elam of Langwathby) who fished the River Eden. In his younger days he had fished the southern chalkstreams, mainly the Kennet, Mimram and Bean, I believe, and he used to tell me how much more leisurely a business dry fly fishing had been down there. He spoke of a uniformly slow strike. We fishers of tumbling northern rivers never have this luxury. I have another northern acquaintance who has told me that whenever he fishes in the South he rarely catches anything because he cannot discipline himself to the local exaggeratedly slow strike. I think we must add to our list of dry fly missers all geographically uprooted fishermen. Those who move from North to South will probably be striking too quickly, while those who move the other way will probably find they are striking far too slowly. What a complicated world!

I have been fly fishing for nearly 30 years and I still get the dry fly strike wrong on occasion. I never get the nymph strike wrong – I miss trout on nymph but only because I fail to detect the take quickly enough: there is a subtle difference. A case in point is the very last fishing trip I made to Yorkshire. I spent a week there, and a pretty disastrous week with dry fly it was too. Basically, the problem was this book. I have spent more time writing than fishing these last two months and have got a little rusty with my fly rod. On the first day of my holiday I had a string of unlucky losses, losing trout in roots or behind rocks. Then my rod tip caught in an overhead branch and the best fish of the day took the opportunity to escape.

A CASE OF NERVES

My wife, who is used to me catching trout with monotonous regularity, could not understand it at all and the gloom of the day even rubbed off on her. She said she could not remember me ever losing and missing so many fish in one day, for by the end of it I was missing droves, simply because I had allowed myself to get rattled and jittery. The next day, though not so bad, was still not good: I was not on song at all. I kept reminding myself that I had caught nearly three hundred trout already in the season and that things like this did not happen to experienced fishermen. But the truth of the matter is that they do. Fishing is a great leveller if Lady Luck decides to flirt with you. By the end of this week I had switched to the upstream worm, whereupon I mercifully discovered I had not lost my knack.

Fortunately, a recent day on the Derbyshire Wye has restored my faith in myself as a dry fly fisherman. Not only did I fish well by my own standards but I had a significantly better day than any other angler on the river. As fishermen we must learn to live with the quirky fluctuations of our sport by being philosophical when things go badly and by efficiently grabbing our chances when it is our day. One of the great things about fishing for wild river trout is that we can never predict whether it will be our day or not. This uncertainty fuels our interest in the sport and keeps us keen.

Before I leave the subject of the difficulty of timing the dry fly strike correctly, here are a few suggestions which beginners, or those rusty or displaced anglers currently experiencing problems in this quarter, might care to consider.

1. Try using a shorter line; indeed always use the shortest possible line (i.e. get as close to your quarry as stealth allows).
2. Try striking more slowly.
3. Try fishing with a different rod, if necessary borrowing those of your friends for an hour or two.
4. Make sure your floating line is not sinking. If it is old, replace it. Dry fly fishing with a poor line is like trying to shoot duck with blank cartridges.
5. Ask another fisherman to watch you for a while. An impartial observer (provided he is not a bighead) can often see what we ourselves cannot. This way you might learn that, for example, you are striking far too fast.
6. Relax. Do not snatch. Take a break. Smoke a pipe or cigar, eat a snack, or look at some wild flowers before fishing the next pool. Even try a snort of Scotch before restarting. (A hip-flask is *always* an essential item of tackle!)

With reference to this last numbered point: I have often struggled to find the correct timing of the dry fly strike but, having had a rest, have suddenly found it. Many such occasions spring to mind, none more curious than a day I had on the Eden in 1978. I left my home in the early hours of the morning and, after a long drive, was on the water in time for the early rise that often takes place on that great river in summer. I had two brace of good fish and then gradually lost my touch. By mid afternoon I could hardly hook a thing. True, some nimble little grayling had begun to take and maybe I was being pestered by these fleet creatures, but I will not let this stand as an excuse. I took a break, had a nap in my car, listened to the six o'clock news, ate something and then went back to the river at a different place.

Now it was an entirely different story. I could not go wrong. I had more fish in two hours than I had had all day. Perhaps fatigue also partly explains my bad patch in the afternoon, for it had been a long day. At any rate, I am a great believer in taking a rest if I find I cannot get the dry fly strike right.

THE SIXTH SENSE

I would now like to come to the sixth sense in dry fly fishing. It is not just nymphing and upstream wet fly which have the monopoly on the impalpable in fishing. There are times when the dry fly fisherman must trust to senses other than his eyes. Two cases serve to illustrate this point. The first occurred some years ago on a small Yorkshire chalk-stream. It happened to be my very first visit to the river, so it was not water with which I was yet familiar. I came to a pool with a bend in it where part of the river was obscured from my vision by the overhang of the bank on which I was standing. As I stood watching this place, a superb trout – the best I had seen all day – idled out from under the 'blind' water beneath the curve of my bank, and took a fly just within my view before slipping back into his shady bower.

I could not ignore such a fish. I cast upstream and let my fly, a Lunn's Particular, dance down my side of the pool. Of course, I was hoping that I would be able to see my fly the whole way down, but currents are difficult things to judge and this pool was unfamiliar. Imagine, then, my concern when my dry fly was swept out of sight into the depths of the overhanging bank. There was no way that I could have seen the trout take. Had the pool been a still one then I might have had some kind of sign – glimpsed a ripple or heard a plop – but the current was both too rapid and too noisy. It occurred to me that I should immediately pull my line off the water but this idea I rejected because I feared frightening the fish. I had to make a split-second decision, since any moment my fly would be over the fish, which was indeed a big one.

RELYING ON GUESSWORK

I made a bold choice: I resolved to strike by guesswork. I had already marked the rough position of the fish and so I had to imagine the progress of my fly coming downstream through blind water. I had to guess both where my fly had reached and where the trout would take it, then give him time before striking, for he had rolled over very slowly in a splendid head-and-tail rise when I had seen him take earlier. It was fishing by instinct or by imagination. I was asking my sixth sense to come to my aid. At any rate, whether by luck or judgement, I successfully hooked that trout. I had a spectacular battle with him – which involved me scaling a barbed-wire fence, climbing down a steep bank, doing a one-handed Tarzan act round a tree and sploshing across a rapid current to gain the opposite bank, all the time with this monster on the line – and finally beached much the best trout of the day. Indeed, despite having since caught many hundreds of fish in this wonderful little river, I have never had one bigger than this particular trout on my first visit.

My other example of a sixth sense at work comes from even further back in the past. I was fishing a small Cheshire trout stream with a friend – a slow, winding, sluggish little river in which some really huge trout resided. As I was walking back downstream in the dusk, I spied a trout below me take a fly in a deep backwater beneath a bush. Because of the vegetation I could not make an upstream cast for this fish, yet a downstream cast was nigh impossible because the pool was so small that if I showed even my rod across it, let alone my head, the trout would be scared, despite the encroaching darkness. There was only one possibility: to fish blind. The trout was making greedy sucking noises as he took. Could I 'strike by sound', I wondered? It seemed worth a try.

I put on a big, fluffy Wickham's Fancy to tempt the fish and cast a snaky downstream line, hoping that I had judged my distance correctly and that I had additionally allowed enough slack to take the fly down over him without drag. A good half of my line lay on the bank: I had no idea whether it might have fouled vegetation and was thus going to hinder my strike. I could see nothing except grass, and even the far side of the stream was invisible, so far back from the brink was I kneeling. I waited, heart in mouth, ears pricked in suspense. Then there came a joyful and clearly audible gulp. Slow water, slow strike. I paused palpably and struck. He was hooked! After a tremendous struggle I netted the biggest trout of the evening.

I have used the 'strike by sound' formula since, but never in such demanding circumstances. Too much line here and I would have caught in the bush beneath which the trout was feeding; too little and he would not have seen my fly. It was not the sort of place where I was going to have several opportunities to get the cast right: the thick vegetation demanded that I get it right first time, which I did.

Such successes show how complex and challenging dry fly fishing can be. They also illustrate two operations which went right; so often attempts involving this degree of difficulty go wrong. I have found that it can be difficult enough to hook a fish when I can see everything clearly, let alone when I can see nothing. The sixth sense, though, is indispensable to all fishermen in all branches of the sport, and in dry fly fishing it is no less important than in any other branch. To the dry fly fisherman it tends to be of most use when eyesight is impaired.

In very turbulent, choppy or rippling parts of the river, or in water where conditions of light are extreme – bright and glary or sombre and gloomy – the dry fly fisherman relies on more than just his conscious eyesight. We have all of us had the experience of raising our rod to make another cast only to find that we have hooked a fish. Such occurrences are sheer flukes where we have relied on no instinct whatsoever, indeed the hooking comes as complete surprise to us, yet there are times when a dry fly fisherman will suddenly quite deliberately strike at some almost impalpable sign and find he has successfully hooked a trout.

AN INSTINCTIVE STRIKE

There must be moments when the angler loses sight of his fly in adverse conditions of light or ripple, yet all may not be lost. At such times the fisherman will suddenly have the overwhelming instinct to strike and on doing so will find that his suspicions were well founded. As to what exactly this instinct or second sight is I am uncertain, but I do have an inkling that it might not be quite the mystery some sportsmen believe it to be. I am happy to call it a sixth sense, though I suspect that it is no more than a barely perceptible combination of some of the other five.

Sometimes, it is the line which we notice without realizing that we have done so: it falters or checks very slightly in the current and this it is that triggers our response. When you have been fishing for some years you become utterly accustomed to the usual flow of a river and any abnormal swirl or ripple, be it only partly glimpsed, or any irregular plash or plip which you only half hear, will immediately arouse your suspicion without your eyes ever being fully aware of any concrete evidence that a trout has taken your fly. This is more a case of perception heightened by experience than the possession of some arcane sixth sense.

I remember a purple patch I had just below Langwathby bridge on the Eden a few years ago. I was out in mid river wading among the weedbeds where the water was quite choppy and subject to the conflict of several different currents brawling down from above. It was a gloomy, grey afternoon yet the water was giving off a flickering, livid glare which made it quite a feat to keep sight of my fly all the time. I was additionally hampered by a downstream wind. This part of the river often acts as a wind funnel with its towering right bank and slightly narrowing neck of water, and what was just a light breeze elsewhere was here quite an annoying gusty current of air – as turbulent as the water itself.

JUDGING DISTANCE

All dry fly fishermen become expert at judging distances: they learn to anticipate exactly where their fly will fall upon the water simply by knowing how much line they are swishing backwards and forwards above their heads. However, a strong downstream wind plays havoc with this judgement. Your fly is blown back a yard or so as it is landing: instead of alighting 15 yards (14 m) ahead of you, as intended, it lands 13 or 14 yards (12–13 m) away, and sometimes well to the left or right of your intended target. On still, smooth, or evenly flowing water this presents no problem because your eye can easily pick up your fly's deviation, but on agitated water or in gloom or glare it is extraordinarily tricky to spot your fly at once. As your eyes frantically scan the surface to locate your fly, it is moving downstream all the time, eluding your search.

In order to combat the wind you put more vehemence into your cast, cutting the rod point down to the surface, and although you may succeed in placing the fly in the exact spot, it lands with such force it sinks! The only solution then, it seems, is to shorten your line to keep the fly nearer your searching eyes, but although this idea is good in theory, in practice it fails because you have not sufficient weight of line out now to make any impression on the wind. Thus instead of blowing back a yard or two (0.9–1.8 m), with a short line it blows back 5 yards (4.5 m) and lands under your rod tip!

On the afternoon in question the wind was not strong enough to cause extreme discomfort of this sort but the combination of strong breeze, rippling cross currents and flickering, difficult light made it a very demanding place for dry fly fishing. The blue-winged olive was hatching and some good fish were on the feed. I rose six trout (to my knowledge) and caught five of them, which weighed 5 lb (2.3 kg), the best scaling 1½ lb (0.7 kg). Four of the five were instinctive strikes – an unusually high proportion. The principal difficulty was catching sight of my dry fly when it landed.

I resorted to twin dry fly, using a big point marker fly as a target for my eye – always a worthwhile ruse on a blustery day. A big Red Sedge on the point ultimately did the trick for me while I rotated a series of flies on the dropper: Blue Dun, Gold Ribbed Hare's Ear and Greenwell's Glory all scoring. In all probability I rose a few more than six fish without realizing it, but that I connected with four via instinctive strikes shows that my sixth sense was working well on that particular afternoon.

A DANGEROUS MANOEUVRE

I remember another occasion on a sister river of the Eden, the Eamont, when this 'extra' sense was an immense help to me. I came to a big, deep pool into which a powerful foaming current rushed from above.

On the far side of this roaring current I rather imagined I had seen a fish rise. It was something of a long shot but there was little else to go on as it was still early in the day and not much was doing yet. I gingerly waded out into the surging current, for it was a hazardous place to wade – indeed so perilous that the big, deep pool just below was called Danger Pool because a luckless salmon fisherman had drowned there while attempting to wade in it many years previously. However, I had a strong instinct that I really had seen a trout poke his nose out over on the other side, and the current had to be negotiated if I wanted to have a cast at him.

With the violent water thrumming round my waders, I cast a snaky line downstream, for a downstream approach was the only one I could manage. I had put on a big, bushy dry Jock Scott and I trotted this tempting morsel down the far side of the current in very rough water. Sure enough, a great neb appeared and my fly disappeared. Making my way back across the violent current while playing a large and powerful trout was not an experience I would willingly repeat, but somehow I managed it. Many leaps and runs later a magnificent one-and-a-half-pounder (0.7 kg) was netted.

No sooner had I creeled this lovely fish and dried my fly than I turned my attention to the strong current in the tail of the pool above. I fished this up carefully, not always able to see my fly clearly, so rough and tumbling was the place. On one of my casts, having momentarily lost sight of the large Jock Scott, some instinct made me strike. After a frantic struggle in very foamy, drumming water I landed a trout of 1 lb 1 oz (0.5 kg). With such a splendid brace in my creel at the start of the day my confidence was sky high and things turned out memorably: ten trout weighing 10½ lb (4.8 kg).

This last occasion illustrates another very useful benefit of the sixth sense: the strong suspicion that you have had a glimpse of a fish in a particular place without having any overwhelming sensory evidence of the fact. This instinct is of supreme value to all fly fishermen whether on river or lake, whether fishing wet or dry. It is an instinct which can make the difference between a fish or two and no fish at all.

TURBULENT WATER

A few springs ago I was fishing the Aberdeenshire Don on a very dour day. Snow-melt had raised the river to such a level that it was barely fishable as a fly water. March Browns had been hatching well but the trout had difficulty in catching sight of them in the tumid water. I had been pacing up and down the river like a caged tiger, trying to find a spot where a trout could take a fly, when I came to a broad, long pool which was normally quite a serene smooth glide, but at this level of water it was a flamboyant, careering race full of ripples and swirls. I stood watching the peaty brew boiling past me when, despite the pock-pitted water surface, I thought I glimpsed the movement of a trout.

On such a day I had nothing to lose so I flicked my Baigent's Brown out across the pool. The first cast elicited no interest, nor did the second, third, fourth or fifth. It was not at all easy to mark a rise in the turbulent, tumescent current, especially one only glimpsed, but I kept casting in the hope that I would get my fly to cover just the right place. All I can say is that I did not leave that spot until I made a cast to my satisfaction, and that as soon as I had made such a cast a trout took my fly.

Up through the thick water came a long pale shadow which engulfed the Baigent's Brown in one wolfish gulp. He weighed 1 lb 5 oz (0.6 kg) and was the only trout any angler caught all day on that stretch of the river. Instinct or a sixth sense had saved me from drawing a blank: without it I never would have located this trout in the roaring, swollen river. It would have been like trying to find a needle in a haystack without the help of my sixth sense.

These last few examples involve the capture of big trout (big at least for northern rain-fed rivers) in rapid, turbulent water, and in my experience big trout often lie in such places. Most of the biggest trout that I have caught on dry fly have come from rapid places in rivers. This is just another attraction of rough-stream dry fly – along with all the others! I love this type of fishing where I can see a bushy fly come bobbing down towards me on a rushing, undulating current.

I quoted William Currie earlier on the two different types of dry fly fishing: rough-stream angling of the type just mentioned and the altogether more delicate art of stalking trout on clear-running streams. Which is more demanding and difficult? Which do I prefer? The answer to both questions is: both! Each art makes its own special demands; and though I love to see a bonny, bouncing dry fly I am also devoted to the stalking of trout in clear water. In my opinion the true dry fly expert should be able to handle each environment with aplomb, though I suspect that he would probably be slightly more adept at one than the other, so different are they as skills. I also suspect that deep down such an expert would probably have a slight preference for either one world or the other, a priority probably dictated by upbringing, so powerful are early impressions on heart and mind. If I looked deep into myself to pose such an unnecessary question I have an inkling that I would take the path along the rough stream, though it would grieve me never to stalk a trout in smooth, crystal-water again.

PROBLEMS OF USING TOO LONG A LINE

I have already mentioned several times the importance of using the correct length of line when fishing, especially avoiding the use of too long a line. If I had to pick out a single criticism of many modern river anglers it would be that they have a tendency to use too long a line. In my view there are four principal drawbacks to this: (a) a quick, clean strike is inhibited; (b) the risk of drag is additionally increased; (c) some fish beneath the line will be quite unnecessarily put down; and (d) the fisherman can perceive less and be aware of less when at a great distance from rising fish, and will in consequence not observe nearly so much as the short-line fisherman who has got much closer to his quarry.

It might *look* elegant to brandish a long line with dexterity but it is not necessarily good fishing to do so. Stalking skill – the ability to use cover and approach fish with great stealth – is more important to a river trout fisherman than great skill in casting. I probably use a consistently shorter line than any other fisherman I have ever met. I can and do use a long line but only when I consider it strictly necessary. I specialize in fishing turbulent water with a short line, and the manipulation of such a line gives me more satisfaction than the control of an elegant long one. I am a crafty fisherman: I try to do nothing which is inefficient, wasteful or unnecessary.

The manipulation of a long line, when distance is genuinely required, is a skill in its own right, a prime skill for the dry fly man. Not only does it require great adroitness and accuracy in the actual casting but also considerable sleight of hand to deal with current and counter current. It also adds complications to the strike: the fisherman must make allowances for distance. It is sometimes necessary to strike immediately, even on very slow water, if a great length of line is used. The whole question of length of line depends on necessity. A skilled dry fly angler will be able to use both a long and a short line, but what is most important, he will know *when* to use which. I get a great kick out of casting right across a river and hooking a trout just inches off the opposite bank, as I am sure all fishermen do, but this is not a mechanical tactic which I employ all the time: for me a long line is the exception not the rule.

STRIKING RATE

The penultimate thing I have to say in this chapter concerns 'the striking rate' in dry fly fishing, by which I mean the ratio of successfully hooked fish to the number of fish actually risen. In fly fishing it is impossible to achieve perfection. All anglers miss fish: we miss them because we are not good enough. Sometimes sheer bad luck intervenes, but most of the fish we miss are missed because of angler error. None of us can stay on our mettle at all moments during a day, especially if we are fishing the water. Fatigue or loss of concentration often mar our fishing. Slow reaction and over-zealous haste also account for many misses. But once an angler has reached a level of some proficiency most of his misses will be the result of mere miscalculation. In dry fly fishing the angler must expect to miss trout on a regular basis and must not become discouraged by this fact.

Perhaps in the southern chalkstreams, where everything is steady and regular, a dry fly fisherman can approach perfection but in the rough and tumble of the North I can vouch for the fact that perfection is but a pipe-dream. Things come at you in such a rush and the unexpected always lurks. What is true, however, is that the good fisherman will rise more trout than the ordinary one; so too he will hook a higher proportion of the fish he rises than will the ordinary angler. But not even the best angler can expect to hook all the fish he rises.

Just what proportion of fish can we miss and still feel satisfied with ourselves? Without analyzing a hooking-rising ratio over several seasons I am not sure I could say with accuracy. I have on odd and completely random occasions noted my striking rate and recorded variations from 100 per cent efficiency to 20 per cent (i.e. missing eight out of every ten fish risen!) The type of water enters the equation as well: some rivers are more demanding than others. On a sluggish, well-manicured chalkstream stocked with big trout it is much easier to attain a high striking rate than it is on an overgrown beck full of small wild fish which zoom like arrows at your fly.

ESTIMATED RATIOS

The following estimates of striking rates are therefore no more than uninformed guesses. On smooth, clear streams where you fish the rise and can select your specimens perhaps your strike ratio could be as high as 3:4 – i.e. you hook three out of every four fish you rise. In the North and West the situation is very different and I am inclined to think that a ratio of 1:3 would represent a pretty competent performance. This means rising 30 trout for every ten caught. Grayling complicate the issue further, especially if they are in the 4–10 oz (0.1–0.3 kg) bracket, for they take a dry fly so quickly that they alter the ratio dramatically – perhaps to 1:6.

Recently stocked trout are a problem as well: they take more swiftly than indigenous fish and the angler must allow for this. Little fish, often parr, also put pressure on the fisherman. All in all, if you average 1:3 when fishing the water on a northern stream in which trout and grayling cohabit you are doing pretty well. A ratio of 1:2 would be very good fishing and a better ratio still would be well above average.

The question of recently stocked trout is worth returning to briefly. Brown trout lately introduced to a river tend to shoal exactly like rainbows. These shoaling stocked fish will take a fly like lightning, far faster than a wild trout – indeed much as if they were taking the pellets on which they have been reared. A quick strike will be required for these newly released trout and the angler who fails to appreciate this fact can find himself bemused. It sometimes takes a practised eye to be able to spot stockies in a river but there are some tell-tale signs. Repeated and fearless attacks on your fly is one sign, and learning to recognize the kind of lie they first favour on introduction is yet another.

Newly stocked fish seem to favour somewhere with some depth tucked away out of the main current, such as the smooth cheek beside a racing stream, the calm angle between two strong currents, or the head of a deep pool into which a powerful run issues. Anywhere basically untroubled but protected by a moving wall of water seems to offer the recently released fish a sense of security, and here he will lie with his peers, craving strength in numbers, until sheer hunger, native curiosity and the increasing call of his predatory genes finally overcome his domestic gregariousness and he begins to venture further afield to learn the lore of the river.

EASY PICKINGS

The unscrupulous angler who stumbles upon such a crowded little pocket can very quickly make a prodigious killing of these unsophisticated boobies, provided he can adapt to the quick strike. The sportsman will not plunder such a place, preferring to allow the naïve inhabitants to acclimatize and become more testing quarry. He always has the option of returning to the spot later in the day and picking up a brace there if his basket has proved meagre.

As for little fish – parr, small trout and wee grayling – if these are plaguing the angler then he could try not even striking at them at all. When he is not sure what size fish has taken his fly, if he strikes as for a decent-sized trout then if the fish is indeed of such size he has a chance of hooking it. If he misses he can console himself with the fact that the fish was small!

Newly stocked fish, grayling and tiddlers do spoil an efficient strike rate and can ruin an angler's confidence in himself: I have probably not caught as many as half of all the trout I have risen on dry fly in my life. Taking all things into consideration – good days, bad days, unlucky days, grayling days, all those days of my bungling apprenticeship and the fact that I have fished a great deal on difficult, overgrown little rivers full of nimble little fish – I would guess that I might have caught only about 20 per cent of all the fish that I have ever risen on dry fly. This is a statistic I will never be able to verify. When we look back on a day we tend to recall its successes and not its failures. We easily remember numbers caught and quickly forget fish we missed. We are none of us as good as we think we are, so my estimate of 20 per cent could be generous; the real ratio could be even more humiliating!

Finally, to return to the theme that opened this chapter – the allure of dry fly fishing. At the furthest extremities of accomplishment in its two different forms (clear-water stalking and rough-stream searching) dry fly is as difficult and as complex as any other branch of fly fishing, in my opinion, for its esoteric skills are elusive and not easily acquired. At the other end of the spectrum, the basics of the art are quite easily learnt. If he keeps his fly afloat and his line both buoyant and short, the beginner will soon start catching trout on dry fly. It is an accessible form of fishing because it is visible and spectacular. Dry fly has been my favourite way of catching trout for quarter of a century and I fancy it will remain so for as long as my eyesight stays keen.

16

Dour and Difficult Days

'All in a hot and copper sky
The bloody sun at noon.'

Samuel Taylor Coleridge

'Blow winds and crack your cheeks. Rage! Blow! You cataracts and hurricanoes spout!'

King Lear

We all experience dour and difficult days from time to time. Sometimes we are subjected to a sequence of them and this can be quite a test of character. The ability to conquer adversity is an important constituent in any sport. Most folk have the character to appreciate good days but it requires rather more fortitude and grit to put up with bad ones. As fishermen we are all of us utterly subject to the vagaries of the elements. Fair-weather fishermen are not true fishermen. Only those prepared to face squall, storm, drought and heat wave with equal resolve can call themselves fully-fledged anglers.

The Chinese have a proverb that says: 'There is no such thing as bad weather but only different types of good weather.' Here is much truth. Farmers praying for rain smile at the first angry drops falling from a sultry sky, while those organizing church fêtes or outdoor wedding receptions sigh with frustration and wonder how God could be so cruel. Within the world of angling there is a similar divergence of desire. The same storm brings hope to the salmon-fishing fraternity as the rivers swell with rain, while the dry fly fisherman grits his teeth philosophically at the flood which has ruined his holiday.

A FLEXIBLE OUTLOOK

One of the good things about trout fishing, and fishing in general, is that if you are prepared to be flexible there are no conditions which rule out a day on the water. Heavy rain which ruins fly fishing on the local river does not prevent fly fishing on the local reservoir, while for those who are not averse to adopting even more ancient methods, the humble worm can give you splendid sport on the river, provided club rules allow it.

However hopeless things look we often manage to conjure up a fish or two. A fish caught in extremely difficult conditions always becomes a special fish, so it can be surprising how those days which look the most unprepossessing at the outset turn out to be most satisfying. There are basically three things which make days difficult: first, the weather; second, the condition of the water; third, the mood of the fish.

There can be other factors such as bulls, midges, inconsiderate passers-by, bad-mannered fishermen, our own tempers or the state of our tackle, but let us concentrate first on the weather. There are four specific difficulties: excessive cold or heat, rain and wind. The condition of the water, always allied to the weather, creates extra problems if it is either too high or too low. The mood of the fish I will not talk about for the present. In the bar of a little pub beside the Teifi many years ago I found the following rhyme which amusingly sums up the problems that confront the fisherman:

> Sometimes too early, sometimes too late,
> Sometimes no water, sometimes a spate,
> Sometimes too muddy, sometimes too clear –
> There's aye something wrong when I'm fishing here!

I memorized this on the spot and it has been a comfort to me ever since!

I shall deal with each of these difficulties in turn. Because I have touched on some aspects of these difficulties already here and there in previous chapters I will be as brief as possible to avoid dull repetition. First, the difficulty of cold, though cold days are not always bad fishing days. It is well known that the iron blue, for instance, will choose very chill and inclement occasions to emerge. Indeed one of the best rises I have ever seen – it was to dark olives – was on an utterly freezing spring day, a day so cold that I had to stop fishing simply because I no longer had the strength to grip my rod handle. The wind-chill factor was so severe that my hands became utterly numb. As I plodded back to the car, with a good creel of fish, the trout were still feeding in a frenzy. It was close to dark and bitterly cold – conditions that on most rivers in April would ensure no activity whatsoever, but on this occasion they prompted a prolific rise. It was a truly bizarre occurrence – the only time in my life, including even during the pursuit of winter pike, that I have ever had to abandon fishing because I was simply too cold to continue.

DOUR TROUT

Cold days when the trout are active are one thing, cold days when the trout are dour are another. If the fish are dour then they will be deep. It seems to me that the angler has a choice of tactics. He can fish deep with a sinking line and weighted nymphs or else employ a big, fluffy dry fly on the surface. The first is to put the fly on the inert fishes' noses, the second is to lure them up to the top to take. A compromise, and the best way of discovering which of the two tactics is best on the day, is wry fly with a heavy nymph on the point (Killer Bug) and a big dry fly (March Brown, Greenwell's Glory, Wickham's Fancy, Gold Ribbed Hare's Ear) on the dropper. This is the approach I would recommend on such days, particularly at midday and early afternoon in spring, and in the morning during the summer.

HIGH VISIBILITY

Hot days bring frustrations of a different sort. Hot bright days, especially in low water, make the angler very visible. Glare can be a problem too. Shady places under trees can be fished to avoid these problems. There is also a certain type of grey overcast day when trout seem to see every movement on the bank very clearly. On either of these types of tricky days it is worth experimenting with the colour of your nylon. Sometimes it is not the fly which needs changing but your leader. The crafty angler will always carry nylon of different tones (clear, green and dark brown, for instance) and will switch colours if he suspects the fish can see his cast. There are days when nylon is more visible to trout than on others – usually in low water on either very bright days or days with a very even grey light – and this is always worth bearing in mind. It also sometimes pays not to grease your dry flies on such days.

After prolonged hot weather, when the water is low, the trout sometimes become lethargic. Oxygen levels drop in the water and fish tend to feed mainly at night. During the day trout will often lie in the runs where the water is better oxygenated than in the placid pools. It pays to search the fast water with a big, bushy dry fly in such weather. The choice of fly can be critical in glare or in the gloom under trees and in areas of dancing light with dappled shadows. In bright places a dark fly such as an Alder or Coch-y-bondhu might be needed in order to be visible, while in gloomy, sombre ones a bright fly such as Jock Scott, Grey Duster, or a big Tup's might be best employed. There is, however, a special category of useful flies which are visible in either light. The Bi-visible series of flies were created specially for this purpose. The Leckford Professor is another useful pattern, as is my invention the Hotspur. Other flies which fish well in differing light conditions are the Coachman, John Storey, Adams, Royal Wulff, various Badgers and the ubiquitous Wickham's Fancy.

FURTHER HOT-WEATHER TACTICS

Upstream or downstream wet fly, too, can be very deadly in runs during hot weather, though I have found it accounts for smaller trout than does the dry fly. Wry fly with a nymph on the point is even deadlier and is the option I often plump for on such days. Twin dry fly is also an excellent tactic, especially if the angler selects two flies of differing colour – for instance, an Alder and a Tup's Indispensable or a Knotted Midge and a Ginger Quill.

A nymph will often score in shady places on hot days. Something which makes an attractive plop when it lands is recommended. The Killer Bug is brilliant. Beetles work well too – for instance, a weighted Kill Devil Spider, Black and Peacock Spider or Eric's Beetle. Smooth flats, sequestered bays and backwaters under low branches are worth exploring – any niche where a big, lazy trout awaits easy pickings. The odd animated twitch of the bug is worth trying too.

The extremities of the day during heat waves are usually good times to fish. Early, before the sun gets hot, fish are still to be found in pool tails after a night's feeding. Nymphs work well in such places. Big trout under overhanging banks might fall to a spent imitation: some spinners are bound to be trapped in eddies and along the edges of the river. Lunn's Particular is a great fly for this job, as is something a little more juicy: a Caperer, Little Red Sedge, Hare's Ear or even a Wickham. Then, late, when the sun is sinking trout might start to become active after a snoozing day. It might well be worth staying on for an hour after dark to drag a big wet fly across the pool tails. Generally, the hotter and brighter the weather the more stealth and guile are required. A few good trout picked up on a difficult hot day are worth much more than a creel filled with ease in a falling flood. On really tricky days satisfaction is not measured by numbers of fish but by the skill required to catch the few you do take.

WET WEATHER

Next, wet days, which are sometimes associated with high and coloured water. Wet days can pose two problems: the physical effects of the falling rain itself and its effect upon the colour of the water. But rainfall is not always bad for fishing – indeed it can sometimes make your day. Some rainy days produce just the right temperature and atmospheric conditions to prompt fly to hatch in quantity. I have often found squally days with passing warm and cold fronts to be good fishing days. I have had good baskets on dry fly on many a wet day.

However, persistent heavy rain makes dry fly fishing very difficult: keeping your fly dry becomes virtually impossible and your wet fingers soak any new pattern you knot on your line. On these occasions you are forced to switch to wet fly or nymph. I usually plump for traditional wet fly, and excellent this method proves to be. On such days the rain-pocked surface of the river helps to hide both you and your line from the fish. Still pools, pool tails and flats where your approach is normally noted by the fish are now quite approachable. If you animate or work your flies through such places you can sometimes pick up splendid baskets.

If rain falls but the water remains unaffected, clear and fishable with fly, then you should have no problems – indeed your basket could be boosted. But if the river becomes coloured then a whole new set of difficulties present themselves. A brief freshet after a cloudburst is one thing; a huge roaring spate after 48 hours of solid rain is quite another. So too there are different stages in a flood. A falling flood with rapidly clearing water is a deadly time to fish, especially with a team of wet flies. A rising flood, too, before the water becomes thick and pasty, can trigger a feeding frenzy among the trout. The angler who stumbles on a situation like this is likely to experience almost unparalleled sport.

AN EXCEPTIONAL RISE

One of the most vigorous, spectacular and prolonged rises that I have ever witnessed took place in just such circumstances. It was back in 1964, when I was only 14, but I remember it as if it were yesterday. My father and I arrived at Sawley Bridge on the Ribble, having driven through heavy rain. However, the day cleared up as soon as we began to fish. We were sharing a rod. I was still a pretty inexperienced fisherman and no doubt received some patient coaching, but this did not prevent us getting an extremely good bag. The river was rising and so were the trout – everywhere. We only fished about 150 yards (140 m) of bank all afternoon but took eight good wild brownies apiece. The trout never stopped rising until the water became too coloured for them to see the olives which had been hatching obligingly all afternoon.

However, we are not always lucky enough to time our visits to rain-affected rivers so well. More often than not we arrive to find a swollen torrent and our hearts sink, but maybe all is not lost. At the height of any big spate there will be a period when the river is completely unfishable with fly, but either side of this period the canny and observant fly fisherman might be able to wangle a brace or so.

I remember a seemingly hopeless situation in 1966 when I arrived at the Eden with my father to discover a great brown spate. With his extensive knowledge of that river, my father reckoned he knew a spot where we might find a fish or two. We walked down a steep hill to a huge long pool and here among the flooded boles of a plantation of pine trees we found some cruising trout. It was not easy fishing but my father, loving instructor that he was, put me into the easiest spots. He had a brace and I had a leash. All were good-sized wild brown trout and all were taken on dry fly.

Even though the river was up very high and dirty, in this tranquil place fish found backwaters and bays where they could actually see the surface. We spent the afternoon scrambling about the steep bank, avoiding the sharp branches and flicking out our flies into the paths of unsuspecting fish. It was wonderful sport and an afternoon I will never forget. To succeed against all odds is always a pleasure and a big water is always a challenge to a thoughtful fisherman prepared to have a go.

SWOLLEN RIVERS

Some of my most memorable days have been on rivers swollen with rain. These have not been days of big baskets or even big fish but occasions when unusual tactics yielded me trout I really had to outwit in unusual places. Any touch of the exotic or different appeals to fishermen accustomed to the normal on their rivers. The chance to ensnare trout in circumstances out of the ordinary is most appealing to the adventurous angler.

When rivers are running high the fisherman need only concern himself with water close in to his own bank. Every bay, backwater, bend, leat, side channel or inlet must be searched – anywhere which affords trout a refuge from the roaring current. They occupy these places out of self-preservation. Not only is it hard work maintaining a position out in the middle of the swift, swollen river, but at any moment a large piece of debris could come sweeping downstream and concuss any fish in its path. These havens from the dangers of the torrent are also traps for food both above and below the surface, so both dry and wet flies will work.

SURFACE FILM TACTICS

The water might look opaque to a fisherman's eye but to a trout's it might be clear enough for him to perceive objects in the surface film. I have quite regularly stumbled upon good rises in these conditions. Dry flies do work then, and although the pattern is immaterial I have found big brownish ones to be best: flies like the Soldier Palmer, August Dun, Ginger Quill and Wickham's Fancy. When visibility is poor for the fish then trout rely on the senses along their lateral line, their useful adipose fin and their olfactory organs. The wet fly comes into its own in this situation. Perhaps the best of both worlds is a wet fly cast with a bushy pattern on the top dropper (March Brown, Invicta, Wickham tied wet). I have saved many a blank day by jinking and dibbling my top dropper fly about in the surface along the edges of swollen rivers. The motion imparted to the flies both below the surface and in the surface film will attract fish. Worked and animated flies often have a distinct edge over static dry flies in tumescent spate conditions.

Your heart need not sink when you find your river in flood. By exploring your bank with a short line you may attract a fish or two, or even more. Trout tend to be rather unsuspecting in these circumstances: they cannot see you nor your line. Even more likely is that you will have the river to yourself. It is great to know that you have caught a basket of trout on a day which all the other, less adventurous members of your club considered to be quite hopeless.

WIND

The fourth weather problem is wind. Unlike the stillwater angler, who likes a nice ripple induced by the wind, the river fisherman prefers the surface not to be ruffled. It is true that sometimes a windy day can help the river angler, especially the wet fly man fishing big, broad pools or the beginner learning to fish upstream who discovers a strong upstream wind coming to his aid. In general, though, strong, gusting wind is a nuisance. Rough, windy days make accurate presentation of a dry fly difficult, make riparian vegetation even more difficult to avoid than normal and create havoc with leaders. On windy days I find I get frequent knots and tangles in my line, which is annoying. Strong downstream winds are a veritable bane.

The fact that some flies are blown off the water on windy days is balanced by the fact that others are blown on to it, especially terrestrials dislodged from bank and branch. In refuges from the wind, such as sheltered bends and backwaters, flies often collect, and in these little food traps the angler can sometimes get good sport on windy days. On days when an insistent wind is blowing across river it may profit the angler to fish the windward bank, for flies will be blown to this side. If the river being fished is a sinuous, winding one the angler can always find spots where he can either use the wind to his advantage or else negate its ill effects: for instance, escaping any downstream gusts by turning a corner and fishing with the wind at his back or side. On long, straight and exposed stretches of river there is less respite, especially from a raking downstream wind, and the fisherman must grin and bear it.

TACKLE FOR WINDY CONDITIONS

One trick I employ on windy days is to use a heavier rod and line then usual. My normal set-up for small stream fishing is a 7½-foot (2.3 m) rod and no. 5 line. When it is windy, however, I usually employ a 9 or 9½-foot (2.7–2.9 m) rod and a no. 7 line if I am fishing an exposed river. This helps casting difficulties. Slightly heavier nylon than normal is also a good idea on windy days. I said earlier that I do not always use tapered casts, but windy days are an exception. I invariably use tapered casts on such days and my tippets are sometimes as heavy as 5 or 6 lb (2.3–2.7 kg) b.s. On swollen rivers and on wind-ruffled ones you can get away with heavier nylon than normal because visibility is impaired for the fish. It is silly to fish fine in such weather: it is unsporting, for you increase the chances of breaking off a fish. In heavy water you may have to hold trout to prevent disaster so you need all the strength you can muster, and in windy weather light nylon is a liability because it becomes strained and weakened by the knots.

Of all four unpleasant elements – excessive heat, cold, rain and wind – perhaps wind, when on its own, is the least serious hazard for the river angler. One of the additional obstacles of windy days, however, is that they are often associated with other climatic conundrums. Windy days are often cold days or wet days, and often come at times when rivers are swollen. Anyone who has any experience of trout fishing in Britain (be it only a couple of seasons) will be acquainted with cold days on flooded rivers accompanied by rifling, eye-watering downstream winds. There is no doubt that combinations of difficulties do add to our vexation but, by way of compensation, they are cause for elation when they are successfully overcome.

THE MOOD OF FISH

So much for weather. Now for fish and their moods. There are times when trout, and grayling, are inexplicably dour. On a cold, dismal day or a torrid, sultry one I think we can understand the reasons for a dour mood but when conditions seem set fair and yet trout are not responsive it is particularly perplexing.

Years ago I had a friend to whom I boasted about some of my best fishing haunts. He was a fisherman who often had bad luck, so, in the hope of turning the tide for him, over a period of several seasons I took him one by one to many of my favourite rivers. However, some Unkind Hand waved a malign wand over this scheme because places which had yielded me hundreds of fish suddenly became inexplicably dull when I took my friend there. It is true we often hit unhelpful weather, too hot usually, but even so the days were all horribly dour. More and more I looked like a fisherman who was all mouth. From my point of view it was particularly frustrating that rivers (including both the Ribble and the Eden) which I knew were so marvellous turned out on this succession of days to be dead as dodos. If this chap ever reads my book I swear he will take it all with a pinch of salt!

I remember another quite different occasion when I took some friends to the Eden. The idea was to have a picnic beside the river and cook some trout. None of these particular friends was a fisherman but they had all heard my glowing reports about the brilliance of the sport there. I was secretly looking forward to showing off my magical prowess as an angler to an admiring and uninitiated audience, and to displaying my culinary skills into the bargain. The day was perfect – a balmy spring morning in mid May with a clear river running at medium height. Dour? I have never known the Eden so ineffably dour. Flies hatched but no fish appeared to take them. I never saw a single rise nor rose a single fish. In desperation I even turned to worm, but that was just as useless. My friends enjoyed lolling about on the bank in the lovely weather but my reputation as a great fisherman was irretrievably tarnished. As for the riverside feast of smoked trout . . . we ended up in the pub!

An added frustration of dour and difficult days is that non-anglers are incapable of understanding the agony of fishermen on such occasions.

They assume that all fishing is like this and that, in consequence, all fishermen must be liars. 'That's a real fisherman's yarn' is a metaphor entrenched in our culture, and in a good few others too, I would guess. Fishing is easy game for a cheap snigger, and dour and difficult days are at the bottom of it all. The agonies of a blank day are incommunicable to the uninitiated. At our most inconsolable the only possible semi-solace can be found over a pipe or a beer with a fellow angler!

Why do such days exist? Who knows? There must be a reason for dourness among fish but if so it is not always clear. Give me a howling wind or phalanx of huge, black, rain-bearing clouds any day than a river in perfect condition, in perfect weather but with invisible, obstinate fish! I can deal with bad weather but sullen, sulky fish are another question. Give me a problem I can solve. A beastly swirling wind or driving rain are not much fun but at least they are honest problems, problems which are evident and can be partially solved. But elusive, irrational, mercurial, bolshy fish defy angling logic. Such irritating days do exist but, thankfully, they are rare, simply because fish must eat to live, and if they are eating they can be duped ... somehow.

EXCEPTIONS TO THE RULE

One of the principal charms of river fishing for me is that however dull and sluggish the fish in general may be, I can usually find the odd trout which is the exception. The same is not true, for me at least, on stillwaters where, when the fish are dull and uncooperative, I find them utterly uncatchable. I have far more blank days on lakes than I do on rivers, indeed a blank day on a river is an extreme rarity for me. I do concede, however, that I am far from being an expert stillwaterman. On rivers it is a different matter for me. On hot bright days in summer, when most fish are lethargic, I can always trust myself to find one or two active chaps on the feed somewhere or other – usually tucked away in some leafy pocket. On cold spring days when most trout are lying deep and doggo it is surprising how I manage to stumble upon the occasional opportunistic fellow whose greed and optimism prompt him to cruise about in some backwater or bay.

Dour and difficult days are ones on which we must be prepared to do a great deal of walking, looking and experimenting. Sometimes it is our observation which is rewarded on such days, sometimes it is our guesswork. If we suddenly get a feeling (that sixth sense again) that a certain nook or corner holds an active fish we must act on that hunch. On such hunches are some tricky days made memorable for us. When roaring gale or thrashing rain makes a lake or reservoir a merciless and gruesome experience, a river can still be fished intelligently. Trees, topographical shelter, bends and protected out-of-the-way places help to give the fisherman hope, and, more important perhaps, variety. It is the variety which river fishing offers that makes this kind of angling my favourite.

NERVOUS FISH

There is another kind of mood which creates problems for the angler and that is when fish are jittery. There do seem to be days when trout appear to be more than usually scared. Any movement on the bank will terrify them. You can clearly see their nervous, edgy behaviour on days of this kind. What is it that makes them so easily spooked? I think Skues put forward one convincing answer in a chapter entitled 'A Problem for the Optician' in his book *The Way of Trout with a Fly*. He describes a day on a little brook where the trout were very jittery and easily scared before they began feeding. Once they had started to feed, however, they were much less shy and he caught 24. He observes:

> Were the trout so infatuated with their food that they did not care about me during the rise, or was it that, with their eyes concentrated on the nymphs and duns coming down to them, they could not see me without a special effort, or without some special cause attracting attention?

The answer is yes to both questions. Subsequent research has proved Skues was, as usual, quite correct in his theorizing. The deeper a fish lies the wider is the cone or window of his vision. A deep-lying trout can see out beyond the water and up onto the land, so that any movement on the bank will be visible to him. A trout lying high in the water scrutinizing the surface for food has a much diminished cone of vision as he concentrates his focus near to him: his view of the bank will be a fuzzy blur. The following diagram has become a standard one in textbooks on trout fishing, but I reproduce it nevertheless. See fig. 13.

On dour days, perhaps when there is not much appearing in the way of fly life, trout will be out and ready to feed but cannot do so for lack of insects. On these occasions, as they lie deep before taking up more aggressive feeding stations, their view of the bank is very clear. Our clumsy, blundering movements on the bank above are therefore very conspicuous on such days. I am not satisfied that this is always the correct explanation for jitteriness in trout, but it is certainly the case on a fair proportion of days.

A GOLDEN RULE

The moral here is to avoid places where trout have a good view of the bank. On all days when trout are difficult and the visibility is good I am sure that the golden rule is: fish the faster-moving and rippling water. In these streamier places trout see you and your tackle less easily. Runs and ripply stretches of the river also have several other crucial advantages over calmer, clearer places. A trout has less time to scrutinize your fly and therefore less time to make up his mind whether to take it

Figure 13 Cross-sectional comparison of fields of vision of surface-feeding and deep-lying trout.

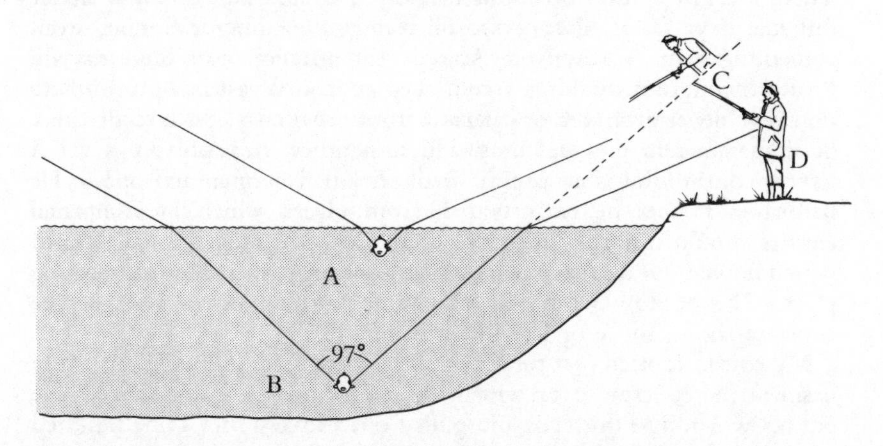

The deep-lying fish has a much wider field of vision than a surface-feeder. Fish A, concentrating on the surface, cannot easily see the angler at D on the bank. Beyond the water its vision is almost exclusively of sky. Fish B, however, though farther from the angler than fish A, can quite clearly see any movement on the bank, although the angler will appear at position C, owing to refraction. It is deep-lying fish like this, with their wide fields of vision, which the angler can most easily disturb as he plods about on the river bank.

or not. A fly flashing past triggers a trout's hunting instinct and his hunger: he has to be both more decisive and less cautious as he takes it. A take in fast water is thus a reflex one and a trout finds that he is hooked before he can have any second thoughts.

By adhering to this golden rule I have scored successes on countless occasions. Not only have I saved difficult days this way but I often choose to fish in the streams on good days, doing even better as a result. In fact I stick so much to this rule that, at a guess, as much as 80 per cent of my fishing time is spent in fast-moving water. Every season I still meet other fishermen who ignore this fundamental precept – very much to their own cost. While they have frittered away their time fishing slow, clear pools, frightening away trout after trout, I have stuck to the faster water, frightened fewer and risen more.

The main thing to do on dour and difficult days is to keep fishing and not give up. At times this is no easy thing to do and I cannot pretend that I always heed such advice myself. Sometimes there really does seem to be no alternative but to pack up. These foul-weathered and bothersome days are as much a test of our temperament as of the fishing. The fisherman who can keep his enthusiasm and confidence buoyed up will always catch more than the angler who loses heart.

INNOVATIVE APPROACH

There are just a few more observations I should like to make about difficult days. It is always worth trying something different, even something daft. A Mayfly in August, for instance, or a huge dry fly floated incongruously down a still, deep pool, or a cast in a place where you have never ever seen or caught a trout previously. Such tactics may be desperate remedies but they will sometimes, freakishly, pay off. I have a cousin who is an expert small-stream fisherman and one of his hallmarks is that he extracts fish from places which most normal anglers would ignore. When we were lads worming a small stream which flowed out of a lake he caught a good trout in a most astonishing place. The outflow from the lake came hurtling down a 45-degree concrete shoot, more or less like a waterfall.

My cousin spotted that the force of the water had hollowed out a tiny basin in the concrete over which the main force of water sluiced. He put his worm into this spot and pulled out a lovely fish. Nine hundred and ninety-nine anglers out of a thousand would never have dreamed of such effrontery, myself included. I also well remember the time I heard cries for help from upstream and, running to the source of the yells, found my cousin lying down with his rod underneath a low strand of barbed wire. He had chosen to fish in a tiny pool, barely 4 ft (1.2 m) in diameter, boxed in by wire and completely covered by branches. Somehow I got my landing net into the tangle of metal and leaves and netted out a wonderful wild brown trout of 1¾ lb (0.8 kg). It was not a pool anyone in their right mind would ever have attempted fishing.

DAPPING

As a boy I used to do a great deal of dapping in overgrown parts of rivers. The set-up was simple. I shortened my leader to a mere 12 or 15 in (30–40 cm) and poked my rod between branches to dibble and buzz my dry fly on the surface. A swan shot pinched on to the top of the leader can help too: it stops the fly line sagging back through the rod rings to drop in useless coils at your feet. In high summer on hot days this tactic has saved me many a time. It is a most exciting way to catch trout and calls for great self-control on the strike. One of the things that I like about this form of fishing is that it is probably the most ancient variant of dry fly angling in existence. With the wind at your back on very blowy days you can practise the art of dapping too. Nor is there any need to alter the length of your leader in these circumstances.

My last two remarks concern choices which can be made before you start fishing. When you arrive at a river you do have a choice as to where to fish first. On good days when the water is boiling with fish it matters not where you begin, but on tricky days a little thought beforehand may pay dividends. It is not just the weather which must be borne in mind, as a recent experience of mine illustrates.

Towards the end of last season I went to fish one of my favourite rivers. It is also a favourite river of many other fishermen and I arrived to find that all the other rods were taken too. (I always make a point of enquiring about how many other anglers will be on the water on the day I have chosen.) This discovery made me plan my day with care. The water here falls into three sections, the middle one being the most popular with its easy access, convenient car park, neat styles and cleared banks. The upper water is not much fished because of difficult access and heavy vegetation, while the lower water is, for reasons which I have never understood, also often ignored by anglers.

I decided to begin on the bottom stretch (which happens to be my favourite part) and had fish straight away. A brace of good grayling was quickly followed by a brace of good trout. By lunch I had half the limit and had seen no other fisherman. After lunch, having taken a picnic on the bank with my wife, who had netted my first few fish and was charmed by the tranquillity of the spot, I went up to the top water. Here I found a hatch of medium olives in progress and had some tremendous sport: completing the limit and getting the best trout of the day. Once again I came across no other fisherman.

THE HERDING INSTINCT

Out of curiosity, just before going I went to have a look at the middle section. The car park revealed exactly where all the other anglers had chosen to spend their day. I walked part of the bank and met them all in turn – all within a few hundred yards of one another. The river certainly looked dour and I gathered it had been a difficult day. Nobody had caught anything of any size to keep. As I passed from fisherman to fisherman the story was the same. I remained non-committal about my day: no point in giving away secrets it had taken me years to acquire. The next time I go there I hope I still get my favourite stretches to myself! What had been a depressing and dismal day for all these other fisherman had been an excellent one for me, simply because I had fished less fashionable parts of the river. The day had turned out well for me because of a decision I had taken before my rod had even been drawn from its case.

I find this herding instinct among anglers rather a difficult phenomenon to understand. I come across the syndrome every season. On this particular day, out of 8 miles (13 km) of river, one rod had had over seven miles (11 km) at his own disposal and the other ten or so had shared barely a mile (1.6 km)! Such a situation is ridiculous. We must never allow ourselves to forget that our quarry is a shy, wild creature and one of the best ways of equalizing the struggle is to try not to advertise our presence. Tramping up and down a confined stretch of river like a herd of buffalo, tangling each other's lines and flogging one another's pools is hardly the way for us to get on equal terms with a character as wily as *Salmo trutta*!

CHOICE OF RIVER

My final point is about another choice. Before we even leave home, let alone take our rod out of its case, we have a choice: which river should we fish? If it is obvious because of the prevailing elements that we are going to encounter tricky and unfavourable conditions wherever we decide to go, then it is only sensible to minimize the risks before we set out. An intelligent choice of river is the first step we can take to beat the weather. If the forecast is for high winds then to select a river with a well-sheltered stretch would appear wise. If the day is clearly going to be hot and bright then a heavily wooded or at least a shady river is surely our target. Some of the bosky upland rivers I visit are at their very best on hot bright days. The branches above the water in such weather teem with terrestrial insect activity and the trout find rich pickings.

Big, wide, lowland rivers are certainly best avoided when it is mercilessly bright. As for very wet days with the threat of roaring, high water then rivers with plenty of backwaters, flats and calm corners should be considered. Big rivers are often the best bet because they offer the most accessible slack water: they also take longer to rise and become unfishable than their tributaries. Conversely, tributaries run off and clear more quickly after big floods than parent rivers do.

Another alternative is rivers which are not normally much affected by rain. Chalkstreams aside, such rivers are rare, but not impossible to find. I know one such stream. It is a small, spring-fed beck which gets coloured only after prolonged torrential rain. Usually, when all the surrounding streams and rivers are running in flood, this little gem still remains clear and perfectly fishable with fly. Needless to say, this beck has proved my saviour on countless occasions.

By a few thoughtful decisions at the beginning of the day we can make a hard day easier. In a way I enjoy dour and difficult days. It is especially pleasing to get a brace of trout in demanding conditions. Such days are good for us; they keep us on our mettle and prevent us from becoming too arrogant. If every day were a great one then perhaps we would give up trout fishing as too easy and take up darts, snooker or table tennis. Even worse, we might become insufferably pleased with ourselves and tiresome to our friends. We should be grateful for these days.

17

The Mayfly

'The river rins gey low, Jock,
And on the gravel stanes,
The May-flee's hatching oot, Jock,
I feel it in my banes.'
Wilfred Walter Morris

It occurs to me that so far I have not said very much about the mayfly. This period in the trout fisherman's calendar (provided he is lucky enough to have access to a mayfly hatch) is an important part of the season: indeed far more than this, as J.W. Hills says: 'It is an event of nature.' Nothing I can say on the subject can rival this great writer, but my efforts must include a few pages on this scintillating phenomenon. The two chapters devoted to mayfly in Hills' delightful book *A Summer on the Test* are the best ever written on the subject and are required reading. If my chapter does no more than direct you to Hills then it has served its purpose.

There is a great deal of bunk talked about the mayfly. For a start there is that misleading epithet 'Duffers' Fortnight'; misleading because during the fortnight of the mayfly there are days when the trout are maddeningly difficult to catch. There is quite a lot of luck about the day you choose to fish during this time. When the fly first appears it takes the fish a day or two to acclimatize to the situation. Likewise at certain points of the fortnight the fish get 'glutted' and ignore the flies. In between there are other days when the trout lack any caution or suspicion and will lunge at anything bushy you offer them. This, then, is the first difficulty of the mayfly: timing your visit to the water so that it coincides with an easy day.

HOOKING MADE EASIER

The second difficulty is that if you do manage to hit the right day with the trout in cooperative mood you may find the fish very difficult to hook when they do take. A mayfly is a big morsel for a trout to pouch and swallow. Some artificials are big, spiky and additionally difficult to mouth. Softer-hackled artificials are recommended. I like the French Partridge Mayfly pattern. The Straddle-Bug or Summer Duck pattern is also absolutely excellent. I would fish with one of these two out of preference – they beat every other pattern in my opinion. Other patterns work without actually being mayfly copies. The Grey Wulff is a brilliant fly at this time of year, but not tied too big: a size 12 hook is large enough. A White Wulff also works well. In the North I have found a John Storey to be an excellent mayfly substitute. A Wickham's Fancy will also do, so will a big Tup's Indispensable. One year I had a fine bag on a rather odd, brightly tied Medium Olive I had bought at some time or other and never before used. When the trout are going mad anything will do!

A slower strike than normal is required, with one exception, which I will come to later. If you are experiencing difficulties hooking trout at mayfly time then my advice is threefold: (i) slow down your strike, (ii) try a soft-hackled fly, (iii) try a smaller pattern of fly. A combination of all three remedies should solve your problems.

I remember one of the first occasions that I ever came across the mayfly: it was a disaster. My first ever encounter had been on the Dove near Ashbourne with my father: we had hit the river just right and did pretty well. But on this later occasion, on a different river, I had terrible problems. I had inherited a box of ancient Mayflies from my grandfather and mistakenly used these patterns. They were very stiff and well varnished, some possessing bulky cork bodies. They looked pretty but I had a dreadful time trying to hook trout with them. Grey and green drakes were coming down in droves and trout were feeding avidly but I missed fish after fish. At one point I vividly remember missing a dozen good trout in succession. I was probably striking too quickly but the unsuitable flies I used could not have helped matters. If I had switched to an ordinary medium-sized fly I might have done better. I did get a small brace but I should have had a hatful of bigguns. I have never had such a bad or frustrating day with the mayfly since, though I have had difficult and taxing ones.

Hooking trout on a mayfly is not always easy, then. I find that I still, almost inexplicably, miss trout at this time. On this problem Hills is instructive:

> But, when all is said, however good your tackle, whatever you do, however accomplished you are, and however long your experience, trout on the mayfly are extraordinarily hard to hook. This remains the eternal difficulty of the mayfly.

So, 'Duffers' Fortnight' is not always the doddle it is made out to be. You have to find the trout in the right mood and get the strike right in order to enjoy any sport at all. Do not develop an inferiority complex, then, if you experience difficulty next time you stumble on a mayfly hatch. Great men have had great difficulties at such times too and this should be of some comfort. But if you get to the river on the right day then you could be in for memorable sport, with the sky full of fluttering fly falling like cherry blossom. It is, as Hills declares, 'an event of nature'.

MODERATE MAYFLY HATCHES

Some of the best mayfly fishing I have ever had has been on little rivers and streams where hatches, while good, are not like the prolific snow-storms just described. Many big northern rivers get no mayfly at all (their equivalent bumper gluts being either the March brown or the stone fly) but it is surprising how many little becks and burns in the North do get very good hatches. Yorkshire is an excellent county in this respect. I remember a visit I made some years ago to a small Yorkshire river, a river where I had seen the odd mayfly in the past, but never a concerted hatch. Furthermore, my reading of nineteenth-century angling literature told me that this river, while only small, had dependable hatches of *Ephemera danica*.

It was 16 June and I was taking a bit of a gamble because if I failed to find the mayfly on this trip I knew that I would be missing out on reliable sport elsewhere. But if you want to broaden your angling horizons, and your network of 'hot spots', you have to take the odd risk. On this occasion the risk I took turned out to be one of the most rewarding I have ever taken. I was fishing by 10 a.m. and the first hour was dour. But around 11 o'clock mayfly duns began to emerge. The next two hours or so were memorable. I took a riparian lunch at 1.30 and by that time I had caught 20 trout on my Green Drake. I had kept a limit creel of excellent fish, choosing only the best trout, one of which was a fine chap for such a small river. I have never had better mayfly fishing than that wonderful day. I might add that I was entirely alone on the water, paid a mere 70 pence for my ticket, and saw a roe deer and two kingfishers, as well as hearing a woodpecker and a cuckoo.

WHEN TO FISH

This experience throws up one of the extra problems facing the lone angler in the wilds at mayfly time: when exactly to go to the river. In big clubs which have water with reliable mayfly hatches, keepers have up-to-the-minute information. The telephone can allow fishermen to keep in touch with events from day to day. But when no such information is available the angler has to take pot luck. In the North on little streams I find the best period is the second or third week of June, but it can vary. In 1988 the mayfly came to the Midlands and North earlier than usual: I was catching trout in May on mayfly. In the South the mayfly really lives up to its name and regularly appears in May, whereas in the North it is more reliably a June fly. But I have experienced wide fluctuations. The earliest good hatch of mayfly I have ever witnessed, with proper fishy interest involved, was on 2 May (1981) on the Cher at Vierzon in central France. The latest full hatch (as opposed to the odd, individual emergence) with corresponding trout activity, was 7 July (1985) on a small Yorkshire beck.

I well remember this last occasion. I was staying with an uncle and aunt in Yorkshire and we had all spent the afternoon watching Boris Becker win Wimbledon for the first time. I felt rather cooped up after the match, and in need of exercise, so I took myself off to the water for the evening. As soon as I approached the river bank I could tell something spectacular was happening: the trout were going mad over some fly or other. Once I had a clear view of the water I saw exactly what was up – a good hatch of green drakes and a thick fall of spent grey drakes. I put on a Grey Drake and began to fish. It was 6.15 p.m. By 9.15 I had caught 15 trout on Mayfly, keeping an excellent creel to present to my aunt.

It was an odd year, 1985 – a very wet one. I had fished on 25 and 29 May on a Midlands river where I can normally count on seeing some mayfly and had seen none. I fished in early June in Yorkshire (on the 2nd, 5th, 8th and 9th) and saw no mayfly whatsoever. I had five days in mid month (the 14th, 15th, 16th, 20th and 23rd) and the picture had not changed. You cannot say I had not tried to find the mayfly! By this time I think you could have forgiven me if I had believed that the mayfly would not appear that year, and indeed I believe I had given up hope. But on 29 June on the upper Derwent above Hackness I came across a small hatch of mayfly, and had some good fish in the space of an hour mid afternoon. There was another hatch, right at dusk, on this day too. However, on 30 June I saw no mayfly at all, although on a different river.

HIGH TEMPERATURE

The end of June 1985 was pretty hot and I believe it was this surge of high temperatures which saved the mayfly that year. Certainly, when I ventured to the river on 7 July I was not expecting to see a good hatch of mayfly. So it pays not to give up hope. Another thing to bear in mind is the timing of the hatch during the day. In pleasant mild summer weather mayfly will usually start emerging before midday, but on cold days the hatch might not start till mid or even late afternoon. On very hot days the hatch might also be delayed by the heat – indeed it might be dusk before you see any mayfly at all. If time is not at a premium it might well pay you to stay to the bitter end on a very hot day. Indeed the ending might be very much more sweet than bitter if the hunch pays off. Nothing is ever guaranteed in fishing but hope is the nearest thing to a guarantee you will ever get!

The day at Hackness on 29 June which I have just mentioned is a case in point. In the early evening the whole river went completely dour after a day of good activity. I had not been alone on the river, but as soon as this dead spell set in there was a mass exodus from the Derwent. My car was the only one in the car park by eight o'clock. I had a rest and some grub, then a smoke by the stream. It had been a very hot day, buzzing with insect life, but now all was still apart from the eternal bubbling of the current. A delicious cool began to fall and with it fell the mayfly spinners. I had the river to myself. The trout went mad at dusk and I took the biggest fish of the day right at dark on a Mayfly. The sudden drop in temperature had encouraged the mayfly to emerge and those anglers who drove home thinking that the day was done never knew what they had missed.

SURGE OF MAYFLY ACTIVITY

One of the great excitements of mayfly fishing is the sudden surges of activity you can stumble upon. I find this particularly true on small rivers, where hatches can be very localized. I was fishing a small tributary with a friend some years ago on a warm day in mid June. Apart from the odd mayfly we had seen no evidence of a proper hatch. Late in the afternoon I ambled some way upstream on my own, just to stretch my legs really, when I came across several big, slow pools in which trout were splashing around madly. It was not a big hatch, just a steady dribble of mayfly duns, but every single fly was being picked off greedily. I had an amazing half an hour or so. Every fly was fought for as soon as it hatched. At times I had three or four trout rising at my Green Drake as soon as it landed. Exciting!

However, when I walked back downstream to join my friend after the fun was over I learnt that he had witnessed nothing of what I had seen. He was almost a little sceptical about my experience. But this type of event is quite common on days when there is no big, general hatch. It pays to move about a bit on days like this. You do not want to be left downstream out of the way while some chap steals all the sport. It is a question of being in the right place at the right time. A good pair of legs and a sharp eye are your best allies on such a day.

I remember getting to the River Manifold early in June on the evening of a hot day. I parked at the bridge, my normal place, and strolled downstream. About 50 or 60 yards (45–55 m) below the bridge there is a long, curving pool and as I gently approached I could see signs of frantic activity right in its tail. I ducked down out of sight, made a wide detour through the meadow, where cows were contentedly chewing the cud, and approached the spot from below. I crept upstream into position and was confronted with something I had never seen before. In the narrow, shallow tail of the big pool there was an amazing congregation of trout. In a little patch of water maybe 3 or 4 yards (2.7–3.7 m) square, an area that normally held at most four feeding fish, there must have been more than two dozen trout. This is only an estimate because the light was wrong from my angle and I could not see into the water. Had I changed the angle so as actually to see the fish I would have scared the whole lot. I think what was happening was that mayfly was hatching just upstream, mid pool, and the trout had come down to the tail to pick off the fly as it was swept into the funnel where the water narrowed. Downstream was a rapid, frothing run, no place to feed contentedly, so the fly had to be intercepted or it was lost.

A FRENZY OF FEEDING

The fish were taking the mayfly as it came to them, whether sunk or emerged. The odd savage swirl or bulge betokened a nymph had been swallowed, while surface splashes showed where emerged fly had been swallowed. The trout were going berserk. Fish were jumping out of the water and descending on fly, standing on their noses and cartwheeling at fly and slashing across the surface like water-skiers after fly. It was an incredible sight . . . you can imagine my pulse rate! It was not unlike watching dolphins doing acrobatics in a marine zoo: a private performance just for me.

I knotted on a Straddle-Bug and cast with heart in mouth. The water was shallow and smooth but very fast as it was constricted into a narrows. Past experience told me it was very easy to frighten fish here. Each cast would have to be very delicate and soft. I also had the problem of drag if just once I allowed my fly line to be caught in the rapids below, by which I crouched. No easy place to fish. In the event I have never found it easier to fish than that memorable evening. Nearly every cast was rewarded with a take or a slash. The strike was a pretty quick one in the circumstances. I missed two or three, hooked one fish and lost him, and caught six or eight in as many minutes. I kept three, none of them big but all plump and above the size limit.

A photograph of the leash in my fishing log book brings back the atmosphere of the evening. I photographed them on the pebbly surface of the country lane in the mellow, buttery light of the sinking sun. (These were not shoaling stocked fish, by the way, but all completely wild fish, driven into one little shoal out of necessity.) Though this catch was not remarkable for the size of the trout, it is memorable for the way in which they were caught. This remains one of the most exciting encounters I have ever had at mayfly time, proving that size of fish matters less than the quality of the fishing.

This entire diversion took no more than 25 minutes from the moment that I first spotted the rise and began to crawl into position, to the moment that I caught my last trout there and decided to move somewhere else. Yet I spent another three hours on the water that night and only added a further brace to my creel. The fishing became progressively more difficult. Nowhere else did I find such a concentrated area of activity. Elsewhere trout were not in such a mood for mayfly. About halfway through the evening fish suddenly switched to smutting greedily and I found them very difficult to rise. I ended up fishing with Buzzers in the surface film. This story serves to illustrate the occasionally patchy nature of mayfly fishing. If you do hit the right place at the right time, though, the patch can be spectacular!

THREE FISH IN THREE CASTS

One of the best 'purple patches' I have ever had at mayfly time occurred five years ago. I went to Yorkshire with two friends in early June to show them the ropes with wild trouting. On our second day I spent much of the morning fishing with them in turn, trying to sort out their problems. We were fishing a small, wooded river full of plump, free-rising brownies of 6–8 oz (0.17–0.2 kg). A few mayfly were about but nothing very encouraging had happened. However, they had each taken the odd fish by hook or by crook, and we smoked them for a genial lunch in the sunshine. Mid afternoon I finally got away for an hour on my own, and, as luck would have it, found this was the very time the mayfly suddenly started to hatch freely. I had a size 12 John Storey on my cast and presented it to the first fish I saw take a mayfly. He took my Storey like a charm. I eased this fish downstream quickly because another trout was taking in the same place: a gorgeous, deep, swirly pool under a huge tree. My very next cast accounted for this other trout. Both were good, above-the-limit fish.

I was about to move on upstream when a mayfly was suddenly engulfed in a narrow channel leading in to the big swirl. The river here was braided by a fallen tree, whose branches separated each channel. In one of these rapid little runnels a good trout was lying. It was no easy place to fish. Absolute precision on the first cast was obligatory. I had lost flies here in the past with imprecise casting. I made my third cast of the session. Bang! He had taken the John Storey. Soon enough he was in my creel, the biggest fish so far. Two fish in two casts has not been unknown and always puts a spring in my step, but three in three casts!

The John Storey was now a little chewed, so I knotted on a Grey Wulff, size 10, and proceeded upstream. Just to bring me down to earth with a bump, I frightened trout in the next two pools, both difficult ones to approach. In the next, a smooth, narrow glide in a tree tunnel, a grand trout was rising. He took the Wulff first cast. I had a good struggle with this fish, because I was cramped in a very unmanoeuvrable position, but when I did get him to hand he proved the best so far. In the pool above, broad and ripply and still in the tree tunnel, three trout were rising. Two of these were really good fish coming half out of the water as they took: probably chasing ascending nymphs. I failed to rise the smaller of these two exhibitionists, then had a crack at the biggun. He took the Wulff in a great thrash of foam and rushed all about the pool like an express train. After a frantic struggle I landed him to discover that he was foul-hooked outside his mouth. Lucky! The biggest trout of the day, getting on for ¾ lb (0.3 kg) – a solid-bronze bar of muscle 12 in (30 cm) long. I was not finished though. In the very next pool I had another rising trout on the Wulff, the second biggest of the day.

This really was some purple patch: six trout in less than an hour, all on mayfly. In this period I had neither missed nor lost a single fish.

Such experiences are rare, at least for me, a fisher for wild brown trout in rough and tangly northern streams. Yet at mayfly time they are always possible. The fisherman must grab these moments when they occur and profit from them, for on any mayfly day the trout can suddenly turn choosy or even go completely down. Such little patches of success are to be savoured: you might not get another one like it that season.

SUDDEN FEEDING CHANGES

I have noticed that at mayfly time trout often suddenly switch from taking big Ephemeroptera to much smaller Diptera: black gnats, smuts or midges. For this reason I recommend you try fishing twin dry fly with a Mayfly on the point and a Black Gnat, Knotted Midge or small Coch-y-bondhu on the dropper. Wry fly with a Buzzer or Black and Peacock Spider fished in the surface film on the dropper is also a realistic option. This might solve the problem of the choosy fish. Curiously, you might find that even during a good hatch of mayfly the trout will prefer your Black Gnat. I have also found the Hare's Ear a good fly at mayfly time and often use this on the dropper – the Gold Ribbed variety too. Plunket-Greene also recommends a winged Iron Blue when the mayfly's up. It is all a question of what you have faith in. One thing I am sure about is that it does not do to be one-eyed when mayfly are hatching: it is pointless to slave away with an exact mayfly copy on your leader when a Black Gnat, Hare's Ear or some other fly works even better.

The switch from mayfly to midge or gnat is often both quick and universal. Trout all over the river suddenly seem to change their mind in unison. I had always idly speculated that this could be something to do with trout's digestion. Just as humans like a dry cracker with cheese and a cup of coffee after a rich meal, so too perhaps trout like a slight change of menu after a surfeit of mayfly. Then, one day when I was reading *Trout and Grayling – An Angler's Natural History* (published 1980) by Norman Maclean, the following reference jumped out of the page at me, and shows that I might not have speculated so idly after all:

> . . . it has been estimated that, at 20°C. [68°F], midge larvae take some four hours to digest, but snails nine hours. Perhaps that is one reason why fish tend to concentrate on one type of food at a time. To do otherwise may give them indigestion!

Fishermen often become puzzled and frustrated when trout switch from one fly to another, especially if it is to ignore some juicy great ephemerids and take tiny little midges. But perhaps it is all just a question of digestion? Perhaps trout are very health-conscious and careful about their diet. But surely it all comes down to taste. To a giant watching us eat, an after-dinner mint might look exceedingly dull and minute, but we know otherwise. As with many problems in Nature, the solution is both simple and mundane.

I said earlier in the chapter that the dry fly strike with a Mayfly was slower than normal, and so it is in general. However, with eager little trout in crowded streams where competition for food is intense, the strike can sometimes be an instantaneous one. When trout are rushing up at your fly in greedy twos and threes you cannot afford to wait: you must strike quickly. Likewise, in streamy water or in smooth rapid pool tails the strike is not such a slow one. For these circumstances it is worth having some smallish, supple Mayflies on size 12 hooks. I suggest some size 12 Grey Wulffs for this kind of job.

A DIFFICULT STRIKE

With nimble, eager little trout you do need a bit of luck to hook them however you strike. I have often seen little trout rush up, seize a mayfly then swim back down to the river bed and continue to chew at their capture. A mayfly is a big morsel and cannot be swallowed whole by trout of under 7 oz (0.2 kg) or so. Small trout have to chew up a mayfly before swallowing it, much the same as they have to chomp at a worm for a while before getting it down. When little fish attack your mayfly, then, do not be depressed if you miss a few, or even a lot. As J.W. Hills tells us, the mayfly strike is not always simple. From time to time you will get it completely right, though. The last purple patch I described to you is an illustration of how, even with tricky little fish, you cannot go wrong on occasion. During that period I did not miss a fish, was striking quite quickly and took trout from 6 to 12 oz (0.17–0.13 kg).

To reiterate, the patterns I would advise you to use for general Midlands, North Country and small-river mayfly fishing are:

1. French Partridge Mayfly
2. The Straddle-Bug or Straggle-Bug (sometimes called Summer Duck)
3. Grey Wulff
4. White Wulff
5. John Storey
6. Hare's Ear
7. Black Gnat or Knotted Midge

I would advise you to have some tyings of the first four patterns on size 12 hooks as well as the more standard 10s.

Finally, in all this chapter I have said nothing about Mayfly nymphs. Frankly, I have hardly ever found it necessary to use a nymph at mayfly time. Active trout can nearly always be induced to take a floating Mayfly. In any case, dry fly is really so much more fun at this exciting time.

18

The Mystery of the Adipose Fin

'The most irrelevant thing in nature.'
Charles Lamb

In all books on freshwater fish you will read that one of the prime distinguishing marks of the salmon family is the adipose fin. All salmonids possess this small, fleshy fin on their backs down near the tail. It is variously described as 'flabby', 'fatty', 'fleshy', 'rayless', 'a short stump of tissue', or by some similar phrase. The word adipose comes from the Latin *adeps, adipis*, meaning 'soft fat'. What is the importance of this fin? What function does it have? If we are to believe most commentators, the adipose fin has no function. It is described almost universally as a vestigial appendage no longer of any use. This generally held view has remained unchallenged. The purpose of this chapter is to challenge it.

The trout is not unique in having two dorsal fins, nor even in possessing an adipose fin. Members of the North American catfish family, which includes the brown and black bullhead, possess an adipose fin almost identical to that of the salmon and trout. Many sea fish have two (or more) dorsal fins. Among freshwater fishes the perch, ruffe, zander and bullhead can also boast two dorsal fins, though their posterior one is rayed. Some fish have a giant dorsal fin which runs almost the entire length of the back, among them lampreys, eels and burbots. The grayling and carp also possess dorsal fins of marked length. May we assume, then, that the trout's two dorsal fins were once joined in one big fin?

Then, take the predatory pike: his dorsal fin is placed far back on his body just above his anal fin, giving him an arrow-like look and the lancing lunge of instant speed he needs. Half-close your eyes and imagine the trout's adipose fin were bigger and you have an arrangement very similar to the pike. *Salmo trutta* is no less predatory that *Esox lucius*.

AN UNRESOLVED MYSTERY

If a trout's adipose fin really is a redundant feature, it has been redundant for millions of years. It has had about 50 million years in which to disappear. Why has the feature remained if it is functionless? No doubt biologists could cite plenty of cases of redundancy in Nature (our own appendix being a good example) but such evidence does not conclude the case of the adipose fin.

I am not the first writer to suspect that the adipose fin is not a redundant feature. Various other authors have ascribed some use to the fin – not many, it is true: I have discovered three.

The first positive reference to the adipose fin that I have ever come across, occurs in *Salar the Salmon* (published in 1935) by Henry Williamson, who writes: 'There was a small, fixed fin, like a pennon, on his back, aft of the dorsal fin, which served to prevent turbulence or eddy when he (Salar) was swimming forward.'

A fascinating idea. If Williamson is right, the adipose fin could have a crucial stabilizing role in the way salmonids swim.

The second reference comes from *A Creel of Willow* (published in 1957) by W.H. Canaway. As far as I am concerned, Mr Canaway must take pride of place in adipose-fin research. He devotes three and a half pages to the topic, as opposed to Williamson's three lines. I cannot quote them in full, but I suggest that you read his marvellous book. I certainly owe my interest in the adipose fin to him. Canaway quotes the Williamson reference I have already given you and then reluctantly pours cold water over the theory. Apparently, when he took the idea to various experts on the behaviour of solid bodies in water they pooh-poohed it – which is not the same as disproving it, I should like to add. Not content with this disappointing response, he continued his search. Next Canaway conjectures that: 'the adipose fin may help somehow in absorbing torque (the tendancy to twist) resulting from the lateral undulations of the tail as he swims'.

But he has a third hypothesis, which he saves till last, referring to it as his 'choicest theory'. He argues that as a trout swims the adipose fin oscillates, giving the fish some idea of how fast he is moving. Canaway gets quite excited about this concept, for: 'it means that the fish possesses a speedometer, which is a really glorious notion'.

He concludes with the wry dig that though he cannot prove this theory he cannot see how anyone is going to be able to disprove it.

The third reference is from a much more recent book, *The New Compleat Angler*, published in 1983 and written by Dr Stephen Downes, a zoologist. He has a completely different but also very engaging theory. He says of the adipose fin:

> The purpose of this weak fin is obscure; it is much larger, in proportion to the other fins, in the newly-hatched young and in the small parr; it may have some importance in the swimming of such small fish, though not in the adults.

A REAR SENSOR

What can I add on this subject? I can offer several suggestions. The first of these is entirely the product of my own thought on the matter; the rest are the result of my discussions with biologists. I would like to put forward the idea that the adipose fin is a rear sensor, an additional sensory organ that helps the trout to be aware of happenings in his vicinity. The whole of the trout's skin is very sensitive to his surroundings, quite apart from his neuromasts, which are even more heightened nodes of sensation along his lateral line. An examination of the rope of nerves which links the brain to the caudal fin shows quite clearly that the adipose fin is connected to the nervous system. The fin cannot be controlled in a muscular way, as can the others, but I believe it can *feel*, and that it could be a receptor which nets in information for the trout.

Trout and grayling, when resting in shallow, streamy water, tend to lie slightly athwart the run of water, allowing the flow to course over one flank and across their tail. If the fish is big enough for you to obtain a good view of his adipose fin, you will see the fin clearly bowed over in the current. It can be seen to undulate in any counter currents or ripple. Is it, I wonder, a kind of 'third eye' which remains open while a drowsy trout rests? Could it be sensible to temperature change as well as vibration? Could it warn the trout of an approaching flood, or detect the presence of either predator or prey? (Such a function would also be of use to a North American catfish, which already possesses important forward sensors in his eight barbels.)

As a relaxed trout rests in the stream his adipose fin winnows softly in the current, ever alert to any changes in the environment. It is a kind of rear radar scanner; at least, this is my theory. When a trout turns quickly to seize a worm or grub which lands on his tail then maybe the adipose fin has played its part in detecting the disturbance created by the alighting creature. Who knows? Maybe we will never know. The fin could even have another important role: as an extra receptor during floods. When debris is being swept downstream, the careless trout always runs the risk of being bashed by a piece of flotsam and concussed. Maybe, rather like a bather testing the temperature of the pool with his toe before taking the plunge, a trout tests the safety of a current with his tail end first, thus avoiding a deadly blow on the head in the swollen, opaque water. Rather a fanciful notion, I admit. Still, before anything can be proved or disproved there has to be a supposition, a hypothesis. I certainly have observed trout under banks flicking their tails out into the current as if to check the water flow.

MULTIPLE FUNCTIONS

It is possible that the adipose fin has more than one function, a function which combines the ideas of Williamson, Canaway, Downes and myself, or is broader still. Could the adipose fin have anything to do with the wonderful navigational powers of the salmon and other migratory salmonids? Is it a detector of freshwater out in the estuary? A thermometer warning of rainwater on its way out to sea? I have discussed this matter with various biologist friends of mine and between them they have supplied the following possible functions for the adipose fin:

(i) The adipose fin could be important in a buoyancy role. Salmonids are relatively long fish with a fairly primitive swim bladder. The position of this organ tends to change the density of the anterior rather than the posterior end of the fish. Migrating to/from waters of differing density (salt to fresh and vice versa) may necessitate this extra rear buoyancy.

(ii) The adipose fin could be important for energy storage – similar in function to a camel's hump. This purpose could aid posterior buoyancy.

(iii) The adipose fin could be important as a fixed stabilizer, like a rigid ship's keel. At times when the main dorsal fin has to be lowered, or is rendered useless (in very rough water, beneath waterfalls or weirs, in tunnels, weed channels or grottoes) or at spawning time in shallows when the principal dorsal fin is *above* the surface and of no hydrodynamic use, then the little fixed adipose fin could come into its own.

(iv) The adipose fin could combine several functions, such as being sensory, hydrodynamic and an aid to buoyancy.

Commentators who say that the adipose fin is redundant and functionless have not, as far as I am aware, put forward any clear proof that this is so, yet they have been believed. I can furnish no proof for any of these hypotheses but they seem to me quite as plausible as the redundancy theory. I prefer to think positive rather than negative. Besides, Nature, the great controller of us all, rarely does anything without a reason.

19

The Hotspur and Other Flies

'The gallant Hotspur.'

Henry IV

Of all the many clumsy experiments I have made with fly dressings over the years there is really only one which I think is worthy of setting down in print. I do not use the word 'clumsy' with false modesty, for in reality I am only a very bungling, amateurish fly-tier. I have always been far more interested in fishing than in fly tying. The two skills are separate, though of course they often go hand in hand. I have found that the tried and trusted patterns are the best, such as Wickham's Fancy, Greenwell's Glory, and Tup's Indispensable, and so I always view allegedly deadly 'new' dressings with scepticism. If a 'new' pattern is really only a plagiarized variation on an already established dressing then why bother with it at all? But this is not the way of the human mind. Many of us suffer from a restive and fastidious urge to improve our lot (or that of others). Some try to improve health or housing, praiseworthy aims, while others seek to improve such relatively inconsequential things as tennis rackets, water-skis or fly dressings.

AN ORIGINAL DRESSING

My best contribution to the world of fur, feather and tinsel is the Hotspur. It was a fly which was conceived well before it was tied. I had been revolving various ideas in my head for some time. Why not produce a fly which is a composite of some of the most successful features found in other artificial flies? Would it be possible to amalgamate features of Ephemeroptera and Diptera in the same fly? Which features? Why not the black hackle of a Black Gnat and the gingery-red hackle used in ephemerid copies such as the Ginger Quill, August Dun, Imperial, or that grand utility fly Wickham's Fancy? A double-hackled fly, then, with a Knotted Midge profile. Something either of dipteran colour but having bushy buoyancy, or ephemerid colour but possessing dipteran outline.

I made some sketches, the first three of which were simply design prototypes. I jotted down some notes underneath my sketches. The last few notes read:

> When trout are feeding predominantly on black gnat in upland streams they will often take a brown ephemerid type copy in preference to a replica of a gnat. Ditto with black ant (Wickham's Fancy the killer). Think I'll try to amalgamate the two concepts to see if the amalgamation is even more deadly.

A combination I often use when fishing twin dry fly is Wickham's Fancy on the point and a Black Gnat on the dropper. After two days of fishing a wooded hill stream in Yorkshire with this successful formula I began to ponder an experiment: combining a Black Gnat and a Wickham in one fly: like fishing 'twin' dry fly but with only one fly. Time passed, and when I did get round to putting my idea into concrete form I rejected the black body of the Gnat and the gold body of the Wickham's. I wanted something bright but matt. Hot-orange silk was my choice. And so a fly was born.

All through the summer of 1987 these notions had been whirling around in my head. When I actually sat down at my vice to tie the first Hotspur, it emerged, after a little practice, as a fly on a long-shank hook with a hot-orange silk body, a black cock hackle at the head and a ginger-red cock hackle at the tail, with the tip of the hackle tied down as whisks. See fig. 14.

I tie this fly in a rather eccentric way. I start at the bend of the hook, wind silk to the eye, tie in the black hackle, continue down the hook till I tie in the ginger hackle, then secure it down at the tail. The tip of the hackle acts as whisks. Having a whipped varnished tail end in no way limits the usefulness of the fly. It is a pretty simple dressing: no wings, no ribbing. In any case, I am too much of a butter-fingers to tie complex patterns!

A SIMPLIFIED VERSION

Nowadays I sometimes simplify the tying of the Hotspur, neglecting the tail whisks. I tie the fly more conventionally, starting at the head. I wind the silk down to the hook bend, tie in the ginger cock hackle, then wind the silk on back up the shank. I tie in the black hackle and finish off at the head. There is no 'spur' of whisks with this dressing, but the fly seems to catch fish just as well. Should any of my readers wish to try the Hotspur they can choose whichever method of tying they prefer.

My first Hotspurs were all tied on size 12 long-shank hooks, but I have since tied some smaller versions on standard size 14 hooks and I think I prefer them. I have a variant dressing too, called the Black Hotspur, which is identical in every way save for the fact that I use black tying silk. A Dutch angling friend of mine, Jacob Keulen, ties the Hotspur with a greeny-gold iridescent body ('Krystal Flash' by Orvis) on small hooks: size 16 and 18. We have both done so well with this variant that I mention it here.

When I first fished with the Hotspur I found it had two particular advantages (which I had anticipated but needed to prove): buoyancy and visibility. The hackle at each end of the hook makes the fly a very good floater, while the dark and paler hackles are easy to see in all conditions of light. In bright, glary water the black hackle stands out; in dark, sombre places the ginger hackle sticks out like a sore thumb. (This is nothing new: the Bi-visible patterns pre-empted the Hotspur by nearly a century.)

The fly has proved a reliable trout taker. The first time I used it I caught ten. It is an excellent floater and is a very visible fly on the water. It fishes well in difficult conditions of light such as bright glare or under trees. It also doubles well as a night-time Bustard variant. Tied big, I believe it would also make an excellent dapping fly. Another advantage it possesses is that you cannot place it on the water the 'wrong' way up. However it falls, the two hackles ensure it sits correctly on the stream. It is therefore excellent for duffers and bad casters!

As for the fly's name, I hit on Hotspur for two reasons. First, the bright ginger whisk looks a little like a spur, while the 'hot' in hot orange becomes a pun. Second, I have long speculated that if any character in Shakespeare is a trout fisherman then it has to be Hotspur. There are countless references to fishermen, fish and fishing in the plays, so many that one suspects that the Bard did go a-angling in his day. There is an apocryphal story about his poaching of a stag on the Charlecote estate in his youth. He was a countryman born and bred, and seems to know so much about everything rustic, with that acquisitive magpie mind of his, so why not angling too?

But why Hotspur? Well, even a quick read of *Henry IV*, Part I, should reveal to you that Hotspur is very interested in rivers. He talks of 'gentle Severn's sedgy bank' and 'swift Severn's flood', which suggests he is a West Midlands or Welsh Borders angler. The Severn is a great trout river and in those days must have been even greater. He also refers to 'the smug and silver Trent', which he wishes to dam, presumably somewhere up in North Staffordshire, to make a good pool for himself.

Hotspur is clearly a great country pursuits man because he makes endless references to horses and hounds. He has a keen eye for terrain, for he mentions maps, and displays a fisherman's preoccupation with the elements as he speaks of 'unruly wind' and 'foul weather'. Bridges and brooks are mentioned, as is the phrase 'sink or swim'. He talks of a 'fathom line', 'the deep' (which shows he was not averse to worming when all else failed) while allusions to moles, ants and ravens show his interest in fly tying and natural history. He exhibits anxiety about the conditions in early season, and when he dies our suspicions that he was a bait angler as well as a fly fisherman are confirmed because he has a discussion with Prince Hal about worms. All in all, I think you will agree that Hotspur was quite clearly a trout angler. What more fitting name for a fly then?

Figure 14 The Hotspur

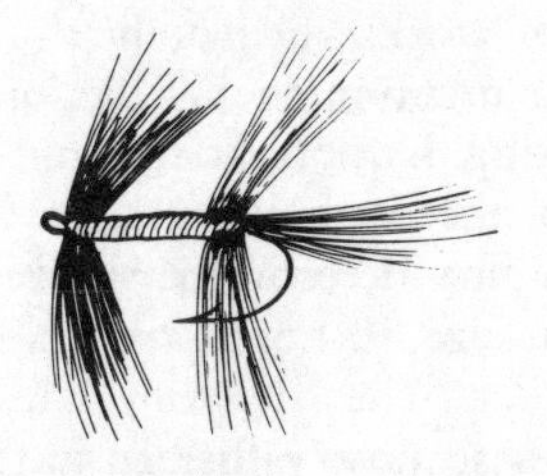

Hooksize: 10–14 (longshank)

Figure 15 Blanchard's Abortion

Hooksize: 12–16

FITTON'S FANCY

I will offer you one other home-made dressing. This fly is an ephemerid copy, more particularly a general olive imitation. It has a bright yellow floss body which when wet goes a nice olive colour. I tie it with two hackles: a small Coch-y-bondhu hackle at the rear of the thorax, then a bigger ginger cock hackle at the head. This bigger hackle provides buoyancy and visibility for the angler, while the small dark hackle gives the fly bulk from the trout's point of view. I have had good results with this fly and I have named it Fitton's Fancy.

To tie this pattern you start at the eye of the hook. Wind yellow silk down the shank to the tail, and tie in the whisks (strands from Ginger cock hackle) and the yellow floss. Wind silk back halfway up the shank, then follow with the floss. Finish the floss and secure. Tie in the first hackle and, in securing it, tie in the second larger hackle: you must leave room for several good turns so that this hackle is substantial. Finish and secure the hackle at the eye of the hook.

One of my friends, a much more sophisticated and knowledgeable fly-tier than me, has suggested that this fly is tied by winding both hackles on together. I have rejected this idea because the smaller hackle needs fewer turns round the hook than the larger, but his advice could be worth considering.

PATTERNS

The three other flies I wish to describe in this chapter are patterns which I mentioned earlier in this book, patterns which do not get much attention nowadays despite their excellence. They are: Frank Sawyer's Killer Bug, Dr Baigent's Brown and Mr Blanchard's Abortion.

Sawyer's Bug is no secret, its dressing can be found in any modern book on fly patterns, yet despite this I rarely come across its use. Quite often anglers I meet show complete ignorance of the pattern, or at best only hazy knowledge of it. This is a strange state of affairs for, in my view, the Killer Bug is the deadliest 'deep' nymph ever invented. On page 60 of Sawyer's *Nymphs and the Trout* can be found a clear description of how to tie this fly. Sawyer is very particular about the type of wool used (Chadwick's 477) but this is now commercially unobtainable. However, any beige shade of wool works adequately.

John Roberts gives the fly a detailed mention in his dictionary of trout flies and his is basically the dressing I quote at the end of the chapter. As Roberts observes: 'It is also one of the easiest flies to tie.' So, no excuse not to have a few in your box. I recommend size 12 for general summer use, plus a few tied on size 10 hooks for cold, dour days.

Next, the Baigent's Brown, which is also now rather an unfashionable fly. Courtney Williams gives a dressing of it, as well as citing Keith Rollo's *The Art of Fly Fishing* in which the rationale of Dr William Baigent's invention is described. Roberts too has a dressing of the fly, though the dressing I quote is that of Alan Bell-Tawse, who was a pupil of Dr Baigent's. On big, rough rivers such as the Aberdeenshire Don this fly is sometimes tied on hooks as large as size 10. I also quote the dressing for the Baigent's Black. The celebrated doctor used to fish twin dry fly with a Black and a Brown Variant on together. (His creations are sometimes called Variants, by the way.)

Finally, Blanchard's Abortion, the most obscure of the three. I can find absolutely no allusion to it in any of my many fishing books. I believe it is a North Midlands fly, for you can buy dressings of it quite easily in places like Ashbourne and Bakewell. I have grown up using the fly and swear by it. For the rough-stream fisherman who needs patterns which are highly buoyant, the Blanchard's Abortion is a must. I place it in my top half-dozen favourite dry flies for this very reason. There exists no better floater. Whoever Mr Blanchard was, he hit on an idea of genius, for his fly has an inspired innovation. In appearance the pattern is very similar to a Pheasant Tail but – and this is the masterstroke – as well as having a strong bunch of ginger whisks for setae it has a great bunch of forward whisks as antennae. With this double set of whisks fore and aft the fly is virtually unsinkable. Try it and I think you will agree. It is also a very visible fly and trout fall for it in droves. I cannot praise the pattern highly enough. It is tied with cock pheasant tail fibres for the body, gold ribbing and a ginger or red cock hackle. See fig. 15.

To conclude this chapter there follow notes on all these dressings.

HOTSPUR

Hook: 10–14 (long-shank or standard hook)
Body: Hot-orange silk
Hackles: Front – black cock
Tail – ginger cock
Whisks: Tip of ginger cock hackle (fly finished off at tail)
(optional)

BLACK HOTSPUR

Same as for Hotspur but with black silk body.

FITTON'S FANCY

Hook: 12–16
Body: Yellow silk underlay, yellow floss overlay
Hackles: Thorax (tied on first) – small coch-y-bondhu
Head (tied adjacent) – ginger cock
Whisks: Strands from ginger cock hackle

KILLER BUG

Hook: 8–14
Body: An underbody of lead or fuse wire is overlaid with three layers of beige darning wool. Fine copper wire is then used to tie in the materials and finish off at the tail. (No tying silk is used at all.)

BAIGENT'S BROWN

Hook: 10–12
Body: Yellow floss silk
Wings: Woodcock or hen pheasant
Hackle: Game cock, dark rusty colour

BAIGENT'S BLACK

Hook: 10–12
Body: Black ostrich and peacock herl
Hackle: Black cock (rusty on one side)

BLANCHARD'S ABORTION*

Hook: 12–14
Body: Brown silk, cock pheasant tail fibres overlay, gold ribbing
Hackle: Ginger cock or ginger-red cock
Whisks: Good bunch of strands from hackle
Antennae: Good bunch of strands from hackle (or the hackle tip itself when tied down)

* Recently I have discovered a reference to Blanchard's Abortion in *A Guide to River Trout Flies* by John Roberts, published by Crowood Press, 1989. Readers seeking more information on the fly should consult this volume.

20

Philosophical

'I love all waste and solitary places.'
P.B. Shelley

I remember once meeting an angler in high dudgeon beside a reservoir – apparently because he had not got his limit of eight fish. He failed to be satisfied with the seven rainbows he had caught. He showed me his catch, remarking that they were miserable small fish hardly worth catching, fish much inferior to those in his local stillwater. With that he stumped grumpily off to the car park. I was surprised at his attitude. Had he obtained no joy from seeing fish, birds, aquatic flies and the marvellous sight of waves frothing across the great grey expanse of water? He could hardly complain of lack of success either – seven rainbows is far from a blank day. True, they were not big fish, but at around 1 lb (0.5 kg) apiece they would have been monsters in some of the little rivers I fish. I had caught nothing and would have been delighted with one brace of them, let alone three and a half. Alas, this kind of attitude is not uncommon nowadays, and it causes me some concern about the direction in which British trout angling is going.

The stocked rainbow is a marvellous fish: he has been a great boon to countless fishermen, myself included. He is a hard, flashy fighter and makes a splendid meal when the day is done. I consider that the small stillwaters are good places to start fishing, for they offer encouragement to the beginner. They offer an easy and friendly environment for beginners to learn how to cast and how to play a fish. They are excellent springboards from which to jump off into the more demanding worlds of river, loch and big reservoir – environments where a fisherman does not always have things his own way.

THE SIZE FACTOR

However, I do think that alongside the spread of the spectacular rainbow has come a series of rather regrettable attitudes. Size is one: there is now an obsession with size of fish in trout angling. Where once the prime sporting factor was the degree of difficulty involved in the capture of a trout, size now seems to be the prime criterion. In addition, the fishing in many of these little stocked ponds is a very easy business, a process far removed from the demanding quest for trout in river and big lake. Trout fishing in these small 'put-and-take' stillwaters is really the *reductio ad absurdum* of the sport. Beginners without any skill, knowledge or experience are catching giant fish regularly, and as their exploits are vaunted in the popular angling press, so angling becomes debased.

These gigantic fish, too, are not like wild trout in appearance: they appear to be a different breed of trout altogether. They are hugely plump and porcine, almost grotesque to look at: more like carp than trout. Many have stumpy, mangled fins and are a travesty of what a natural brown or rainbow trout should look like. They have never had to work for a mouthful in their lives but have been pampered in pens like tame geese. They are Billy Bunteresque, milksop trout with no idea of the fate which will probably befall them within a few days or even hours of their release. If they do survive uncaught they will not be able to find an adequate food supply to keep their huge, bloated bodies satisfied, so they wither, become black and lank, and die. This, in my view, is cruel – a cruelty arising out of the modern angler's insatiable desire to catch ever-bigger fish.

Even more ridiculous (and unfair) is the prospect of catching trout under floodlights, which is a facility now offered in some areas. Such a rule is unsporting and against Nature, in my opinion, and can only bring our pastime into disrepute. We need fishermen in the vanguard of our sport, pushing back its frontiers, but we also need wise and experienced voices to remind us of traditions and principles which we ignore at our peril. Fishing, like anything else, must progress, but not at any price.

THE ROLE OF THE PRESS

The existence of these small stillwaters in themselves worries me less than the disproportionate space they have created for themselves in the angling press. Some fishing journalists make no attempt to distinguish between the various degrees of difficulty needed to take fish in the different places they write about. Again, the main concern is size. Banner headlines proclaim the capture of some new monster nearly every week. Indeed, totally undiscriminating journalism has much to answer for, in my opinion. It does seem that traditional skills, gained over seasons and seasons of observation and practice, are being muscled out of the public view. This is the 'new' trout angling, for those who want the old traditional game fishing in the modern, convenient way.

I am not alone in my condemnation of some of the aspects of our stillwater scene. A prophetic note was sounded as long ago as 1958 by Frank Sawyer:

> when one hears of really big trout being caught in places where the natural food supply is too sparse to support fish more than half a pound [0.2 kg] in weight, I wonder if this sort of thing is not becoming something of a farce.

If Sawyer detected a farce in prospect then, I wonder how he would view the situation today, some 30 years on? In that time our small stillwaters have multiplied tenfold, and so has the population of giant bred rainbows.

More recently, in 1980, the angler and biologist Norman Maclean observed that this type of angling management 'may produce hungry, easily caught, fish but in the long run it must lead to a type of fishing which is increasingly boring and unnatural'.

AN ESCAPE

The older I get the more important the environment becomes to me when I am fishing. I would prefer, any day, to fish a stream where the trout are small but the location is wild, uncrowded and lovely, than visit a more popular, less attractive water where the fish are large. This is why the rocky, tangly hill streams of the North and the West appeal more and more to me. In a way I suppose the world of wood, rock and swirling water is an escape for me from modern artificiality and convenience, back to the purity of how things were in the beginning. I am a lucky being to have found such a comforting and complete diversion. This is one of the reasons I wrote this book: to share this marvellous world with you. I am proselytizing, spreading the gospel about fishing in the wild.

To conclude my philosophical meanderings, I leave you with ten axioms which have evolved and guided me during the time I have spent fishing:

1. No man is infallible and especially no fisherman.
2. The best (or only) fish of the day always takes when you are not paying proper attention to your line.
3. He who covers the most amount of water most thoroughly catches most fish.
4. All fishermen should be your friends. If you sometimes find that this rule has been broken, be sure it is not you who has broken it.
5. He who is most certain is least right.
6. Look before you cast.
7. Read, think and listen.
8. To catch the most or the biggest fish is not the only aim of angling.
9. I would rather catch 10 oz (0.3 kg) wild trout than a 10 lb (4.5 kg) stocked one.
10. Thank Providence that you have become an angler.

21

The Last Cast

'He watereth the hills from above: the earth is filled with the fruit of thy works.'

Psalm 104

Some people love the sea. Others fall under the spell of lakes or pools. I love rivers. To me, the lure of a river is irresistible. The ever-moving, liquid stream is a mesmeric delight. I can watch a river for hours just for the hypnotic beauty of its flow. Watch a river closely for some minutes, then look quickly up at the trees: they too will flow, swaying as if drunk. Slowly they will sober up and soon become proper trees again. Your eye tires of static Nature and you turn your gaze once more on the moving water.

A river's motion is not tidal as with the sea, nor wind–driven as with lakes, but a simple, remorseless gravitational pulse downhill, ever onwards. A river is always the same yet always different. It maintains the same shape but each cubic inch that passes downstream is unique and will never pass again, yet we unthinkingly refer to it, along with the millions of other cubic inches, by the name 'river'. We refer to it with this single, simple word as if it were a single,. finite entity. True, it is an unchanging blue ribbon on a map; true, it has a fixed name; true, you can walk beside it and recognize it as palpably the same river you visited last year. And yet there is something shifting, irresponsible, perpetually different about a river.

THE PULSE OF NATURE

A little river is in some ways even more of a miracle, for you have intimate contact with every corner of it as you fish quietly upstream. Whatever happens on either bank comes within the compass of your gaze. No kingfisher or weasel will pass by unnoticed. No wild flower will go unseen either. Here you can keep your finger on the pulse of Nature.

A few seasons ago in spring I saw a pair of wrens giving their two tiny chicks a first lesson in flight. On another occasion I was suddenly aware of movement out of the corner of my eye. I turned, and there at eye level, no more than a yard (0.9 m) from my head, was a tiny shrew. He was right at the top of a grass stalk, chewing at the seed pods and completely oblivious to my presence. I see stoats and weasels quite regularly but a few years ago I saw something which I have never seen before or since. Tripping along the riverbank towards me, for all the world like a family in their Sunday best on their way to church, came Mrs Stoat, her three little stoatlings, and bringing up the rear, a wise and watchful Mr Stoat. They trooped sinuously past me at no more than 4 yards (3.7 m) distant and never noticed me at all. On all three of these occasions I was wading out in midstream, a place where the angler really does seem to be invisible to wild creatures as they scurry about their business on the riverbank.

I began fishing little rivers and streams when I was a boy and I have never lost the love of them: they exert an irresistible fascination still. Much of my knowledge about trout behaviour has been gained along their banks. Though rain-fed, many of the becks, burns and streams of the North and the West run clear as chalkstreams for much of the summer, so to the observant they are a laboratory full of trout. In fact, one of the principal charms of the little rivers and streams I fish is the sheer visible number of trout supported by each. It is the frequency with which they rush up at my fly, keeping me constantly occupied and on my toes, that gives this kind of fishing its appeal.

CAREFUL HANDLING OF FISH

In order to keep these Lilliputian populations thriving, we who venture into the wild must be scrupulous in the way we approach the killing and handling of these bonny little trout. We must kill no more than we need – and we should keep our needs within the sensible limits of one or two brace. We must also be very careful when unhooking and returning fish. If we use barbless hooks and unhook the fish while they remain in their element, so much the better. If we have to handle fish out of the water, we must do so as quickly and gently as possible – and always with a wet hand, as this is kinder to their essential dermal mucus than a dry hand.

These little wild brownies, so abundant in the remoter streams and small rivers of our islands, now have an invaluable extra importance: they inhabit the last truly unspoilt environment for wild river trout fishing and are the only remaining truly wild strains of river trout. High up the tributary system, they lie beyond Man and his pollution and beyond the ravaging reach of the stocked trout. The pure native blood of these indigenous fish has not (yet) been watered down with cross-bred invader stock.

In his excellent book *The Wild Trout* (published 1989), Dr Malcolm Greenhalgh argues a forceful case for the diligent preservation of all our wild strains of trout. We should heed this message before it is too late. His hope that his book 'will help anglers more fully appreciate the wild trout' is similar to my hope for my book. It is vital, too, that as well as anglers, all landowners and fishing-club committees respect the environment of the wild trout and ensure his survival.

CATCH LIMITS

I have stated elsewhere in this book that I incline towards the creel-filling mentality. Certainly this was the North Country tradition in which I was brought up. As a lad I did bring home some pretty big baskets – a dozen fish was not unusual. In those days this was quite legitimate. Some rivers had limits of 20 fish, while others had no limit at all. Nowadays I do not keep anything like so many fish. Several rivers that I visit still permit five brace of wild trout to be kept per day, but I never keep my limit. A couple of brace at most suffices for me, though I often keep less than this. I seem to kill fewer and fewer trout per season. I do not think that I will give up killing altogether, though, because I do enjoy cooking and eating my catches.

However, I have become aware that our stock of wild trout is something very precious and special, something to be treasured and preserved and not abused. I now carry a box of barbless flies and if I am experiencing a day when trout are taking well, I switch to barbless hooks. I find many trout anglers put all their fish back nowadays and some fish barbless all the time too. I am contemplating a permanent switch to barbless hooks myself.

For many years now I have been very careful about the number of grayling I keep. I have never regarded them as vermin. I limit myself to a brace, or occasionally a leash, per visit. *Thymallus thymallus* is a truly wild creature which has little or no fish-farming industry to ensure its survival. The grayling survives through its own sheer fertility and guile.

ENSURING THE SURVIVAL OF STOCKS

The policy of 'catch and release' in rivers which hold wild stocks of trout, grayling and char is certainly a sensible, safe and sure way of helping to conserve stocks of indigenous species. In this respect our American cousins are far more environmentally advanced than we are. But, in my view, 'catch and release' is not the only way to ensure that the wild survive. Provided fishermen are not greedy and thoughtless, and kill only a few fish per visit, then stocks will not be endangered by angling.

Trout fishing is part of the game-fishing tradition: that is to say, trout are 'game', just like pheasants, partridge, wildfowl, deer and salmon. If trout fishing becomes exclusively 'catch and release' in this country then I believe that it will lose its traditional character as a fine old British field sport. It is up to us to make sure that we are not forced into this corner by our own greed. It would be some comfort to think that the threat to the wild trout does not come from the angling community.

This book is not the Truth, nor the last thing in advice on how to catch trout. It is just another step along the path of discovery. Even when all the rivers have evaporated and no trout, nor humans, live any longer on our cold, lifeless planet, there will remain vital questions still unsolved about trout behaviour. The vital question: What does a trout really believe an artificial fly to be? will never be answered. We are all of us in pursuit of an unobtainable grail. Still, the comfort of a brace of trout in the creel is superb compensation.

As William of Baskerville says in that remarkable novel by Umberto Eco, *The Name of the Rose:* 'Books are not made to be believed but to be subjected to inquiry.'

Subject what I have written to inquiry. Subject everything you read (or are told) to inquiry.

It only remains for me to wish you success and, to express the hope that on your next foray into the wild, as you stand there surrounded by the marvels and the majesty of Nature, you pause for a cast or two and thank whatever you believe to be your Providence, that you have learnt how to catch trout. No luckier humans live than those who fish.

Bibliography

All fishing book titles mentioned in the text are collected here. Occasionally I have referred to an author but not to the book's title; these titles are also to be found below.

BRIDGETT, R.C.: *Dry Fly Fishing*, 1922
CANAWAY, W.H.: *A Creel of Willow*, 1957
CLAPHAM, R.: *Trout Fishing on Hill Streams*, 1947
CURRIE, W.B.: *Gamefishing*, 1962
The Art of Trout Fishing, 1963
The Guinness Guide to Game Fishing, 1980
DEWAR, G.: *The Book of the Dry Fly*, 1897
DICKIE, W.H.: *From Tyrone to Test*, 1947
DOWNES, S.: *The New Compleat Angler*, 1983
EVANS, J.: *Small-River Fly Fishing*, 1972
GODDARD, J.: *John Goddard's Waterside Guide*, 1988
GREENHALGH, M.: *Trout Fishing in Rivers*, 1987
The Wild Trout, 1989

HALFORD, F.M.: *Dry Fly in Theory and Practice*, 1889
HILLS, J.W.: *A Summer on the Test*, 1924
River Keeper, 1934
JOYCE, H.S.: *Holiday Trout Fishing*, 1943
KITE, O.: *Nymph Fishing in Practice*, 1963
Elements of Nymph Fishing, 1966
LA BRANCHE, G.M.L.: *The Dry Fly and Fast Water*, 1914
LAWRIE, W.H.: *Border River Angling*, 1939
LEE, A.: *Fishing Dry Flies for Trout*, 1983
MACLEAN, N.: *Trout and Grayling: An Angler's Natural History*, 1980
MAUNSELL, G.W.: *The Fisherman's Vade Mecum*, 1933
NELSON, W.: *Fishing in Eden*, 1922
OVERFIELD, T.D.: *Fifty Favourite Dry Flies*, 1980
PLUNKET-GREENE, H.: *Where the Bright Waters Meet*, 1924
PRITT, T.E.: *Yorkshire Trout Flies*, 1885
North Country Flies, 1886
RANSOME, A.: *Rod and Line*, 1929
RITZ, C.: *A Fly Fisher's Life*, 1953
ROBERTS, J.: *The Grayling Angler*, 1982
The New Illustrated Dictionary of Trout Flies, 1986
ROLLO, W.K.: *The Art of Fly Fishing*, 1931
SAWYER, F.: *Nymphs and the Trout*, 1958
SKUES, G.E.M.: *Minor Tactics of the Chalk Stream*, 1910
The Way of a Trout with a Fly, 1921
STEWART, W.C.: *The Practical Angler*, 1857
'THREE ANGLERS': *How to Catch Trout*, 1888
TURNER, E. HORSFALL: *Angler's Calvacade*, 1966
WIGGIN, M.: *Teach Yourself Fly Fishing*, 1958
WILLIAMS, A. COURTNEY: *A Dictionary of Trout Flies*, 1949
WILLIAMSON, H.: *Salar the Salmon*, 1935
WILSON, D.: *Fishing the Dry Fly*, republished, 1987
WOOLLEY, A.: *Thoughtful Practice with a Dry Fly*, 1949
WOOLLEY, R.: *Modern Trout Fly Dressing*, 1932

RIVER FISHING GUIDES

BARR, D.: *The Haig Guide to Trout Fishing in Britain*, 1983
BRADLEY, T.: *The Yorkshire Angler's Guide*, 1894
ORTON, D.A.: *Where to Fish*, published annually

WILSON, T.K.: *The Northern Angler's Handbook*, 1949

RECOMMENDED BOOKS NOT MENTIONED IN THE TEXT

'B.B.': *The Fisherman's Bedside Book*, 1945
FALLODEN, VISCOUNT GREY: *Fly Fishing*, 1899
FARSON, N.: *Going Fishing*, 1942
FOSTER, M.C.: *Muriel Foster's Fishing Diary*, 1980
HARRIS, J.R.: *An Angler's Entomology*, 1952
LUCE, A.A.: *Fishing and Thinking*, 1959
PROFUMO, D. & SWIFT, G.: *The Magic Wheel*, 1985

(Some of these titles are now out of print, but can still be obtained second-hand. Specialist booksellers, who will find these books for you, advertise in the classified section at the back of magazines such as *Trout and Salmon*.)

Appendix

Detecting the Upstream Wet Fly Take

Though I prefer to use wry fly (dry fly on top dropper, Spider wet fly on middle dropper and Killer Bug on the point) rather than traditional upstream wet fly, it may be of interest to readers to consider the difficulties of detecting the upstream wet fly take.

The principal difficulty for the angler in upstream wet fly fishing lies in detecting that the fish has taken a fly. It's curious how even expert fishermen, when they come to write about these signs, often fail to do so in sufficient detail. For instance, W.C. Stewart, the fisherman who championed and popularised the technique, is so brief upon the subject that he almost evades the issue:

> In fishing up, the rise of a trout is by no means so distinct as in fishing down. They frequently seize the

> fly without breaking the surface, and the first intimation the angler gets of their presence is a slight pull at the line. The utmost attention is therefore necessary to strike the moment the least motion is either seen or felt.

This is glossing over a tricky area far too quickly. I have therefore drawn up a list of fifteen pointers: visual indications which suggest that a trout has taken an upstream wet fly. I believe you can expect one of the following visible manifestations as you fish upstream:

1. Your fly line might suddenly check or stop. This can be either quite noticeable or rather hard to spot. It could be that a fly has fouled weed or caught in a rock, although this possibility should never be allowed to defer an immediate strike.
2. Your fly line might suddenly quiver slightly.
3. Your fly line might twitch forwards or slide away from you smoothly.
4. In the case of a really savage take by a strong fish, your whole line will shoot forwards, making quite noticeable V-shaped ripples – a godsend of a take guaranteed to encourage a beginner, especially if the fish is subsequently hooked.
5. Without your fly line registering any movement, your nylon might suddenly move. This could be either a twitch or a jerk, or, even more difficult to perceive, merely a smooth pull as if the leader were being sucked underwater.
6. Without noticing any motion in your line, you might suddenly catch sight of a flash underwater. This flash could be either the silvery sheen of light reflected from scales or else the glimpse of the actual colour of the trout's flank, anything from buttery yellow to bronze. This is what Skues referred to lovingly as 'the little brown wink underwater'.
7. You might suddenly pick out a brief white splash of light against the dark background of water. This signifies the opening of a trout's mouth.
8. You might see neither line movement nor flash of a fish but suddenly be aware of an underwater commotion – a heaving or bulging of the water surface as if something has moved sharply below it. (A short sweep of hand beneath bath water produces this kind of surface disturbance.) This sort of agitation in the water often means that more than one trout has gone for your fly – a competition that the biggest fish usually wins. Such a sign often signals a big trout, so it is an opportunity not to be missed.
9. Better still, you might see a fish actually break the surface, especially early in your cast.
10. Sometimes the fish itself is invisible but there is suddenly a great boil on the surface in the vicinity of your flies.

11 A calmer form of this is just a little dimple on the surface, similar to a trout sipping in a dry fly. This means the fish has taken so near the top that the surface is disturbed in his wake.

12 You might possibly spot a trout lying in the water and try for him. It is not always easy to see if he has actually taken your fly, but any of these pieces of behaviour could indicate that he has done so:

   a) you might see his mouth suddenly open and close;
   b) he might suddenly move forwards a little, or sideways, or up and down, or even turn downstream;
   c) you might see the trout suddenly quiver slightly, wagging his tail quickly;
   d) you might be lucky enough, if the light is just right, to see your fly actually swallowed.

13 You might spot a trout, cast over him and just as you think he's going to take your fly, a bigger fish shoulders past him. If this happens more or less as soon as your cast lands it probably means that the bigger fish has taken your fly. Sometimes, and this is unfortunate, it will be a smaller, quick-silvery fish that beats a better fish to your fly.

14 You might perceive a combination of two or more of these visual clues.

15 It might be something even more subtle or imperceptible than any of these pointers. You might have nothing more than a suspicion or an inexplicable awareness that a fish has taken. Trust your instinct and strike.

As soon as you sense any of these clues you must, of course, strike immediately.

These, then, are the signs I look for when I fish upstream with a wet fly. Pointers *6*, *7*, *12* and *13* are only relevant when the water is clear and untroubled. In coloured or rippling water it is the other signals that I have come to expect.

In places where the current is very rapid but smooth (such as pool tails or areas where a stream narrows) you should be able to rely on sight alone. It is the broken runs and ripply streams which cause the most extreme problems – even to experienced anglers on occasions. Visual clues *1*, *4* and *9* are the most likely ones in such turbulent locations, and here touch comes more into operation.

Thus in upstream wet fly you rely on both sight and touch to sense the take of a trout. The smoother and stiller the water, the more you rely on sight; the more rapid and troubled the water, the more you rely on touch. If when fishing down you strike at ninety five percent of trout by touch and five percent by sight, then in fishing up you probably strike at seventy percent by sight and thirty percent by touch – though of course these proportions depend on the type of water you are fishing.

Index

Page numbers in *italic* refer to illustrations.

Index

Index